Modern Spain

Modern Spain

A Documentary History

Edited by
JON COWANS

PENN

University of Pennsylvania Press
Philadelphia

Publication of this volume was assisted by a grant from the
Program for Cultural Cooperation between Spain's Ministry of
Education and Culture and United States Universities

Printed in the United States of America on acid-free paper

10 9 8 7 6 5 4 3 2 1

Published by
University of Pennsylvania Press
Philadelphia, Pennsylvania 19104-4011

Library of Congress Cataloging-in-Publication Data

Modern Spain : a documentary history / edited by Jon Cowans.
p. cm.
Includes bibliographical references and index.
ISBN 0-8122-3717-X (cloth : alk. paper)—ISBN 0-8122-1846-9 (pbk. : alk. paper)
1. Spain—History—20th century—Sources. 2. Spain—History—19th century—Sources.
I. Cowans, Jon.
DP233.M59 2003
946.08—dc21 2003040217

Contents

INTRODUCTION

In the history of some countries, a single moment, usually involving a war or revolution, so dominates our perceptions of the country's past that it threatens to orient our thinking about all previous and subsequent moments. In the case of modern Spain, of course, it is the Civil War of 1936 to 1939 that plays such a role, and indeed the explicit or implicit question that seems to underlie so many studies of Spain's history in the nineteenth and early twentieth centuries is how the country ended up in such an outburst of fratricidal violence. Unfortunately such a teleological approach to the history of Spain before 1936 can distort our understanding of events requiring attention on their own terms, and similar comments could be made about interpreting Spain's history after 1939. Yet despite the drawbacks of viewing all of modern Spain's history through the lens of the Civil War, that conflict continues to elicit more attention than any other moment in Spanish history, and it inevitably looms large in this collection as well.

If the Civil War dominates Spain's twentieth-century history, the events of the Napoleonic era certainly cast a long shadow over the country's political and social landscape in the nineteenth century. Before 1789, Spain had been taking tentative but significant steps toward social, political, religious, and economic reform, as the Bourbon dynasty installed at the beginning of the eighteenth century brought to Spain a new spirit and new ideas and policies rooted in the Age of Enlightenment. Yet if it is possible to discern in the eighteenth century the beginnings of the country's division into two camps later associated with the "left" and the "right," it was only with the events of the revolutionary period, and particularly the years of Napoleon Bonaparte's occupation of Spain, that such divisions really became visible. The toppling of Spain's monarchy and the installation of Napoleon's brother Joseph as ruler of Spain in 1808 led not only to a wave of nationalistic popular uprisings against French rule—including the first uses of the term "guerrilla" warfare—but also to the emergence of a new group (and term), the "Liberals." This group of mostly young, educated, and relatively prosperous Spaniards emerged within the Cortes, a provisional assembly formed in 1810 in the unoccupied southern town of Cádiz, and as that body proceeded to write a virtually revolutionary constitution—the first national constitution in Spain—the Liberals pushed for a sweeping set of reforms that soon provoked opposition from religious conservatives. Those divisions persisted, and the concepts of "left" and "right" became increasingly crucial, even if new parties and movements soon proliferated and individuals shifted partisan allegiances over time.

In the aftermath of Napoleon's defeat and departure from Spain, the Bourbon king Ferdinand VII returned from exile, and though his political views were not immediately clear to many Spaniards, he soon revealed his sympathies by criticizing the Liberals and their constitution in a public declaration in May 1814. What ensued over the following years was a multisided conflict among liberal and conservative monarchists divided into various factions and parties. The most significant group on the right consisted of the supporters of Ferdinand's brother Carlos, who claimed the right to inherit the throne and whose forces fought a series of civil wars known as the Carlist wars. Over the course of the nineteenth century, major elements of the Liberal program gradually gained wider acceptance, though the Carlists and many devout Catholics remained staunchly opposed. In these conflicts, various branches of the military also played a major role, launching a long tradition of political involvement with an intervention on behalf of the Liberals in 1820.

By the latter half of the century, new groups seeking even greater change arose to the left of the Liberals, including republicans, socialists, and anarchists. A major impetus for the rise of these new groups was Spain's urbanization and industrialization, which created a small but steadily growing industrial working class while also calling new attention to the old problems of rural poverty and inequality. The anarchists showed particular interest in the plight of Spain's rural poor, making major inroads through energetic campaigns to spread their ideas and start a social revolution. Both the socialists and the anarchists continued their growth well into the twentieth century, and when a republic was proclaimed in 1931, those groups (along with other new parties such as the Communists) sought to capitalize on a long-awaited opportunity.

Another political force that took shape in the nineteenth century consisted of various regional movements, primarily those of the Catalans and Basques. The Catalans in particular had a long history of distinct institutions and ways, having enjoyed considerable autonomy under the Habsburgs during the sixteenth and seventeenth centuries, but the advent of the Bourbons, with their centralizing and absolutist tendencies, had undermined the region's autonomy, especially after the Catalans fought on the losing side in the War of Spanish Succession (1701–1713). Yet at least some Catalans continued to recall the region's tradition of self-government and cultural distinctiveness, and by the middle of the nineteenth century a new Catalanist movement inspired by the romanticism and nationalism then in vogue in Europe gained increasing strength. If the movement's boldness derived in part from the comparatively advanced state of the Catalan economy—the region being on the forefront of Spanish industrialization—the same can be said for the Basque region, another relatively industrialized region where ethnic nationalism inspired the growth of regionalist, even separatist, movements by the late nineteenth century. The continuing rise of these and other movements alarmed Spanish nationalists—particularly military officers—and the tensions between these rivals not only produced sporadic violence in the early twentieth century, but also helped provoke the military uprising that began the Civil War in 1936.

Although political violence had been chronic throughout the nineteenth century, that violence seemed to be reaching new levels in the first decades of the twentieth century, and in 1923 General Miguel Primo de Rivera led a movement that seized power and promised to restore order. Many Spaniards welcomed Primo de Rivera's seizure of power and continued to support his government throughout the 1920s, but by 1930 economic difficulties and persistent political opposition from groups on the left weakened the general's position, and having lost the king's confidence, he stepped down in 1930. A year later, in the wake of municipal elections that featured republican victories and mass demonstrations in many cities, it was Alfonso XIII's turn to step down. A coalition of parties of the left and center then proclaimed a republic and set to work on a new constitution and a legislative agenda of reforms in the areas of regional autonomy, workers' and women's rights, education, the role of the Church, and land tenure. Spain, however, remained deeply divided between left and right, and political violence only escalated in these years amid shifts of power between parties of the left and right. Finally, after the election of a "Popular Front" of parties of the left in February 1936, the military began plotting an uprising, which it finally launched in July 1936. The conspiring officers had counted on seizing power swiftly, but as the Republic's partisans and others on the left mounted unexpectedly strong resistance, Spain soon found itself divided into two zones of roughly equal size.

The Civil War thus represented the culmination of more than a century of political conflict, but one of the reasons why it became so bloody was the involvement of various foreign governments and individuals, who viewed the war as the beginning of a showdown between the competing ideologies of the era. General Francisco Franco, who soon emerged as the leader of the Nationalists, received critical support from the Italian Fascists and German Nazis, while the Republicans, whose political leadership remained much more unstable amid bitter political infighting, benefited from military aid from the Soviet Union, but the legally elected government failed in its repeated efforts to secure French, British, and American assistance. But if the governments of the democracies refused to help the Republic, thousands of ideologically motivated volunteers from around the world came to Spain to help fight fascism, playing a significant role in helping the left hold out for three years against the superior weaponry of their foes. By 1939, however, Franco's forces had prevailed.

When the war ended, some still thought Franco, who lacked prior political experience, might step aside for either a restoration of the monarchy or some other political arrangement, but it soon became apparent that Franco would not relinquish political power, and he moved to consolidate his regime through a series of new decrees and laws. Franco organized his state along authoritarian and corporatist lines reminiscent of Europe's fascist regimes (while also borrowing heavily from fascist symbolism and spectacle), but in many ways Franco's regime owed more to traditionalistic Catholic ideologies and regimes, and his refusal to join World War II on the Axis side probably prevented an Allied invasion of Spain during the war. As it became increasingly clear that Germany and Italy would lose the war, Franco took steps to distance himself from fascism, portraying his system as a traditional, Catholic regime in a country culturally and historically unsuited for democracy and liberalism.

Life under Franco proved particularly harsh for anyone who had supported the Republic, and the human-rights abuses inflicted on leftists had much to do with Spain's international isolation. Yet life was not just difficult for those on the left, as the combination of the physical destruction of the Civil War and the lack of access to foreign markets, supplies, and credit led to severe food shortages and poverty long after 1945. Franco's regime gained important support in 1953 through the signing of a concordat with the Vatican and agreements to allow American military bases in Spain (in exchange for U.S. aid), and, with the government promoting tourism and other economic activities, Spain's economy began to improve markedly by the 1960s. Inside the country, Franco still faced opposition and resistance from workers, students, monarchists, and eventually even some members of the Church, but with the continuing support of many propertied Spaniards, most of the Catholic Church, and—most important—the military, Franco's hold on power was never seriously threatened. Although Franco often hinted of restoring the monarchy, the regime only ended with Franco's death in 1975, almost forty years after the start of the Civil War.

Since 1975, Spain has undergone a startling transformation, making a remarkably successful transition to democracy (despite an attempted military coup in 1981, thwarted in part by King Juan Carlos's timely intervention) and registering stunning economic gains both before and after gaining admission to the European Community in 1986. Spanish society has also changed dramatically in areas such as the role of women, the nature and content of the mass media and public debate, the extent of personal freedom, and the level of Spain's cultural and intellectual achievements. Problems certainly remained at the end of the twentieth century, most notably persistent unemployment, political corruption, terrorism carried out by the Basque organization ETA, and the question of the treatment of immigrants entering the country from North Africa, but Spain, which for most of the past two centuries had struck Spaniards and others alike as a backward country that was barely part of Europe, had by the 1990s become a remarkably prosperous country very much at home in Europe. It is perhaps a mark of how far the country has come since 1975 that both the Civil War and the Franco years seem to be passing from memory to history.

The introductions to the documents in this volume seek to provide background information both on their authors and on the relevant historical context. In the hopes of leaving as much space as possible for the documents themselves, however, we have tried to keep the introductions brief, so those desiring lengthy, detailed discussion of historical context should consult one of the many fine histories of Spain listed in the Bibliography. Moreover, the introductions refrain from summarizing each document's content, instead allowing the figures from Spain's past to speak for themselves.

Regarding the translations, which are the work of the editor unless otherwise noted, special care has been taken to make the English texts comprehensible to contemporary readers, including those who may be unfamiliar with Spanish history. In documents translated by others, some changes have been made, bringing language up to date and using contemporary American spellings. Of course modes of expression change over time, and when choices had to be made, we have favored clarity over strict adherence to the linguistic styles of the past. In many passages, discussions of obscure matters have been omitted (indicated by ellipses), while in others brief explanations (in brackets) have been inserted into the text. In the treatment of proper names, we have generally tried to use the Spanish versions, but in those cases where individuals are already well known by their English-language names—Ferdinand VII, for example—we have followed common practice.

Those who read Spanish should be aware of several excellent published collections of historical documents to which this work owes a great deal. One is a series of books edited by Fernando Díaz-Plaja, entitled *Historia de España en sus documentos* (see citations in the Bibliography). Also of immense value is the massive collection known as the Biblioteca de autores españoles, which began publication in the nineteenth century and now runs to over three hundred volumes. Finally, Alfonso García-Gallo's *Manual de historia del derecho español* presents an enormous number of well-chosen documents in a single volume.

In any collection such as this, one ultimately has to leave out many worthy subjects and documents, and no two historians would agree precisely on which documents to include. The book does not include selections from Spanish literature, not because literature is unimportant for understanding history, but on the contrary, because it is so important that it deserves full treatment elsewhere. For the more recent decades, many potentially valuable documents cannot yet be reprinted, though the selection presented here should nonetheless provide a good picture of the main issues of the period. We hope that this collection will contribute to people's understanding of the history of one of Europe's most important and fascinating countries.

Acknowledgments

I would like to thank several people who have helped make this project a reality. For their careful comments and suggestions on the manuscript, I am indebted to Professors Antonio Feros of New York University, James Boyden of Tulane University, and Victoria Enders of Northern Arizona University. I would also like to express my gratitude for a grant to support publication of this book from the Program for Cultural Cooperation between Spain's Ministry of Education and Culture and United States Universities. Thanks are also due to those publishers and organizations that were kind enough to allow me to reprint material under copyright. I also wish to thank the librarians and staff at the New York Public Library, New York University's Bobst Library, Rutgers University's Alexander and Dana Libraries, Columbia University's Butler Library, and the Instituto Cervantes in New York. I am grateful to the Cultural Office of the Embassy of Spain in Washington, D.C., for answering questions and helping me secure permission to reprint documents. Finally, I would like to thank everyone at the University of Pennsylvania Press for their diligent work on this project. Special thanks go to Alison Anderson for her expert and cheerful response to my many inquiries during the editing process, and, most of all, to Jerry Singerman, who was so helpful in answering questions, in offering advice, and in seeing this project through from the outset.

1. Joachim Murat, Report on the Madrid Revolt (1808)

In 1807, Napoleon Bonaparte, leader of revolutionary France, was at war with Britain and other European countries, including Britain's longtime ally Portugal. The Spanish government, however, had decided that Britain posed a greater threat to its interests than France did, mostly because of British encroachment upon Spain's colonies in America, so it had made peace with France and had gone to war against Britain. When Napoleon asked Spain's king, Charles IV, for permission to send troops through Spain on their way to Portugal, Charles agreed.

Napoleon, however, kept sending troops into Spain even after he had defeated Portugal, and the royal family, fearing French intentions, fled south from Madrid. In the town of Aranjuez, crowds, fearing that the king might be fleeing to the colonies (as the Portuguese royal family had done) rioted in protest upon the king's arrival. (These crowds had been incited by noble supporters of Charles's son Ferdinand, who wished to wrest power from his father and his father's chief minister, Manuel de Godoy.) Charles IV then abdicated in favor of Ferdinand, but he soon changed his mind, creating a serious conflict over the Spanish throne. In response to Napoleon's offer to mediate the rivals' claims to the throne, the two went to the French town of Bayonne, where they were promptly detained and replaced by Joseph Bonaparte, Napoleon's brother. At the news of this treachery, crowds in Madrid began rioting on May 2, 1808. French troops in fear for their lives then reacted, as the French military commander Joachim Murat explains in this letter to Napoleon.

SOURCE: Comte Joachim Joseph André Murat, *Murat, lieutenant de l'empereur en Espagne 1808 d'après sa correspondance inédite et des documents originaux* (Paris: Plon, 1897), 318–20.

Murat's Report to Napoleon

Madrid, May 2, 1808, six in the afternoon.

Sire: Public tranquility has been disturbed this morning. For several days people from the countryside have been gathering in the city; pamphlets stirring up rebellion have been circulating; a price has been put on the heads of the French generals and officials staying in the city; in sum, everything has been pointing to a crisis. Since eight o'clock this morning the rabble of Madrid and its surrounding areas has blocked the access to the castle and filled the patios. One of my aides-de-camp, whom I had sent to greet the queen of Etruria, and who was going to get into the coach, was detained at the castle gate and would have been murdered by the frenzied populace if not for ten or twelve grenadiers of Your Majesty's guard that I sent to liberate him. Moments later a second aide-de-camp whom I sent with orders for General [Emmanuel de] Grouchy was assaulted by stone throwers, resulting in injury. The alarm was immediately sounded, Your Majesty's guard took up arms, and all the troops received the order to march on Madrid to occupy the posts that had been designated for them in case of alarm.

Meanwhile, a battalion of the guard that was lodging in my palace, protected by two cannons and a squadron of Polish infantrymen, marched toward the castle, attacking the masses gathered there and dispersing them with rifle fire. General Grouchy gathered his troops in the Prado and received the order to go by way of the Calle de Alcalá to the Puerta del Sol and the Plaza Mayor, where more than twenty thousand rebels had gathered. Isolated soldiers who were trying to join their units were murdered in the streets. . . .

[Murat then describes the deployment of troops throughout the city.] After these measures were taken, I ordered General Grouchy to go to the Puerta del Sol and Colonel Grouchy to march to the same place by way of Calle de la Platería, to disperse the populace with cannon fire. These two columns set in motion and managed to clear the streets, not without difficulty, because these wretches expelled from the streets took refuge in the houses and fired upon our troops from the crossroads, while the majority headed for the Arsenal to seize the cannon and the rifles. But General Lefranc, who was in the Puerta del Fuencarral, went there with bayonets drawn and managed to take control of the arsenal, recovering the cannons from the rebels who had taken hold of them. Later, the columns had headed to the Puerta del Sol, the Puertas de Toledo, Segovia, and Fuencarral. General Grouchy gave the order to enter the houses from which shots were coming, having all who were found inside put to the knife. All the streets have been cleared. The peasants who had managed to escape the city have run into the cavalry and been attacked with saber blows.

The cannon and the rifle fire had ceased to be heard, and upon receiving the reports that no one was left in the streets, I headed to the palace to speak with the prince, Lord Antonio [Infante Antonio Pascual, younger brother of Charles IV], and to tell him that the city must be disarmed immediately. At this point the proclamation was being made, and soon it will be sent to the provinces. The captains general, the district magistrates, the mayors, and the high-ranking clergy will be responsible for this being executed and for the tranquility of the kingdom.

Sire, many people have died; the infantrymen of your guard have lost several men. Colonel Daumesnil has, as always, behaved bravely, confronting the masses twice with his infantrymen. He had twenty men put out of action; he had two horses killed, and he was moderately wounded in the knee. Tonight I will send Your Majesty a more precise report on these events, once I have received the detailed reports from the various commanding generals. In a wink of an eye everyone was at his post, and I must offer the greatest praise to all of Your Majesty's troops, especially General Grouchy.

Proclamation to the French Troops

In crushing the May 2 uprising, the French executed a number of the rebels in Madrid—an event the painter Francisco Goya recorded in one of his most famous canvases. (The precise number executed is unknown, but some historians estimate that several hundred were shot, mostly on May 3.) Murat issued the following decree during the campaign to crush the uprising.

SOURCE: *Diario de Madrid,* May 4, 1808.

Soldiers: The population of Madrid has rebelled and has even turned to murder. I know that good Spaniards have lamented this disorder; I am far from confusing them with those wretches who only want crime and pillage. But French blood has been spilled, and it demands vengeance; consequently, I order the following:

Article 1. General Grouchy will convoke the military commission this evening.

Article 2. All those arrested in the uprising, arms in hand, will be shot.

Article 3. The ruling junta will disarm the residents of Madrid. Any inhabitants found with weapons, and lacking permission, will be shot.

Article 4. Any gathering of more than eight persons will be considered seditious and will be dispersed by rifle fire.

Article 5. Any place where a Frenchman is killed will be burned down.

Article 6. Masters will be responsible for their servants, guildmasters for their workers and officials, parents for their children, and heads of monasteries for their monks.

Article 7. Authors, sellers, and distributors of printed or written manuscripts provoking rebellion will be considered agents of England, and will be shot.

Decreed at general headquarters in Madrid, May 2, 1808
Signed, Joachim Murat

2. Napoleon Bonaparte, Message to the Spaniards (1808)

Having put down the Madrid uprising of May 2, the French soon found themselves facing outrage and resistance all over Spain. Hoping to regain control of public order, Napoleon issued the following message on May 25.

SOURCE: *Gaceta de Madrid*, June 3, 1808.

From Napoleon, Emperor of the French. . . .

Spaniards: after a long agony, your nation was going to perish. I have seen your troubles and I am going to remedy them. Your grandeur and your power are part of mine. Your princes have ceded to me all their rights to the Crown of Spain; I do not wish to reign in your provinces; but I wish to acquire eternal rights to the love and recognition of your posterity. Your monarchy is old; my mission is to rejuvenate it; I will improve your institutions, and I will see to it that you enjoy the benefits of reform without your experiencing conflicts, disorder, and disturbances.

Spaniards: I have convoked a general assembly of representatives from the provinces and cities. I myself want to know your desires and needs. At that point I will transfer all my rights, and I will place your glorious crown upon someone else's head. I will assure you a constitution that reconciles the proper and desirable authority of the sovereign with the liberties and privileges of the people.

Spaniards: remember what your ancestors were, and look at what you have become. It is not your fault, but rather that of the bad government that ruled over you. Place your fullest hopes and confidence in the current circumstances; for I want even your descendants to remember me and to exclaim: He was the regenerator of our fatherland.

3. Calls to Arms (1808)

After Napoleon lured Charles IV and his son Ferdinand to the French town of Bayonne (with a promise to mediate their quarrel over the throne), he forced them both to abdicate, kept them in France, and installed his brother Joseph on the Spanish throne. Most Spaniards, however, rejected the French ruler and yearned for Ferdinand to return, and all over the country leading citizens soon formed committees, known as juntas; these juntas began issuing public appeals to their countrymen to take up arms against the French. Ironically, despite these juntas' conservatism and their goal of restoring Spain's royal sovereign, their members legitimated their actions by invoking versions of the doctrine of national sovereignty, which was so strongly associated with the French Revolution. These are but two of the many such declarations that appeared at the time.

SOURCE: *Demostración de la lealtad española: Colección de proclamas, bandos, órdenes, discursos, estados de exército, etc.*, vol. 1 (Madrid: Imprenta de Repullés, 1808), 15–20.

Proclamation of Seville, May 29, 1808

Spaniards: Seville has been unable to resist the impulses of the heroic loyalty it has demonstrated in all centuries. The king to whom Seville had sworn loyalty and whom it had greeted with a happiness greater than any in memory has been seized and taken. The fundamental laws of the monarchy have been trampled on; our property is being threatened along with our customs, our women, and everything else that is precious to the nation. Our holy religion, our only hope, is going to perish or be reduced to vain forms, being without support or protection; and all of this by a foreign power, and not by force of arms but rather by deception and treachery, using our own people against us and making those who are called heads of our government instruments of these atrocities — those who have not been reluctant to sacrifice their country, either out of their own baseness or their infamous cowardice, or perhaps for other reasons that time and justice will reveal. It was thus necessary to break free of those burdensome obstacles that were preventing Spaniards from awakening and using the generous determination and glory they have demonstrated in all centuries, defending the honor of the nation, its laws, its monarchs, and its religion. . . .

A governing junta that was barely formed before it violated the kingdom's most sacred laws; a president named without proper authority, and one who, if he ever had any legitimacy, soon hastened to lose it . . . could not stop us from showing our loyalty or make us break the sacred obligations we swore as Spaniards, vassals, Christians, and men free and independent of any foreign authority. . . .

All of Europe will applaud our efforts with great pleasure and will hasten to come to our aid. Italy, Germany, and all of the north, suffering under the cruel empire of this nation, will enthusiastically seize this happy occasion that Spain is presenting it to break that empire and recover their liberty, their laws, their monarchs, and everything else they have had stolen. . . .

Spaniards, the fatherland, along with all of your property, your liberty, your monarchs, your holy religion, and the hope of an eternal life that this religion alone promises . . . is in clear, immediate, and urgent danger.

Seville, May 29, 1808, by order of the Supreme Junta of Government.

Proclamation of Galicia (no date)

SOURCE: *Demostración de la lealtad española: Colección de proclamas, bandos, órdenes, discursos, estados de exército, etc.*, vol. 2 (Cádiz: Manuel Ximénez Carreño, 1808), 123–25.

Spaniards,

Between bearing the chains of infamous slavery and fighting for liberty there is no middle ground. The monster of France resolved in his heart to tyrannize our independence by the most despicable means, of which there is and has been no example in the world. His infamies have been witnessed, his betrayal discovered, and the kidnapping of our precious king confirms this for us. Ah, sufferers of a thousand misfortunes! The tyrant will fatten himself on your blood, if our courage does not prevent him. And will we allow this thief to carry out such treacherous intentions on our Ferdinand? Will we allow his armies to come with impunity to rob our homes, to outrage our families, and to despoil our God of sacred items, as he has just done in Portugal?

Spaniards: this cause is that of the All-Powerful; it is necessary to pursue it, or else to leave an infamous memory to all future generations. Under the banner of religion our forefathers managed to liberate the soil we walk upon from the Mohammedan armies, so will we now be afraid to attack a horde of vile atheists, led by the protector of the Jews? [The reference is to Napoleon; the French Revolution had ended discrimination against Jews and other religious minorities both inside France and in territories the French conquered.] Our venerable fathers, those heroes who so gloriously spilled their blood against the Muslims, would raise their heads from the grave and would cry out furiously against our cowardice, disowning us as their children.

The tyrants of France, Italy, and the other countries of the Continent; those enemies of humanity, vomited up from the waves of the isle of Corsica

[Napoleon's birthplace], are the same ones who tyrannized our young Ferdinand, seduced by alluring promises that that young monarch had published, as you have seen. Under these same false pretenses, after they had lit the voracious fire of discord among our royal family, they treacherously imprisoned all of them; with the same tricks and deceptive happiness that they promise you they wish to imprison and enslave the entire nation, mocking its valor, energy, and steadiness in its labors. It is true that a few spurious men are submitting to their infamous ideas, and a few submitted with impunity a few days ago, just as other vile and fickle Frenchmen have done.

No, it is not the illustrious and generous French who are responsible for this or who assist these vile and abominable acts of treachery of their tyrant. Their soldiers are taken from the most infamous of the subjugated nations; the guiding principles of their leader are conquest and the extermination of the same men who made that conquest possible with their blood.

Do not be unaware that they have hoped to see such conduct among our brothers and countrymen, seeking to mix them together with the godless and vile slaves they have brought to Spain imprisoned between hard masters.

Noble Galicians; wise priests; pious Christians of this unfortunate soil: you are the first and the ones most obligated to shake off the yoke of such vile rabble: you, who shelter the body of the patron saint of Spain, Santiago; honored with the sacred trophies of the Most Holy Sacrament, which adorns your standards, do not be afraid, do not fear the bandits who lay waste our court and our lands up to the French border. Hasten to take up arms; join with the other provinces, under the auspices of our constant faith and of the patron Santiago: take up your invincible standards, and hurry, being sure of the victory in the fields of glory, the only means of attaining liberty and not bearing the chains of infamous slavery.

4. Decrees of the Cádiz Cortes (1810–1814)

When Napoleon imprisoned Spain's Charles IV and his son Ferdinand and put his own brother Joseph Bonaparte on the throne of Spain, many Spaniards felt they were without a king. At that point Spaniards began forming local committees, or juntas, which soon formed a central junta to govern unoccupied Spain. Several military defeats in 1809 led that junta to flee from Seville to Cádiz, but doubts about the junta's competence led it to call for the formation of a Cortes and to cede its powers to a five-man regency, or temporary government. The Council of the Regency, run by conservatives, hesitated to convoke a Cortes, but news of rebellions in the colonies, combined with pressure from liberals gathered in Cádiz, led the council to give in. Elections were held wherever possible, while districts under French occupation were represented by citizens from those districts present in Cádiz. The General and Extraordinary Cortes (or "Cádiz Cortes") first met on September 24, 1810.

Amid the sudden political vacuum, the term "Cortes" helped give the entire endeavor a certain historically based legitimacy, but there were many fundmental differences between this body and the traditional representative institutions that had advised Spanish monarchs in the Middle Ages. Unlike the Cortes of the past, for example, this one did not contain separate chambers for commoners and nobles. The new Cortes soon began writing a constitution and issuing legislation on various topics (regardless of its ability to implement that legislation in a country still largely under French rule). Among the most urgent issues facing the Cortes was the problem of the colonies, which had long been linked to Spain primarily by obedience to the king, and which were now witnessing the formation of independence movements. Also, many of those gathered at Cádiz shared the Enlightenment view that the Inquisition represented an obstacle to progress in Spain, though they did not want to be mistaken for atheistic radicals like those of the French Revolution.

SOURCE: *Colección de los decretos y órdenes que han expedido las Cortes generales y extraordinarias desde su instalación de 24 de setiembre de 1810 hasta igual fecha de 1811* (Madrid: Imprenta Nacional, 1820), 1: 1–3, 10, 72–73; 3: 211–12, 215–19; 1: 193–96; 4: 76, 220–21.

Decree of September 24, 1810: The deputies who make up this congress and who represent the Spanish nation declare themselves legitimately constituted as General and Extraordinary Cortes, and [they declare] that national sovereignty resides in it.

The General and Extraordinary Cortes of the Spanish nation, . . . in full conformance with the general will, pronounced in the most energetic and obvious way, recognizes, proclaims, and swears once again in favor of its sole and legitimate king, Ferdinand VII, . . . and it declares null and without value or effect the ceding of the crown that is said to have been made to

Napoleon, not only because of the violence that intervened in those unjust and illegal acts, but primarily for having lacked the consent of the nation.

Given the impossibility of the legislative, executive, and judicial powers convening together, the General and Extraordinary Cortes declares that it reserves for itself the exercise of the legislative power with all its implications. . . .

The Council of the Regency . . . will recognize the national sovereignty of the Cortes and will swear obedience to the laws and decrees that shall emanate from it, for which purpose it will move, immediately after this decree is made known, to the meeting hall of the Cortes, which is in permanent session and is awaiting this recognition.

It is declared that the formula of recognition and the oath that the Council of the Regency must use is the following: Do you recognize the sovereignty of the nation represented by the deputies of this General and Extraordinary Cortes? Do you swear to obey the decrees, laws, and constitution that are established according to the holy purposes for which it has met, and also to command that they be obeyed and to have [those decrees, laws, and constitution] executed? To preserve the independence, liberty, and integrity of the nation? The Roman, apostolic, Catholic religion? The monarchic government of the kingdom? To reestablish our beloved King Ferdinand VII . . . upon the throne? And to look after the well-being of the state? If so, may God help you; and if not, you will be responsible to the nation with regard to its laws.

On the Colonies

Decree of October 15, 1810: The General and Extraordinary Cortes confirms and sanctions the . . . concept that the Spanish domains of both hemispheres form one and the same monarchy, and one and the same nation, and a single family, and that in the same way, those who come from the European or the overseas domains are equal in rights to those from this peninsula; and it is the responsibility of the Cortes to work opportunely, and with particular interest, doing everything that can contribute to the happiness of those overseas. . . . The Cortes thus orders that as soon as the territories across the seas, which have experienced agitation, recognize the legitimate sovereign authority that has been established in the mother country, there will be a general amnesty for everything that has taken place in those territories, without infringing on the rights of third parties.

Decree of February 9, 1811: The General and Extraordinary Cortes, remaining faithful to the principles declared in the decree of October 15 of last year, and wishing to permanently assure the [Spanish] Americans as well as the Spaniards, as native inhabitants of those vast domains of the Spanish monarchy, of the rights they must enjoy as integral parts of that monarchy, decrees:

1. That their competent representation in the national Cortes being one of the principal rights of all of the Spanish peoples, the representation of the American part of the Spanish monarchy in all of the Cortes that will meet from now on will be entirely equal in mode and form to that which is established in the peninsula, with the arrangements concerning this national representation on foundations of perfect equality having to be specified in the constitution, in accordance with the aforementioned decree of last October.

2. That the natives and inhabitants of [Spanish] America may plant and cultivate whatever nature and human effort shall allow them in those climates, and may similarly pursue all manufacturing industries and crafts with all their ramifications.

3. That the [Spanish] Americans, including Spaniards and Indians alike and the children of both classes, have opportunities equal to those of the European Spaniards to pursue any kind of work and destiny, in the [royal] court as well as in any other place in the monarchy, whether in the ecclesiastical, political, or military profession.

On Religion and the Church

Decree of February 18, 1813: Convents [and monasteries] that do not have twelve members may not be reestablished or remain in operation, unless it is the only one in a town, and [in that case] the governing prelate will have to replenish the ranks with members of the same order.

In towns where there were many convents of the same order, a single one should be established for all the members from that town.

The regency will refrain from authorizing new orders for the establishment of convents, and the prelates [will refrain] from granting habits until the resolution of the whole matter.

Decree of February 22, 1813: The Cortes, . . . wanting article 12 of the constitution [which established Roman Catholicism as the country's "only true religion"] to have its fullest effects and to be assured of the most faithful observation of such a wise disposition, declares and decrees:

1. The Roman, apostolic, Catholic religion will be protected by laws in conformance with the constitution.

2. The Tribunal of the Inquisition is incompatible with the constitution.

3. As a consequence, the law is . . . reestablished granting bishops and vicars the power to investigate matters of faith according to sacred canon and

common law, and also to secular judges to declare and impose upon heretics penalties that the law prescribes or that they will in the future indicate. The ecclesiastical and secular judges will proceed in their respective spheres in conformance with the constitution and the laws.

4. Any Spaniard has legal standing to make accusations of the crime of heresy before the ecclesiastical tribunal. . . .

9. When ecclesiastical judgment has been rendered, the findings will be forwarded to the secular courts, with the criminal being turned over to those courts so that they may impose the penalties the law prescribes. . . .

Chapter 2, article 1. The king will take all appropriate measures so that neither prohibited books nor writings, nor those contrary to religion, are introduced in the kingdom through the customs houses of the ports or borders, subjecting those that circulate to the following dispositions, and to those of the law on freedom of the press. . . .

5. The king, after the Council of State has issued its dictates, will circulate the list of the denounced writings that must be prohibited, and will, with the approval of the Cortes, have it published; and it will be observed as a law throughout the monarchy, subject to the penalties established.

Decree of February 22, 1813: The General and Extraordinary Cortes, considering that by virtue of article 305 of the constitution no penalty that is imposed for any kind of crime should fall on the family of the one who suffers it, but rather must have its full effect on the one who merited it; and considering that reminders of the punishments inflicted by the Inquisition, which are preserved in public places, cast infamy on the families of those who suffered them, and even cause those of the same surname to be exposed to a bad reputation; has decided to decree and does decree:

All the paintings, pictures, or inscriptions indicating the punishments and penalties imposed by the Inquisition that exist in churches, cloisters, and monasteries, or in any other public place in the monarchy, shall be erased or removed from the respective places in which they are located, and destroyed in the prompt period of three days, counting from the receipt of the present decree.

On Society and the Economy

Decree of August 6, 1811: The General and Extraordinary Cortes, wishing to remove the existing obstacles that may stand in the way of a proper regime, the increase of the population, and the prosperity of the Spanish monarchy, decrees:

1. Seigneurial jurisdictions of any kind and condition are from now on

taken over by the nation. . . . [This article refers to very old arrangements, often called "feudal," by which the lord of an estate held judicial and other powers over those living and working on it.]

4. The titles of vassal and vassalage and their attributes, royal as well as personal, that owe their origins to a jurisdictional title, are abolished, with the exception of those that emanate from a free contract, following the customs of the sacred right of property.

5. Territorial and manorial domains are from now on classified along with the other forms of private property, if they are not of the kind that by their nature must be incorporated into the nation, or of those that have not fulfilled the conditions upon which they were granted. . . .

6. Similarly, the contracts, pacts, or agreements that have been made based on right of usufruct, lease, quitrents, or others of this kind reached between the so-called lords and vassals must from now on be considered contracts between private individuals.

7. Those privileges known as exclusive, private, and prohibitive that have the same feudal origin, such as the rights of hunting, fishing, the use of ovens, mills, access to water, forests, and other such things are abolished, and are now free to be used by each district's inhabitants, in conformance with common law and the municipal rules established in each district. The owners should not consider themselves deprived of the use of the ovens, mills, and other properties of this kind as private individuals, nor of the common use of the waters, pastures, and other things, to which they may have rights as residents of the district. . . .

10. Prior to the compensation that must be paid to the possessors of said exclusive privileges as repayment for great services recognized, this status must be proven in the corresponding territorial tribunal, which will consult with the government, forwarding the original documents. . . .

13. No demands or appeals impeding the prompt fulfillment and execution of all that is ordered in the previous articles will be allowed. . . .

14. From now on, no one will be able to call himself lord of vassals, to have [feudal] jurisdiction, to name judges, nor to use the privileges and rights included in this decree. . . .

Decree of May 26, 1813: The General and Extraordinary Cortes, acceding to the wishes that various towns have expressed, has seen fit to decree the following as a general rule: the town councils of all the towns shall proceed, without causing any injury, to take down and demolish all signs of vassalage that capitular houses may have over their entrances or any other places, given that the peoples of the Spanish nation do not recognize and will never again recognize any other lordship than that of the nation itself, and its noble pride will not put up with having to see a continuous reminder of its humiliation.

On Justice

Decree of September 8, 1813: The Cortes, . . . convinced of the usefulness of abolishing those laws by which degrading punishments are imposed upon the Spaniards, punishments that have always been a symbol of the ancient barbarism and the shameful relics of paganism, has decided to decree:

1. The punishment of whipping is abolished throughout the territory of the Spanish monarchy. . . .

3. The ban on whipping is extended to public houses or establishments of correction, seminaries, and schools.

4. Given this abolition of whipping throughout the monarchy, the parish priests in the overseas provinces shall not be allowed to use that penalty either as a means of punishing the Indians or for use against criminals, or for any other purpose whatsoever.

5. Diego Muñoz Torrero, On Freedom of the Press (1810)

Although many of the members of the Cádiz Cortes held liberal views, not all did. Here, in a debate on freedom of the press, a leader of the liberal deputies addresses his more conservative colleagues, who had proposed that works intended for publication first be submitted to a board of censors.

SOURCE: Conde de Toreno, *Historia del levantamiento, guerra y revolución de España*, vol. 2 (Paris: Baudry, 1838), 241–43.

The matter in question has, in my view, two aspects, one concerning justice and the other concerning necessity. Justice is the vital principle of civil society, and the offspring of justice is freedom of the press. The right to bring the government's actions under examination is an inalienable right that no nation can give up without ceasing to be a nation. What did we do in the memorable decree of September 24? We declared the Bayonne decrees [in which Ferdinand VII abdicated under pressure from Napoleon] illegal and null. And why? Because the act of abdication had been made without the nation's consent. To whom has the nation now entrusted its fate? To us; we are its representatives, and according to our customs and ancient fundamental laws, we can take very few actions without the approval of our constituents. But when the people placed power in our hands, did they thus deprive themselves of the right to examine and criticize our actions? Why did we, on September 24, decree that the executive power was responsible [to the Cortes]? . . . Why did we assure ourselves the power to inspect its actions? Because we placed *power* in the hands of *men*, and men can easily abuse it if there is no check of any kind to restrain them; there was no more immediate check on the executive power than the power of the Cortes.

But are we [in the Cortes] perhaps infallible? Can the people, who so recently saw us assembled, place such unlimited confidence in us that they abandon any precautions? Do the people not have the same right over us that we have over the executive power, that is, to inspect our way of thinking and to condemn it? . . . And what means do the people have of doing this? They have only the press; for I do not suppose that those who disagree with my opinion would grant [the people] the right of insurrection, the most terrible and dangerous right any nation can exercise. But if they allow the people no legal and opportune means of making claims against us, what difference does it make if it is one person or five or twenty or a hundred who tyrannize them? The Spanish people have always hated civil wars, but perhaps they will unfortunately have to resort to one. The way to avoid this is to permit the solemn manifestation of public opinion. We still do not fully grasp the immense power of a nation to oblige those who govern it to be just. . . . But if you deprive the people of the freedom to speak and write, how can they express their opinion? It is, then, one of the rights of man in modern societies to enjoy freedom of the press, a system as wise in theory as it is proven in experience. Look at England: it is mainly on the free press that the preservation of its political and civil liberty, as well as its prosperity, depend. England knows what such a powerful weapon is worth, and England has therefore protected the press, just as the press has conversely protected England. . . .

We are starting out on a new path, and we must fight a powerful enemy, so we must necessarily turn to all the means that support our liberty and destroy the enemy's schemes and maneuvers. To this end it seems essential to bring together all of the nation's forces, and that would be impossible without concentrating its energy in a unanimous, spontaneous, and enlightened public opinion, to which freedom of the press will contribute greatly. . . .

The difference between me and those who disagree with me is that they see the evils of liberty as many and the advantages as few; I, on the other hand, believe that the evils are few and the advantages are many. All have spoken out against their dangers. . . . But however horrible this picture might be, can we forget the good aspects of civil society? . . . We are fallible men here, with all the mixture of good and bad that goes along with being human. . . . In sum, I believe that we would betray the people's desires and we would give weapons to the arbitrary government we have begun to overthrow if we did not decree freedom of the press.

The Cádiz Cortes passed the following law on the press.

SOURCE: *Colección de los decretos y órdenes que han expedido las Cortes generales y extraordinarias desde su instalación de 24 de setiembre de 1810 hasta igual fecha de 1811*, vol. 1 (Madrid: Imprenta Nacional, 1820), 14–17.

The General and Extraordinary Cortes, considering that the individual right of the citizens to publish their political thoughts and ideas is not only a check on the arbitrariness of those who govern, but also a means of enlightening the nation in general, and the only way to have true public opinion made known, has decided to decree the following:

1. All groups and private individuals of any condition or status have the freedom to write, print, and publish their political ideas without needing any prior permission, editing, or approval, subject to the restrictions and responsibilities that are expressed in this decree.

2. All current tribunals of the press and of prior censorship of political works are therefore abolished.

3. Authors and printers will be responsible for abuses of this liberty.

4. Libelous pamphlets, slanderous writings, those [texts] that are subversive of the fundamental laws of the monarchy, [and] those that are licentious and contrary to public decency and good customs will be punished with the weight of the law. . . .

5. The judges and tribunals will see to the investigation, judgment, and punishment of the crimes that are committed by the abuse of freedom of the press, following the guidelines of the laws and of this regulation.

6. All writings on matters of religion are subject to prior censorship by the regular clergy, as established by the Council of Trent.

7. Authors, under whose name that of the publisher or editor will appear, will not be obliged to put their names on the writings they publish, although they do not therefore escape being subject to the same responsibilities. Therefore, the printer must take note of who the author or editor of the work is. . . .

8. Printers are required to put their names and surnames and the place and year of publication on everything printed. . . .

9. Authors or publishers who, abusing the freedom of the press, violate these regulations will not only suffer the penalties indicated by the laws according to the gravity of the crime, but the crime and the punishment imposed on them will be published along with their names in the government newspaper. . . .

12. Printers of writings on matters of religion that lack prior approval of the clergy shall suffer the fines that are imposed on them in addition to those established by the laws, which they have incurred due to their excesses.

13. To assure freedom of the press, and at the same time to contain its abuses, the Cortes will name a Supreme Committee of Censorship . . . composed of nine individuals, and there will be another similar committee composed of five individuals named by them in each provincial capital.

14. Three of the members of the Supreme Committee of Censorship shall be clergymen, and two of the five on the provincial committees, and the rest will be laymen, educated subjects who have the virtue, probity, and talent needed for the grave task entrusted to them.

15. It will be their task to examine the works that have been denounced to the executive or judicial powers. . . .

16. The author or printer shall be allowed to ask for a copy of the censorship decree and to contest it. If the [provincial] committee confirms its prior decree of censorship, the interested party will have the right to demand that it be forwarded to the Supreme Committee. . . .

November 10, 1810

6. The Congress of Venezuela, Declaration of Independence (1811)

By the late 1700s, the residents of Spain's American colonies had reasons to resent the existing colonial order. Among the grievances of the wealthy Creoles (those born in America) were the domination of political offices by Spaniards born in Iberia and the Crown's taxes and trade restrictions. Given these resentments, one might have expected the arrival of Enlightenment ideas and the news of the American and French Revolutions to provoke independence movements, but because Creole elites in areas such as Venezuela lived in multiethnic societies where rebellions of slaves and people of color remained a constant threat, they refrained from challenging Spanish rule before 1808.

What finally triggered independence movements in the colonies was Napoleon's invasion of Spain, and particularly his decision to replace Charles IV and his son Ferdinand (taken to the French town of Bayonne) with his brother Joseph Bonaparte. With its true king absent, Spain no longer seemed an effective guarantor of social order in the colonies, and Creoles throughout the colonies began to meet and consider their options. In Venezuela, the news of ongoing political instability in Spain soon led to the creation of a junta that held elections for a Venezuelan Congress. That body, dominated by Creole elites, issued the following document in July 1811.

SOURCE: Daniel Florencio O'Leary, *Bolívar y la emancipación de Sur-América: Memorias del general O'Leary,* vol. 1, *1783–1819* (Madrid: Sociedad Española de Librería, 1915), 104–10.

In the name of Almighty God. We, the representatives of the united provinces . . . that make up the American Confederation of Venezuela in the Southern Continent, gathering in a Congress to consider the full and absolute possession of our rights, which we have justly and legitimately recovered since April 19, 1810 as a consequence of the [Bourbons'] journey to Bayonne and the occupation of the Spanish throne by the conquest and succession of another dynasty constituted without our consent, want—before using these rights of which we have been deprived by force for over three hundred years, and which the political order of human events has now restored to us—to explain to the whole world the logic that has emanated from these very events and that authorizes us to make free use of our sovereignty, as we intend to do.

Nevertheless, we do not want to start alleging the rights that every conquered nation has to recover its own property and independence. . . . We shall only point to the true and notorious facts that were bound to separate one world from the other and the upheaval, disorder, and conquest that have already dissolved the Spanish nation. . . .

It is contrary to the natural order . . . and has dreadful effects for America for a country infinitely larger and with an incomparably greater population to be dependent on and subject to a peninsular corner of the European continent. The surrenders and abdications of Bayonne, the [royal family's] journeys from El Escorial and Aranjuez [and other events] . . . force Americans to make use of those rights they have so far sacrificed in the interests of the Spanish nation's unity and integrity.

When the Bourbons agreed to the invalid Bayonne stipulations, abandoning Spanish territory against the will of the people, they betrayed, disrespected, and trampled on the sacred duty they had contracted with the Spaniards of both worlds. . . . By this action they rendered themselves unqualified and incapable of governing a free people, whom they turned over like a flock of slaves.

The usurping governments that appointed themselves as national representatives [in Cádiz] underhandedly took advantage of the attitude that good faith, distance, oppression, and ignorance created among the Americans against the new [Bonaparte] dynasty introduced by force in Spain; and, violating their own principles, they encouraged our illusions in favor of Ferdinand in order to destroy and harass us with impunity while promising us liberty, equality, and fraternity in pompous speeches and clever phrases. . . .

After various ruling powers in Spain were dissolved, replaced, and destroyed again, the stern law of necessity forced Venezuela to protect itself . . . against the evils that threatened it. . . . [Spanish authorities] then ignored all our prior conduct and, abandoning their own principles, denounced as insurrection, betrayal, and ingratitude the very things that served as principles for governments in Spain. . . . Despite our protests, our moderation, our generosity, and the inviolability of our principles, we were said to be in a state of revolt; we were blockaded and attacked; agents were sent to foment mutinies among us; and they sought to discredit us in the eyes of all the world's nations. . . .

In this painful situation we have spent three years, in a state of indecision and political ambiguity that is so harmful and dangerous that it alone would suffice to authorize our resolution, which the faithfulness our promises and the bonds of fraternity had obliged us to put off, until necessity forced us to go beyond what we had intended, impelled by the hostile and unnatural conduct of the Spanish authorities. . . .

In light of all these solid, public, and indisputable political reasons, and persuaded by the need to recover our natural dignity. . . ; and using the imprescriptible rights that all peoples have to destroy any pact, agreement, or association that does not fulfill the purposes for which governments were created, we believe we cannot and must not maintain the bonds that tied us to the government of Spain; and we believe, like all the peoples of the world, that we are free and entitled to depend on no other authority than our own and to take up a position as an equal among the countries of the earth, a position assigned to us by the Supreme Being and by nature, as well as by the course of human events and our own well-being and utility. . . .

As representatives of the United Provinces of Venezuela, we invoke the Supreme Being as witness of the justice of our actions, . . . believing in and defending the holy, Catholic, apostolic religion of Jesus Christ, as the first of our duties, . . . in the name of and according to the will of the virtuous people of Venezuela, and we solemnly declare to the world that our united provinces are and shall be from now on practically and legally free, sovereign, and independent states, absolved of any subjection and dependence on the Crown of Spain or those who claim to be its agents or representatives. . . . And as a free and independent state we have full powers to give ourselves the form of government that corresponds to the general will of the people. . . .

Given in the Federal Palace at Caracas, signed by our hands, . . . on the fifth day of the month of July 1811, the first year of independence.

7. The 1812 Constitution

In 1812, the Cortes formed two years earlier in Cádiz finished drafting its new constitution. That text featured a strong parliament that would share power with the king as soon as he returned, and it proclaimed many fundamental rights. Despite a certain ideological affinity between Spain's new constitution and the ideas of the French Revolution of 1789, the French, who still occupied much of Spain, rejected this assertion of Spanish authority, so the text had limited effect throughout much of the country. Nevertheless, the 1812 constitution—the most liberal in Europe at the time—provided the foundation for the government of unoccupied areas, and it also helped clarify and publicize the new political ideas, as well as serving as a model for both future Spanish constitutions and European revolutionaries of the nineteenth century.

SOURCE: *Colección de los decretos y órdenes que han expedido las Cortes generales y extraordinarias desde su instalación de 24 de setiembre de 1810 hasta igual fecha de 1811*, vol. 1 (Madrid: Imprenta Nacional, 1820), 98–101, 118–22, 125–29, 155–56.

In the name of God the Almighty, the Father, the Son, and the Holy Spirit, the author and supreme lawgiver of society.

The General and Extraordinary Cortes of the Spanish nation, firmly convinced, after the most careful examination and due deliberation, that the ancient fundamental laws of this monarchy, accompanied by opportune fortune and precautions, which assure its complete fulfillment in a stable and permanent way, will be able to fully achieve the great object of promoting the glory, the prosperity, and the well-being of all of the nation, decrees the following political constitution for the good government and the proper administration of the state:

On the Spanish Nation

Article 1. The Spanish nation is the sum of all the Spaniards of both hemispheres.

Article 2. The Spanish nation is free and independent and is not nor can be the property of any family or person.

Article 3. Sovereignty resides essentially in the nation, and therefore the right to establish its fundamental laws belongs exclusively to the nation. . . .

On the Spaniards

Article 5. The following are Spaniards:

First. All free men born and residing in Spanish territory, as well as their children.

Second. Foreigners who have obtained naturalization papers from the Cortes.

Third. Those who, lacking those papers, have lived for ten years under the laws of any part of the monarchy.

Fourth. Freed men, from the moment they acquire the liberty in Spanish territory. . . .

Article 7. Every Spaniard is obligated to be faithful to the constitution, to obey the laws, and to respect the established authorities.

Article 8. Every Spaniard, without any distinction, is also obligated to contribute, in proportion to his means, to the state's expenses.

Article 9. Every Spaniard is similarly obligated to defend the fatherland by arms whenever summoned by the law. . . .

On Religion

Article 12. The religion of the Spanish nation is and will always be the Roman, apostolic, Catholic religion, the only true one. The nation protects it with wise and just laws and prohibits the exercise of any other.

On the Government

Article 13. The goal of the government is the happiness of the nation, given that the end of any political society is nothing other than the well-being of the individuals who make it up.

Article 14. The government of the Spanish nation is a moderate hereditary monarchy.

Article 15. The power of making laws resides in the Cortes, with the king.

Article 16. The power to have the laws executed resides in the king.

Article 17. The power to apply the laws in civil and criminal trials resides in the courts established by the law. . . .

On the Cortes

Article 131. The powers of the Cortes are:

First. To propose and decree laws and to interpret and repeal them whenever necessary.

Second. To receive the oath of the king, the prince of Asturias, and the regency. . . .

Third. To resolve any doubt of fact or law concerning the succession to the Crown.

Fourth. To elect a regency or regent of the kingdom when the constitution calls for that, and to indicate the limits under which the regency or regent must exercise royal authority. . . .

Seventh. To approve treaties of offensive alliance, subsidies, and special commercial treaties prior to their ratification.

Eighth. To allow or deny the admission of foreign troops in the kingdom. . . .

Eleventh. To give orders to the army, navy, and national militia in all their branches. . . .

Twelfth. To determine the expenditures of the public administration.

Thirteenth. To set levels of taxation annually. . . .

On the Formation of the Laws and the Royal Sanction

Article 132. Any deputy has the power to propose bills to the Cortes, in writing, offering the reasons on which the proposals are based. . . .

Article 142. The king has the power to sanction the laws. . . .

Article 144. The king shall refuse laws by this formula. . . . "Return [this law] to the Cortes," sending along with his message of refusal an explanation of his reasons. . . .

On the King

Article 172. The restrictions on the king's authority are as follows:

First. The king may not, under any pretext, prevent the Cortes from meeting at times and under circumstances indicated in the constitution, nor may he suspend or dissolve it, nor harass its sessions and deliberations in any way. Those who would advise him or assist him in any such attempt are declared traitors, and will be prosecuted as such.

Second. The king may not leave the kingdom without the consent of the Cortes, and if he does so it will be understood that he has abdicated the Crown.

Third. The king may not alienate, cede, renounce, or transfer royal authority, nor any of its prerogatives, in any manner.

If for some reason he should wish to abdicate the throne in favor of his immediate successor, he shall not be allowed to do so without the consent of the Cortes.

Fourth. The king may not alienate, cede, renounce, or transfer any province, city, town, or place, nor any part, no matter how small, of Spanish territory.

Fifth. The king may not form any offensive alliance or special commercial treaty with any foreign power without the consent of the Cortes. . . .

Article 173. The king, upon his advent to the throne, and if he be a minor, when he begins to govern the kingdom, shall swear an oath before the Cortes, using the following text:

"I (here his name), by the grace of God and the constitution of the Spanish monarchy, king of Spain, do swear before God and the Holy Apostles that I will defend and protect the Roman, apostolic, Catholic religion, without permitting any other in the kingdom; that I will protect and see to the protection of the political constitution and laws of the Spanish monarchy, seeking nothing other than its well-being and prosperity; that I will neither cede nor dismember any part of the kingdom; that I will never demand any part of its products or money or any other thing other than that which the Cortes has decreed; that I will never take anyone's property; and that above all I will respect the nation's political liberty and the personal liberty of each individual; and if I should violate any part of what I have sworn, that I will not need to be obeyed, but rather what I have done that contradicts it shall be null and void. So may God help and defend me, and if I do not [respect this oath], may I be accountable to Him." . . .

On Public Education

Article 366. In all the towns of the monarchy, primary schools will be established, in which children will be taught reading, counting, and the catechism of the Catholic religion, . . . as well as a brief account of civil obligations.

Article 367. Similarly, it will be arranged that a number of competent universities and other educational establishments judged proper for the teaching of all the sciences, literature, and the fine arts [shall be established].

Article 368. The general educational plan will be uniform throughout the kingdom, with the political constitution of the monarchy having to be explained in all the universities and literary establishments in which ecclesiastical and political subjects are taught.

Article 369. There will be a general directorate of studies, composed of persons of known instruction, to whom the inspection of public education will be entrusted. . . .

Article 371. All Spaniards have the freedom to write, print, and publish their political ideas, without any need of license, review, or any prior approval for publication, subject to the restrictions and responsibilities established by the laws.

8. Ferdinand VII, Declaration on the Constitution (1814)

When Charles IV abdicated in 1808, few Spaniards knew much about his son Ferdinand, though hopes in his ability to regenerate Spain ran high. During the years of his captivity in France, Ferdinand remained the object of countless Spanish hopes for the future. What was unclear was how he would react to the work of the Cádiz Cortes, and whether he would accept the position marked out for him in the Constitution of 1812.

In 1813, Napoleon, defeated by the British in Spain, was concentrating on Central Europe, and after signing a treaty of alliance with Ferdinand, he allowed him to return home. Upon his return, Ferdinand refused the Cortes' call for him to come to Madrid, staying instead in Valencia in the company of army officers opposed to the Cortes and its liberal constitution. Ferdinand issued the following statement to the nation from Valencia on May 4, 1814.

SOURCE: *Gaceta extraordinaria de Madrid*, May 12, 1814.

Ever since Divine Providence placed me on the throne of my predecessors, by means of the spontaneous and solemn abdication of my august father, . . . and ever since that splendid day [in 1808] when I entered the capital amid the most sincere demonstrations of love and loyalty with which the people of Madrid came out to greet me, . . . I have felt a real desire to respond to such loyal sentiments, to satisfy the great obligations that a king has toward his people, and to dedicate all my time to the fulfillment of such august functions and to repair the damage done by the injurious influence of an impostor [Joseph Bonaparte] during the previous reign. My first acts concerned the restoration to office of various officials and other persons who had been arbitrarily separated from their proper destinies. . . .

[In 1808] I had sought to protect my people from the cruel effects of the difficulty of the situation and the treachery of Bonaparte, by going to Bayonne. . . . With the royal family gathered there, such an atrocious offense was committed against it, and particularly against me, that the history of civilized nations offers no parallel. . . . With the highest and most sacred of people's rights being violated, I was deprived of my liberty and the government of my kingdom and transferred with my very dear brother and uncle to a palace that served as a glorified prison for almost six years. Throughout this time of suffering, I always kept in mind the love and loyalty of my people, and a large part of my suffering was my awareness of the endless evils to which they were exposed; [my people were] surrounded by enemies, were almost completely without means of resisting them, were without their king and without a previously established government that could mobilize and bring together the forces of the nation, guiding them and taking advantage of the resources of the state to combat the considerable powers that were simultaneously invading the peninsula. . . .

From among the deputies that the [provincial] juntas had named a central junta was formed, which in my royal name exercised all the powers of sovereignty from September 1808 to January 1810, when the first Council of the Regency was formed; [the council] continued to exercise that power until September 24 of that year, when the Cortes known as the General and Extraordinary Cortes was installed, . . . swearing and promising to preserve all of my domains for me as its sovereign. . . . But this Cortes was convoked in a way that has never been seen in Spain, even in the most trying times; . . . the estates of the nobility and the clergy were not called even though the central junta had ordered it. . . .

In this way everything came under the power of the Cortes, which on the very day of its installation and as the basis of its acts deprived me of the sovereignty that those very same deputies had just recognized in me, as they attributed it, in theory, to the nation while actually appropriating it for themselves. Then based on that usurpation of sovereignty, the Cortes gave the nation the laws it saw fit, imposing on it the yoke of a new constitution. . . . This first attack on the prerogatives of the throne, abusing the name of the nation, was the basis of many more that followed. And despite the opposition of many deputies, perhaps the majority, laws . . . were adopted amid the shouts, threats, and violence of the spectators attending the sessions in the hall of the Cortes, intimidating and terrorizing [the deputies]. So what was really the work of a faction was dressed up with the specious name of the general will; and so the work of a few subversives in Cádiz, and later in Madrid, went out to cause concern and sorrow for good people. These facts are so notorious that there is hardly anyone who is not aware of them, and the very *Journal of the Cortes* gives ample testimony of all of them. A method of lawmaking that is so foreign to the Spanish nation gave rise to the changing of laws that in other times had made that nation so respected and happy. In truth, almost the entire form of the old constitution of the monarchy was changed; and copying the revolutionary and democratic principles of the French constitution of 1791, . . . [the Cortes] passed laws that were not those of a moderate monarchy, but rather of a popular government with a chief or magistrate, a mere delegate, as executive. . . . With the same lack of liberty, this new constitution was signed and sworn to, and everyone knows . . . the penalties threatened against those who would not sign or swear to it.

Then to prepare people to accept such enormous novelties, especially those relating to my royal person and the prerogatives of the throne, they sought to make the idea of royal power hateful, giving all of the rights of majesty the name of despotism, making the terms king and despot synonymous and calling kings tyrants; [they did this] through the means of the public newspapers, for some of which various deputies of the Cortes worked, abusing freedom of the press, which the Cortes had established. And at the same time they cruelly persecuted anyone who had the strength to contradict or even dissent from this revolutionary and seditious way of thinking. All this was done under the name of democracy, and they took away the title of "royal" from the army, the navy, and all the establishments that had long been called that, instead calling them "national," thus flattering the people, who, in spite of such perverse schemes, retained . . . the good sentiments that always marked their character.

As soon as I happily entered the kingdom, I began to learn of all this, in part through my own observations and in part from the newspapers, in which even in those days very crude and infamous things were imprudently said about my arrival and my character—things that would be very serious offenses worthy of severe punishment even if they were said about someone else. Such unexpected things filled my heart with bitterness; only partly was this lessened by the demonstrations of love by all those who were waiting for my arrival so that with my presence I could put an end to these evils and to the oppression that was facing those who still harbored in their souls the memory of my person, and who yearned for the true happiness of the fatherland. I swear and promise to you, true and loyal Spaniards, that as I suffer from the evils that have plagued you, you will not be disappointed in your noble hopes. Your sovereign wishes to be that for you, and in this he places his glory, in being the sovereign of a heroic nation, which with immortal acts has earned the admiration of all, preserving its liberty and honor.

I revile and detest despotism. The nations of Europe now no longer bear it; nor were Spain's kings ever despots, nor did its good laws and constitution authorize it, even if unfortunately we have sometimes seen, as in all countries, . . . abuses of power that no constitution could have prevented. . . .

I will work with representatives of Spain and the Indies, in a Cortes legitimately formed . . . as soon as order and the good customs by which the nation has lived are reestablished . . . so that my vassals may live in prosperity and the happiness of a religion and an empire closely united in unbreakable bonds. . . . Individual and royal liberty and security will remain firmly guaranteed through the means of laws that, assuring public tranquility and order, . . . distinguish a moderate government from an arbitrary and despotic government. . . . Also, everyone will enjoy this just liberty, communicating their ideas and thoughts through the means of the press, within those limits that sane reason . . . prescribes for all so that they do not degenerate into license, for no civilized government can reasonably allow the respect that is owed to religion and to the government—and that men owe each other—to be trampled on and broken with impunity. All suspicions about the wasting of the revenue of the state will also cease, as we separate the money that is assigned . . . for the expenses that the dignity of my royal person and family demand from those of the nation I have the glory of commanding. . . . And the laws that must duly serve as guidelines for the actions of my subjects will be passed with the agreement of the Cortes. And so that those laws will serve as a sure announcement of my royal intentions in the government I am going to lead, making known to all not a despot or a tyrant, but a king and a father of his vassals.

And so, I have heard what respectable persons . . . have unanimously told me, and that which has been expressed in representations sent to me from various parts of the kingdom, representations in which repugnance and disgust for the constitution drafted by the Cortes . . . have been expressed; [and I have heard] how the other newly introduced political establishments are seen in the provinces, and the damage and evils that have arisen from them, and how much they would increase if I were to authorize that constitution with my consent by swearing to it. In conformance with the decisive and general expressions of the will of my people, which is just and well founded, I declare that my royal will is not to swear to or accept that constitution or any decrees of the . . . Cortes currently in session, namely, those that are prejudicial to the rights and prerogatives of my sovereignty, established by the constitution and laws under which the nation has long lived. I also declare that constitution and those decrees to be null and void, now and at all times, as if those acts had never been passed, . . . so that my people and subjects of any class or condition are not obligated to fulfill or keep them. And whoever wishes to retain them and to contradict my royal declaration . . . , attacking the prerogatives of my sovereignty and the happiness of the nation and causing disturbances and worries in my kingdoms, I declare guilty of treason. The penalty of death shall be imposed upon anyone who . . . dares or attempts, . . . by writing or speaking, acting or inciting, or in any way exhorting and arguing that the said constitution and laws should be kept and observed. . . .

This is my will, which both the well-being and the happiness of the nation demand.

9. Army Proclamation of 1820

After Ferdinand VII returned from exile in France in 1814, he reversed most of what the liberal Cádiz Cortes had done, overturning the 1812 constitution and reasserting royal prerogatives. The king's government, however, proved rather inept, and the country's economy stagnated. Among those Spaniards most upset about the restoration of royal "absolutism" were members of the urban middle classes, along with many army officers. The officers had some political differences with Ferdinand's regime, but they were also angry over matters such as salaries, promotions, and favoritism toward nobles within the military.

In 1820, after several other military revolts had failed, a group of officers led by Major Rafael de Riego decided to launch a campaign to restore the liberal constitutional order. The rebels issued this proclamation in January in Cádiz, hoping to rally a widespread movement, and though the proclamation met a somewhat disappointing response, few showed any enthusiasm for supporting Ferdinand's government either. When the troops arrived in Madrid, the king gave in and accepted the restoration of a constitutional order. This revolt helped establish a precedent in Spain for the *pronunciamiento,* in which officers "pronounced" their will (often proclaimed to be the will of the people) and urged others to help overturn an existing government or regime.

SOURCE: *Correo Universal de Literatura y Política* 1 (April 1820): 18–19.

The national army, in declaring its support for the constitution of the Spanish monarchy proclaimed in Cádiz by its legal representatives, is in no way seeking to sabotage the legal monarch's rights as recognized in the constitution. Nevertheless, convinced that all the government's policies have come to naught, in a way that is as lamentable as it is incomprehensible, and have caused the downfall of a nation that made so many sacrifices to support the monarchy, [the army] believes that this coup alone can save both the nation and the prince from the current predicament.

The army has no intention of endangering the security of property or persons, nor does it seek to make innovations contrary to the equity, justice, and faith of our fathers. We reject any kind of subversive spirit; the motives behind this action are not merely transitory babblings. Only the purest patriotism [and] the most ardent yearning for the country's well-being have led to the most solemn of oaths, that we will offer our last drop of blood to ensure that we attain these goals. The rest of the Spanish army, which has spared no sacrifice in promoting the nation's salvation, honor, and glory, and the entire nation, which has provided the world with such shining examples of heroism, will not resist applauding the citizens' feelings and staunch determination. This gratifying ideal will be the reward for their efforts, and all of those in whom a noble and magnanimous heart beats will follow this example.

People of Spain: it is up to you to follow this example; it is up to you to live up to your past glories or to descend forever into an abyss of shame. The choice is clear, and all of Europe, which is watching you, will not lose the respect it holds for the nation that six years ago cast off its lethargy and determined its own fate.

Ordered at headquarters, in the absence of the commander in chief.
Chief of the military staff, Felipe de Arco Agüero.

10. Ferdinand VII, Manifesto of October 1, 1823

After the military's seizure of power in 1820, Ferdinand VII cooperated very reluctantly with the liberal constitutional order the army had reinstated. In 1823, however, the French, now under the conservative rule of a restored monarchy, sent troops into Spain to topple the liberal regime and restore Ferdinand to full power. Once French troops gained control of the situation in Spain, Ferdinand made the following declaration to the nation.

SOURCE: Don Antonio Pirala, *Historia de la guerra civil, y de los partidos liberal y Carlista*, 2nd ed., vol. 1 (Madrid: Imprenta de los Señores F. de P. Mellado y C., 1868), 580–81.

The scandalous events that preceded, accompanied, and followed the establishment of the democratic constitution of Cádiz in the month of March 1820 are only too well known to my vassals. The most criminal situation, the most shameful cowardice, the most horrendous disrespect to my royal person, and the most inevitable violence were the elements used to fundamentally transform the paternal government of my kingdoms into a democratic code, a fertile source of disaster and misfortune. My vassals, accustomed to living under wise and moderate laws adapted to their customs and traditions—laws that for so many centuries had made their forefathers happy—quickly gave public and universal proof of their disdain, disapproval, and disregard for the new constitutional regime. All of the country's classes felt resentment toward institutions that they could see would lead to their misery and misfortune.

Everywhere, the general wish protested against the tyrannical constitution, clamored for the suspension of a code that was null because of its origins, illegal in the way it was formed, and unjust in its content. It clamored, finally, for the support of the holy religion of our elders, for the restoration of fundamental laws, and for the preservation of my legitimate rights, which I inherited from my forefathers, and to which my vassals had sworn with all due solemnity. . . .

Now seated once again on the throne of San Fernando by the wise and just hand of the Omnipotent, by the generous resolution of my powerful allies, and by the daring efforts of my cousin, the duke of Angoulême and his courageous army; wishing to offer a remedy for the most urgent needs of my people and to demonstrate my true liberty to the entire world, I have decided to decree the following:

1. The acts of the so-called constitutional government . . . that has dominated my people from March 7, 1820 until today, October 1, 1823 are null and

void. I declare that throughout this entire period I have not been free, [but rather] forced to sanction laws and expedite orders, decrees, and regulations that this government considered and proclaimed against my will.

2. I approve everything that has been decreed by the provisional junta of government and by the regency of the kingdom, . . . with it being fully understood that until I am fully informed of the needs of my people, it can make laws and dictate policies more suited to creating true prosperity and happiness, the constant object of all my desires.

11. The Carlist Movement (1833)

Ferdinand VII, despite his attacks on liberals, soon found himself under pressure from rich merchants and others to liberalize his system of rule, so despite his own conservative inclinations, he gradually oversaw a regime incorporating aspects of liberalism. Yet doing so brought opposition from Spain's most conservative elements, known as the *apostólicos,* who favored measures such as the restoration of the Inquisition. Those conservatives, concentrated in rural areas in the north, eventually took up arms in a rebellion against the Crown. After that rebellion was defeated, the *apostólicos* began rallying around Ferdinand's brother Carlos, who shared their views.

As Ferdinand grew older, Carlos and his conservative followers, known as "Carlists," took heart, knowing that because Ferdinand had no children, Carlos stood first in line to inherit the throne. In 1830, however, Ferdinand and his fourth wife had a daughter, raising the possibility that Carlos might be denied the throne. At that point, Carlos and his followers pointed out a law, known as the Salic Law, under which the first Spanish Bourbon, Philip V (reigned 1700–1746), had declared that no woman could inherit the throne. Unfortunately for Carlos, it turned out that Charles IV (1788–1808) had secretly abrogated that law. The Carlists denied the legitimacy of that abrogation on the grounds that no Cortes had ratified it, but the disagreement persisted. In the following letter from 1833, Carlos explains his position to his dying brother.

When Ferdinand died, his wife María Cristina became regent until their daughter, Isabella II (reigned 1833–1868) was old enough to become queen. The Carlists then took up arms, fighting a civil war that ended in their defeat, but the movement persisted for another century.

SOURCE: Don Antonio Pirala, *Historia de la guerra civil, y de los partidos liberal y Carlista,* 2nd ed., vol. 1 (Madrid: Imprenta de los Señores F. de P. Mellado y C., 1868), 592–93, 599–600.

My very dear and beloved brother, Ferdinand, mine for life. It was with the greatest pleasure that I saw from your letter of the 23rd [of April] . . . that you are well, as are Cristina and your daughters; we are also well, thanks to God. . . .

What you would like to know is whether I have the intention of swearing loyalty to your daughter as princess of Asturias [i.e., heiress to the throne]. How I wish I could do so! You must believe me, for you know me, and I am speaking from the heart, that the greatest pleasure I could have had would be to swear and not to cause you this displeasure and the others that result from it; but my conscience and honor do not permit me to do so; I have legitimate rights to the Crown if I survive you and you do not leave behind a male heir; I cannot overlook these rights, which God gave me when it was his will that I be born, and only God can take them away by giving you a male child, which I desire as much as you do, perhaps even more than you do. Besides, I am defending the rights that those who will come after me will have, and so it is that you see me needing to send you this declaration. . . .

I, Carlos María Isidro de Borbón y Borbón, heir to the throne of Spain, finding myself fully convinced of my legitimate rights to the Crown of Spain, if I should survive Your Majesty and you do not leave behind a male heir, do state that neither my conscience nor my honor permit me to swear to or to recognize any other rights [to the Crown]; this I declare.

The Carlists, whose following was strongest in Catalonia, Navarre, and the Basque country, sought to rally their troops in the civil war through posters such as this one, which appeared unsigned and undated in the Basque region of Guipúzcoa:

Spaniards: While all of Europe finds itself armed for the defense of the legitimacy of Henry V, a demagogic faction, originating in the filthy classes of Paris to submerge us in the abyss of atheism and heresy, is trying to usurp the throne of Carlos V, summoned by the fundamental law of the monarchy to be the successor of San Fernando, whose virtues he imitates, and whose zeal for religion constitutes one of the beautiful traits that make up the character of this singular prince, chosen by heaven many years ago, and tested in various ways for being a king, according to the heart of God. Spaniards: Ferdinand, already declared incapable, not by men but by God himself, who has him lying on his deathbed, from which he will not rise, and even by himself, in that he named his spouse to govern, [is] legally disqualified. Ferdinand, who is dying, now no longer reigns legally or in fact, for he is dead in a civil sense. The faction that has taken over his governing spouse has thrown the whole kingdom into turmoil. A tyrannical separation of the government from the capitals of the king's good vassals, substituting those most complicit in the revolutionary system of the constitution and the [parliamentary] chambers; an ill-advised amnesty, contrary to all the principles of civilized nations; the impending imposition of the French charter, which has touched off revolution all over Europe; minority seated on the throne; the call to the French to assist in Cristina's usurpation; the toleration of all religions; the extinction of the Carlist volunteers, the Jesuits, and the religious orders; finally, the extermination of the clergy and the religion of Jesus Christ; this is the sad portrait that the very government of Cristina has already presented to you in just a few days. The legitimate granddaughter of María Luisa, she seems destined, like her mother, to bring foreign domination into our midst.

Will you put up with this, brave men of 1808? You, who without arms, without armies, without resources, and having lost the fortresses, opposed the armies of the tyrant Bonaparte? You, who defeated the so-called invincible, will you fall to the ground at the sight of impotent threats from a bloodthirsty sect? I do not believe so; Carlos, the unconquered and virtuous Carlos, is worthy of your sacrifices, and with him as our leader, victory will crown your efforts, and his generous hand will repay your courage. To arms, royalist volunteers: long live the absolute king, with Carlos V ruling, and legitimacy. Death forever to the atheists and the heretics, enemies of our God.

12. Joaquim Rubió y Ors, The Catalan *Renaixença* (1841)

Reflecting the growth of nationalism in the wake of the French Revolution, as well as the rise of the Romantic movement, a resurgence of interest in the Catalan language and culture known as the *Renaixença* (Renaissance), took place during the nineteenth century. Although knowledge of the language had declined in recent centuries—particularly under the centralizing rule of the Bourbon dynasty established in the early eighteenth century—the publication of Bonaventura Carles Aribau's "Ode to the Fatherland" in Catalan in 1833 helped renew interest in Catalan culture, and soon a handful of writers such as Joaquim Rubió y Ors (1818–1899) sought to promote Catalan culture and pride by publishing works in the language. The following passage is the introduction to a collection of poems Rubió published under the title *Lo gaiter del Llobregat*, "The Piper of the Llobregat." (The Llobregat is a river in Catalonia.)

SOURCE: Joaquim Rubió y Ors, *Lo gaiter del Llobregat*, 2nd ed. (Barcelona: Librería de Joseph Rubió, 1858), v–xii.

The ardent love I have and have always had for the things of my fatherland, the enthusiasm with which I would like my compatriots to know more fully our ancient, melodious, and rich language, which is unfortunately being lost day by day, despite being a slab of marble upon which our glories are inscribed, . . . and finally the desire to awaken that noble and praiseworthy sentiment in others are the only reasons that have moved me, the author of these poems, to bring them to public light, hoping not that my compatriots will judge them for what they are in themselves or for their artistic merit, but rather that they might view them as the outpouring of a young heart still surrounded by all the illusions of life, by one who has wanted to unburden himself by leaving on the paper everything he was feeling, just as the flower casts to the winds the scents it has in abundance. In publishing them, I seek only to inspire palpitations in the hearts of those true Catalans who will take the trouble to read them. . . .

I know that some will reply that there are serious difficulties in wanting to write verse in a tongue of which the grammar is almost unknown; also that one can sing of our ancient glories and the deeds of our forefathers in Castilian [Spanish] without losing the same effect. But can it be that our language is so rough and poor that it does not more than repay the effort spent in studying it? . . .

It was a century and a quarter ago, in the attack on Barcelona (September of 1714), that our forefathers fought for fourteen consecutive hours in defense of their ancient privileges, and their blood flowed copiously from the walls, plazas, and temples of this city, in order to be able to transmit to their grandchildren the heritage and language that their ancestors had left them. And though so little time has passed, not only have their descendants forgotten all of this, but some of them, ungrateful toward their forefathers, are even ashamed to be caught speaking Catalan, like a criminal caught in the act. But this will stop, at least so the author of these poems has promised himself . . . in light of the growing affection that is beginning to take root among our compatriots toward everything related to our history.

As for those who reply that Castilian can also awaken similar sentiments in us, as long as one seeks to celebrate the glories of our fatherland, the author of this collection will be content to respond to them by asking them to place their hands over their hearts, and to judge afterward based on what this says to them.

One cannot deny that despite being Catalans we have to overcome certain difficulties to be able to write verse easily in our language, but one can deny that this is sufficient motive to excuse us from singing in it. Those who find it harsh, poor, and badly suited for poetry do not really know it. Catalan is sweet in spite of the exotic words that have been introduced into it and the extent to which it has been corrupted by our neglect and abandonment of it; it is as rich as any other of the languages descended from Latin, among which it was the oldest; and it is just as easily, or more easily, adapted to use in verse as the others, except for Italian, because it still retains many of the constructions of the Latin, and because of the great number of single-syllable words that make it elastic, concise, energetic, and harmonious.

I speak in this way not out of a spirit of provincialism or because others whose authority I respect have said this, but because I am convinced of it. No one can better evaluate the wealth of a mine than one who works in it . . . and who has gone down into it to touch the vein. As soon as I heard the word "troubadour," which was unfortunately very late; as soon as I heard young friends speaking . . . of these young minstrels who went from castle to castle [in the Middle Ages] to entertain the barons in times of peace, and who put down their soft caps for helmets in times of war; these young musicians, who were both poets and knights, who so swiftly came to lay at the feet of their ladies the wreath of silver they had won in a literary contest, like the embroidered band with which the queen of a tournament had rewarded their bravery; these young musicians, in sum, who spent their lives singing of love, religion, and chivalry, I was seized with a burning desire to know more about them—a desire that has continued to grow, and which I have in part had the chance to fulfill. . . .

I have searched and continue to search the entire gallery of troubadours from William of Aquitaine to the modest Aribau, who seems to have wished to place the seal on our poets' songs with his "Ode to the Fatherland." . . . I have examined and am still examining, part by part, these venerable and gigantic monuments of the past centuries. . . . I have studied and continue to study these poems written in an almost unknown language, in which such painful suffering, such passionate sentiments, such secret palpitations are expressed; those that seem to be . . . epitaphs written on the tombs of the same ones who sang them, and that are of interest for the very reason that no one remembers them; my limited talent is to blame if they do not yield the profit they should, and if my poems, instead of being a practical argument for what I have just said in favor of my language, only serve to contradict that. . . . I hope that my compatriots will treat the work generously . . . for the effort it took and for the intentions with which it was made, as long as it is promised that others whom the heavens have favored with greater talents will take up the task of studying our language enthusiastically. . . .

Catalonia can once again aspire to independence, not in a political sense, since it carries little weight in comparison with other nations, which can throw into the balance, in addition to the bulk of their history, armies of many thousands of men and fleets of hundreds of ships; but rather in the realm of literature. . . . Over the course of two centuries, Catalonia was the master over other peoples in letters. Why, then, can it not cease to play the humiliating role of disciple or imitator, creating for itself a literature of its own that is distinct from that of Castile? Why can it not reestablish its *Jocs Florals* [Floral Games, a medieval poetry contest] . . . and once again surprise the world with its love songs, tensons, sirventes and aubades [genres of medieval song and poetry]? A little bit of effort would be enough for it to regain the literary importance it enjoyed in other times, and if God should permit this idea to be realized one day, and if the Catalan geniuses were to pick up the harps of the troubadours that have been so long forgotten, the Piper of the Llobregat, however weak his forces may be, would henceforth be committed to help it find the place it deserves, even if it be in the last rank, and to win the crown of poetry that our fatherland so shamefully allowed to fall from its head and which the other peoples picked up and took over.

In the meantime, from this day on, the author of these meager efforts, the product of two years' worth of work and study, will consider himself more than rewarded with all he might merit from his compatriots if they will say to each other what Doctor Ballat said to himself at the end of his work on grammar: "So speak in Catalan, God has given it glory."

13. Fernando Garrido, On Communism (1848)

Always attuned to events in the rest of Europe, Spaniards watched closely as a wave of revolutions swept across Europe in 1848. In that same year, Karl Marx and Friedrich Engels published their *Communist Manifesto.* Although Spain's industrial working classes remained far too small to pose any real threat to the liberal regime, the beginnings of a politicized working-class movement were sufficient to create concern among Spain's property-owning classes.

Here, one writer addresses those fears and offers his own ideas on how Spain should proceed. Fernando Garrido y Tortosa (1821–1883), born in Cartagena and raised in Cádiz, was an early socialist and republican who founded various publications. Garrido spent much of the 1850s in political exile, but he was elected to Spain's Cortes after the revolution of 1868.

SOURCE: *La Organización del Trabajo* 6 (April 27, 1848): 129–30.

Communism is for many a terrible and bloody specter. Rejected everywhere by the governing powers, viewed with horror or disdain, to speak its name is to condemn it. Persecution and violence are used to annihilate it, and in the hands of the powerful and of dominators of all kinds, it has come to be what a scarecrow is to birds in the fields, the bogeyman with which one frightens honorable, peaceful, and ignorant people. "Communist" is a synonym for traitor, for cannibal, and according to [the newspaper] *La España*, [communists] are advancing with a leveling ax through the mountain passes of the Pyrenees, using a seductive and enchanting melody to fool the unwary. Today, any citizen who has anything to lose and any governing power is on guard against this wild monster. But how? How do they hope to conjure away their siren song or their leveling blows? With persecution, with ridicule, declaring it a crime of treason against society to be a communist.

But what is this communism that is agitating so many minds against it? Where has this lethal specter come from? We are going to explain and to try to show how far people are from understanding it and from freeing themselves from it by the means they are using.

Communism, despite all its variations and in all its aspects, is nothing other than the logical result of the social disorder in which we are living, the consequence of so many centuries of disorder, oppression, hypocrisy, legal theft, immorality and exclusivism, monopolies, the cornering of markets, and miseries of all kinds produced all at once by the clash of interests. And so, insofar as these evils grow, insofar as civilization advances by these false paths, communism progresses despite the sermons, the worrying, the opposition, and the ridicule that is pitted against it. The results of its application will be horrible, all the more so if the opposition it encounters forces it to use oppression and violence to establish itself; but when the greatest number suffers the evils that the past centuries have left us, by what right will one seek to subject them to one's domination? How can one not see the abundance that the communist society promises in an enchanting light? Isn't it ridiculous to ask those who lack bread or who cannot give their children the things they need to ponder the duties and joys of the family and to consider it the basis of all social order? What father would not prefer to separate from his family—if, as it is supposed, communism demands that of him—if it meant that he could see them have what they needed? It is said that communism will take away the freedom they now enjoy; but is this true? Does this liberty really exist other than in theory for the greatest number of men, condemned to ignorance and even to being made stupid, to misery, to dependence, to enslavement by the rich and the intelligent? If we suppose that communism will take away this illusory right, wouldn't they gain by exchanging it for security of subsistence, for the reassuring confidence in the future that the communist society guarantees them?

What is said about the family can also be said about property: however sacred this right may be, when only a small number of privileged people can use it—and generally to the detriment of the greatest number who own nothing—is it not natural for [the greatest number] to view it as an enemy of their well-being?

This is why, despite the persecutions the communists suffer throughout Europe, we are sure to see their ideas spread rapidly, flowing over the dikes built against them, inundating all the working classes and no small part of the middle class, at least if this state of social disorder and incoherence continues. Neither then nor now will we hold them responsible for their ideas or their conduct, which are only the consequences of the social chaos in which we are living. This is why we are proposing an association that, by fulfilling the needs and desires of *all*, will keep the masses away from this dangerous path toward which the ignorance of the powerful—who only know how to be powerful at the price of the people's blood and misery—is pushing them.

The only effective means of ending uprisings and revolutions once and for all is the satisfaction of the needs of those who are kept from that satisfaction by injustice and misery. Those who think this can be accomplished through persuasion are fooling themselves badly. Fooling themselves even more seriously are those who think that by applying palliative and partial measures such as undertaking public works in which the hungry earn a meager salary, or increasing and organizing charity, or gathering the disadvantaged in institutions, or persecuting vagrants, that they are thus fulfilling their duties and that they have therefore earned the people's gratitude and can demand that the people reject communism, given that they would no longer have the right and would no longer need anything else; these people, we repeat, are also fooling themselves. Those crumbs, those rags for which they make the people pay so dearly, and because of which the sellers seem to be so satisfied with their good works—as if this were some great deed—do nothing more than highlight the injury and stir up the hatred, by humiliating those who receive them. May all beware; we are saying this loud and clear for all to hear; if they really wish to free themselves from this enemy, which is much closer than they realize, if they want to chase away this terrible specter, which they claim to disdain but which frightens them so; if they do not want, sooner or later, but inevitably, to fall prey to it, and thus to see the ruin of their property and their families, let them look seriously at our program; let them listen to our fraternal and reconciling voice, which cries out to them: *association*.

Let them consider and observe nature, and they will see this formula, this condition of life in general, incarnated in all the movements of creation. The misfortunes of all kinds that afflict men amid the harmonious arrangements of nature will not stop until one applies to human societies the law of nature: the principle of *association*.

We have said it before, we repeat it now, and we will not stop saying it; social incoherence is the cause of the evils of past and present and those that threaten our future—terrible, incalculable evils from which we can only be freed by a harmonizing of interests, the complete *association* of *capital*, of *labor*, and of *talent*.

14. Juan Donoso Cortés, On Religion and Liberty (1849)

By the middle of the nineteenth century, few Spaniards still believed that absolutism remained a viable system. The Carlists certainly did, but those conservatives unwilling to join the Carlists generally began reconciling themselves to ideas such as parliamentary representation, constitutions, and some measure of political liberty. Consequently, conservatives competed for positions in a parliamentary system about which they still had great misgivings. Those who chose to participate in that system, however, used their powers to try to guard Spain against what they saw as dangerous innovations—especially any measures designed to weaken the Church's authority in Spain.

The following speech is by a leading spokesman of the conservatives in Spain's Cortes in the middle of the nineteenth century. Juan Donoso Cortés (1809–1853), from Estremadura, was elected to the Cortes in 1833 as a Moderate, but by 1849 he had broken with the liberals and sided with the most conservative deputies in the Cortes.

SOURCE: Juan Donoso Cortés, *Oeuvres de Donoso Cortés, Marquis de Valdegamas, ancien ambassadeur d'Espagne près de la cour de France*, vol. 1 (Paris: Librairie d'Auguste Vaton, 1858), 325–37.

The cause of all your errors, gentlemen [addressing the benches on the left], consists of not knowing in what direction civilization and the world are going. You believe that civilization and the world are progressing, when in fact the world and civilization are regressing. The world, gentlemen, is heading rapidly toward the construction of a despotism, the most gigantic and destructive that men can remember. . . . To announce these things I do not need to be a prophet. It is enough to consider the frightening conjunction of human events from the only reliable point of view: from the Catholic heights.

Gentlemen, there are only two possible kinds of repression: one internal and the other external, one religious and one political. It is the nature of these that when the religious thermometer is high, the thermometer of repression is low, and when the religious thermometer is low, the political thermometer, the level of political repression, tyranny, is high. This is a law of humanity, a law of history.

And if you do not believe this, gentlemen, look at what the world once was, look at what society without the cross was, and tell me how it was when there was no internal repression, no religious repression. It was then a society of tyranny and slaves. Show me a single people from that time in which there were no slaves and no tyranny. This is an incontrovertible fact, this is an undeniable fact, this is an obvious fact. Liberty, true liberty, the liberty of all and for all only came to the world with the Savior of the world. (*"Very good!, Very good!"*) This is also an undeniable fact, a fact recognized even by the socialists, . . . [who] call themselves his successors. His successors, holy God! They, those men of blood and vengeance, successors of the one who lived only to do good; . . . of the one who in the space of three years made the greatest revolution that the centuries have seen, and carried it out without having spilled any blood other than his own! (*Lively and general applause.*) . . .

In the ancient world, when religious repression could not go any lower, because there was none, political repression went to where it could go no higher, for it reached the point of tyranny. But then, with Jesus Christ, with whom religious repression was born, political repression disappeared completely. The society Jesus Christ founded with his disciples was the only one that has existed without a government. Among Jesus and his disciples there was no government, only the love of the master for his disciples and the love of the disciples for their master. This is to say that when internal repression was complete, liberty was absolute. . . .

Then came the Middle Ages, and at that time religion was still at its peak, but it was ruined to a point by human passions. What happened at this time in the political world? A real and effective government became necessary, but the weakest of all possible governments, and so the feudal monarchy was established, the weakest of all monarchies. . . .

Then came the sixteenth century. In that century, with the great Protestant Reformation, with this intellectual and moral emancipation of peoples, the following institutions arose: in the first place, feudal monarchies turned absolute. . . . The thermometer of political repression had to go higher, because the religious thermometer kept going lower. And what new institution was created? That of permanent armies, . . . and a soldier is a slave in a uniform. . . . It was not enough for governments to be absolute; they also asked for and obtained the privilege of being absolute and also having a million men in arms. . . .

[In time] the religious thermometer continued to go down, so the political thermometer had to go up. . . . Governments said: "It is not enough, in order to repress, to have a million arms. We also need a million eyes." So the police were created. . . . Still it was not enough for governments to have a million arms, to have a million eyes; they also wanted to have a million ears. So administrative centralization was invented, through which all demands and complaints made their way to the government.

Well, gentlemen, that was still not enough; with the religious thermometer still falling, the political thermometer had to go even higher. And it did go higher. Governments said: "In order to repress, it is not enough to have a million arms, a million eyes, and a million ears; we need even more. We need the privilege of being everywhere at the same time in our empire." And they got it, as the telegraph was invented. (*Great applause.*)

Gentlemen, such was the state of Europe and the world when the first outbreak of revolution announced to all of us that there was still not enough despotism in the world. [And there is still not], for the religious thermometer remains below zero. . . .

Either a religious reaction will happen or not; if there is a religious reaction, you will see how, as the religious thermometer starts to go down naturally, spontaneously, without any effort on people's part, or the government's part, the political thermometer will point to the liberty of peoples. ("*Bravo!*") But if, on the contrary, . . . the religious thermometer keeps going down, I don't know where we'll end up. . . .

Only one thing can prevent a catastrophe, only one. It will not be avoided by giving more liberty, more guarantees, new constitutions; it will be avoided . . . by provoking a healthy, religious reaction. . . . Gentlemen, here I speak with the most profound sadness; I do not believe this likely. I have seen and known many individuals who lost their faith and returned to it; unfortunately, gentlemen, I have never seen a single nation that returned to its faith after having lost it. . . .

From the beginning of the world until now it has been debatable whether it was better to avoid revolutions and unrest through a system of resistance or a system of concessions . . . but [as of 1848] it is no longer a question of that kind. . . .

If it were a matter of choosing between liberty and dictatorship, there would be no disagreement; for who could refuse liberty and choose to bow before dictatorship? . . . The question is one of choosing between the dictatorship of revolution and the dictatorship of the government; placed in these terms, I choose the dictatorship of the government as a less burdensome one. (*Applause from the deputies of the majority.*) It is a matter of choosing between a dictatorship that comes from above or a dictatorship that comes from below, and I choose the one from above, because it is purer and more serene; it is, finally, a matter of choosing between the dictatorship of the dagger or that of the sword: I choose the dictatorship of the sword, because it is nobler. ("*Bravo!*") You, gentlemen [addressing the left], you, as always, will vote for what is most popular, and we, gentlemen [addressing the right], we, as always, will vote for what is most salutary.

15. Liberal Principles (1868–1869)

In the mid-nineteenth century, two parties, the Moderates and Progressives, competed for power in Spain's parliamentary, constitutional monarchy. Both groups tended toward a rather cautious liberalism, though the Progressives, who drew support from the urban middle and lower-middle classes, were more anticlerical and more open to reform. Many Moderates were wealthy conservatives who feared change but considered participation in the system their best means of limiting it. Military officers, who by this time were well accustomed to the idea of involvement in politics, could be found in both major parties; the military's political involvement, however, went beyond participation in the leadership of parties, for in a system in which the Crown and its favored politicians held enormous powers to engineer election results and keep rivals out of power, disgruntled officers looked to the tradition of the *pronunciamiento* as a means of forcing political change. Overseeing the system was Queen Isabella II (reigned 1833–1868), who generally used her influence to help the Moderates.

Over time, the socioeconomic changes Spain was experiencing, including a midcentury economic boom based on the construction of railroads, generated social and political tensions and spurred the growth of politically conscious elements in the lower-middle and working classes. Emerging to represent such growing forces was a new party known as the Democrats, and many Progressives also began to resent the existing political arrangements. The combination of these broad forces and movements with the unpopularity of a queen known for her promiscuity helped bring about a successful military uprising in September 1868. As the queen fled Spain, the movement's leaders, Generals Juan Prim and Francisco Serrano, formed a provisional government backed by many Progressives, Democrats, and others; the new government oversaw elections for a Constituent Cortes, which quickly began drafting a new constitution. In the first document in this reading, the provisional government states the principles of the "Glorious September Revolution"; excerpts from the 1869 Constitution follow

SOURCE: *Gaceta de Madrid*, October 26, 1868.

As a starting point for the proclamation of its general principles, the revolution has begun by pointing to the necessary foundation of its reconquered liberties. That foundation is the dethroning and expulsion of a dynasty whose open opposition to the spirit of this century has been an obstacle to all progress. . . . With this obstacle now having been removed and the path cleared, the revolution has established universal suffrage, as the most evident and tangible demonstration of the sovereignty of the people. In this way all the new powers will be strengthened by the contribution, absolute and precise rather than limited and fictitious, of general opinion, and our institutions will enjoy the vigorous support of the whole nation, the arbiter and author of its destiny.

Having proclaimed the principles on which our future governmental regime must be based, that is, on the broadest liberty, . . . the provisional government now proceeds to bring together the various expressions of the public spirit in a single doctrinal statement. . . .

The most important principle of all, because of the essential way in which it alters Spain's secular organization, is that concerning religious freedom. The passage of time, which modifies and renews everything, has profoundly altered the conditions of our existence. . . . Deeply implanted faith will not be threatened just because we are allowing the free and calm exercise of other religions alongside the Catholic one; in fact it will be strengthened through the competition. . . . Besides, religious freedom is a necessity of our political state and a protest against the theocratic spirit that had pervaded the essence of our institutions. . . .

Freedom of education is another of the cardinal reforms that the revolution has demanded and that the provisional government has hurried to realize quickly. The excesses committed in recent years by the movement of unrestrained and blind reaction against spontaneous expressions of human understanding have been put forth by the Church without respect to legal and legitimately acquired rights, and [this religious movement has] pushed even into the sanctuary of the home and the conscience; this dark inquisition relentlessly exercised against professional thought, which had been condemned to perpetual servitude or shameful punishment by governments turned into submissive auxiliaries for obscure and unaccountable powers; this state of decline to which public instruction had come in Spain resulted from monstrous plans imposed not for the needs of science but rather for narrow partisan and religious outlooks. . . .

And as a natural result of the freedom of education, the revolution has also proclaimed freedom of the press, without which those other conquests would be no more than illusory and vain. The press is the durable voice of intelligence, a voice that is never extinguished. To try to enslave it is to seek the mutilation of thought; it is to tear the tongue away from human reason. The Spanish mind, weakened and closed in by narrow limits that were a mockery of rights expressed in our constitutions, . . . had been gradually losing spark, originality, and life. We hope that now that its chains have been broken it may emerge in freedom, revived and radiant, like Lazarus from his tomb.

Freedom of peaceful association, which is a permanent source of activity and progress, and which has contributed so much to the political and economic growth of other peoples, has consequently been recognized as a basic dogma by the Spanish revolution. . . . In this way, nations learn to govern themselves, to maintain and exercise their rights. . . . [Through this freedom] the individual, the municipality, the province, and the nation will be able to develop themselves independently within their proper spheres, without the daunting intervention of the state. . . .

Thus armed with all the political rights and public liberties, the Spanish nation will no longer be able to complain justly about the unbearable pressure of the state. Having grown up and been emancipated from official tutelage, it has before it an open road. . . . Liberty leads to movement and thus to responsibility. From now on the Spanish people are responsible because they are free, and their steadiness, their energy, and their labor . . . can and must make up the time lost through their prior servitude.

The following are excerpts from the new constitution issued in July 1869.

SOURCE: Don Antonio Pirala, *Historia contemporánea*, vol. 1 (Madrid: Manuel Tello, 1875), 676ff.

Title 1: On the Spaniards and Their Rights

Article 2. No Spaniard or foreigner can be detained or imprisoned without proof of a crime.

Article 3. Anyone detained must either be freed or turned over to judicial authorities within twenty-four hours of being detained. . . .

Article 5. No one can enter the home of a Spaniard or a foreigner residing in Spain without their consent, except in emergencies of fire, flood, or similar danger, or of illegitimate aggression coming from inside, or to bring assistance to a person asking for assistance from within. Other than in these cases, entry into the home of a Spaniard or a foreigner residing in Spain can only be ordered by a judge and can only be carried out during the day. . . .

Article 7. In no case can mail or telegraph messages be detained or opened by governing authorities. But on the orders of a judge these kinds of correspondence can be opened, in the presence of the interested party to whom they are addressed. . . .

Article 13. No one can be deprived, either temporarily or permanently, of his property and rights, nor disturbed in his possession of them, unless based on a judicial sentence. . . .

Article 16. No Spaniard entitled to full use of his civil rights can be deprived of the right to vote.

Article 17. Nor can any Spaniard be deprived of the right to express his ideas and opinions, either orally or in writing, using the press or other similar means; or of the right to gather peacefully; or of the right to associate for all the purposes of human life that are not contrary to public morality; or finally, of the right to present individual or collective petitions to the Cortes, the king, and the authorities.

Article 21. The nation is obliged to maintain the worship and ministers of the Catholic religion. The public or private exercise of any other religion remains guaranteed to foreigners residing in Spain, with no other limitations than universal rules of morality and law. If some Spaniards should profess a religion other than the Catholic religion, everything stated in the previous paragraph applies to them as well.

Article 22. Censorship cannot be established. . . .

Article 24. Any Spaniard may found or maintain establishments of learning or education without previous license or approval except for inspections by competent authorities for reasons of hygiene or morality. . . .

Title 2: On the Public Powers

Article 32. Sovereignty resides essentially in the nation, from which all the powers emanate.

Article 33. The form of government of the Spanish nation is monarchy.

Article 34. The power to make laws resides in the Cortes. The king approves and promulgates the laws.

Article 35. The executive power resides in the king, who exercises it through his ministers.

Article 36. The courts exercise the judicial power.

16. *El Estado Catalan*, On Federalism (1870)

The tradition of asserting Catalonia's right to govern itself had a very long history, but with the advent of the Bourbon dynasty in Spain in 1700, the region lost most of its powers. In the first half of the nineteenth century, intellectuals and writers launched the Catalan cultural movement known as the *Renaixença* (see reading 12) but that movement had few political repercussions at first. By the second half of the century, however, political Catalanism was beginning to reemerge.

The conditions conducive to this political shift included widespread discontent throughout Spain with the liberal monarchy headed by Queen Isabella. When that discontent culminated in the Glorious September Revolution of 1868 and the ouster of the queen, Constituent Cortes were formed throughout the country, and remarkably clean elections were held for a new parliament. Although the moderate liberal monarchist party known as the Progressives secured the largest group of seats, those elections saw the rise of new parties committed to ending monarchy altogether, and many of these republican deputies came from Catalonia. Some of the Catalan deputies also began speaking of "federalism," a less centralized political system. Such ideas alarmed many, who accused the federalists of threatening the very existence of Spain, and indeed the outbreak of violent uprisings in Catalonia and other regions in 1869 raised the general level of anxiety in much of the country.

Replying to such charges, a recently founded Catalan newspaper, *El Estado Catalan* (headed by Valentí Almirall, among others), published the following article. In retrospect, the paper's outlook may seem mild compared to later separatist voices—the newspaper itself was published in Castilian, not Catalan—but for its time, the paper articulated ideas that were undoubtedly shocking to many.

SOURCE: *El Estado Catalan*, March 10, 1870; the text also appears in Albert Balcells, ed., *Cataluña contemporánea*, vol. 1 (Madrid: Siglo Veintiuno Editores, 1977), 187–90.

On many occasions, including only a few days ago, more or less official voices have been raised in Madrid, saying, in accusing tones, that Catalonia was trying to proclaim itself independent.

Upon hearing this, parliamentary deputies and newspapers have felt duty-bound to protest, denying that this was true.

These deputies and newspapers are mistaken. It is now time to set aside these diplomatic hypocrisies that lead nowhere, and instead speak frankly. In the wake of the emergence of a federalist party whose strength derives from the minds within it, it has become clear that this party constitutes a majority—and a very large majority—of opinion in the country, so no one can doubt that the idea of independence lives powerfully in this classic land of liberty.

The banner of the Catalans is "Independence of Catalonia within a Federation of Spanish States," and this banner, varying by region, is that of all Spanish federalists.

It can be no other way. Those who believe that federation can be formed from above are quite mistaken. Only those who have liberty to do so can form contracts, and only peoples who are in possession of their sovereignty can sign federal pacts.

Federation cannot thus be constituted unless the states have sovereignty in advance; each one of them has to have the necessary liberty to cede to the agglomerate that part of its sovereignty it sees fit to cede; otherwise, were it imposed from above, the federation would be wrongly constituted, and it would lack one of its essential principles, and that would lead it to fall apart.

Therefore, federation must be constituted by each one of the units that together make up a state issuing a cry of independence and convoking its own representation and its own Constituent Cortes to draft its own constitution. Only afterward will the formation of a federal pact take place.

We know of no other way to arrive at the result we seek. A federation in theory is unacceptable, . . . for within it the rights and duties imposed on the states would have to clash among themselves, and the central government would undoubtedly want to intervene in the interior organization of the states, thus killing federation.

From all of this it results that the only policy that can lead to a federal republic involves giving life to the idea of independence that is latent in all of the provinces of Spain, as well as giving life to the provincial spirit that has been the only one that has achieved great things in Spain.

Liberty in its most perfect form must be the basis of the constitutions of Spain, and it follows from this that they must adopt the form of a democratic republic. This must be at once a means and an end. The goal guiding all of us is to regenerate Spain and lead it to prosperity and greatness. The means is the creation of a federal democratic republic, but as long as this is not established, its creation must be the goal, the immediate object of the federalists' efforts.

Given that this is the immediate end, one must strive to reach it by the most direct route. Therefore, vacillations are not possible. . . . Anything that pushes us off course takes us further from the goal. . . .

Within the current form of Spanish unity our principles do not fit, so federalists can accept nothing of what is done within that framework. That would have the precise consequence of leading us to a dead end, and so our duty might be either to refuse to accept public positions within the institutions we are combating or to refuse to recognize the current political unit, and thus to refuse to send federalist deputies to the Cortes [in Madrid].

The party's membership has thus far thought in ways very different from our own; but the party's rank and file should think about what advantages their representatives in the Cortes can hope for through the triumph of the federal idea [in its current form], and they will find that there are none. . . .

In the current Constituent Cortes one cannot see the reflection of the provinces. The idea of independence produced as a deputy's accusation against Catalonia has not produced that which Catalonia's federalist representatives have declared: It is true, this is what Catalonia wants, because without independence there can be no federation, and without federation there can be no salvation for Spain.

Did the Catalan federalists in the Constituent Cortes fear that this would cause a storm? Did they fear that for this reason the government's anger would be unleashed on Catalonia?

If they feared this, they did poorly.

They are in the Cortes because they were named by the federalist democratic republican party to keep the banner unfurled, and in these solemn moments, they should declare themselves very clearly.

17. Justo Zaragoza, On Slavery in the Spanish Antilles (1872)

Spain lost most of its American empire in the 1820s, but as of the late nineteenth century it still retained the Philippines and two very important islands in the Caribbean—Cuba and Puerto Rico. In the latter region, also known as the Spanish Antilles, slavery still provided the labor supply for the colonial economy—most notably the cultivation of sugar—but international pressure to abolish slavery kept building throughout the century, and British-led efforts to stop the international slave trade began to stem the flow of Africans to the Americas in the 1860s. Because the slave population in Cuba and Puerto Rico tended to decline without a continuing influx of new slaves, the days of slavery appeared numbered there.

In 1868, Spanish colonialism faced a new threat from a nationalist uprising in Cuba, and though many planters (and slaves) showed little enthusiasm for the uprising, Spain struggled to end it. Among the partisans of empire who grappled with these challenges was Justo Zaragoza (1833–1896), a writer and historian who published a book on the subject in 1872. Note that Zaragoza uses the term "philanthropist" not in the narrow sense of a giver of charity, but in the broader sense of a "friend of humanity."

SOURCE: Justo Zaragoza, *Apuntes para la historia política de esta isla en el presente siglo* (Madrid: Imprenta de Manuel G. Hernández, 1872), 289–96.

In truth, we are in no way [seeking] . . . to declare ourselves champions of slavery, for we would certainly be foolish to commit to an anachronism and to pursue an opinion that is so suspect in the times in which we are living, but rather to prove that the Negro race, which is quite inferior in its intellectual capacities, needs to be directed, needs to be prodded to work, needs to rely on a superior race, just as the poor have always needed and will always need to live subordinated to the rich, the man lacking in intellectual gifts to the man of talent, the ignorant man to the wise man, and the unfortunate to those whom fate has favored. We believe and are profoundly convinced that Negro slavery has within it something very bad, and that is its name, which today no longer sounds good. Bring that slavery, the slavery of the Spanish Antilles . . . to the European proletariat, along with the healthy daily provisions the Negro enjoys, with the protection he receives from having two new changes of clothing each year, with the conscientious medical care, with the prudent rest he gets from his work, and with the usufruct of the . . . small garden he cultivates for himself, . . . and with the [supposed] tyranny of that slavery most of the Spanish proletariat will disappear, soon transforming itself into a middle class, as the individuals in it pass into a situation much more comfortable and happy than the difficult one in which they now live. But at the same time bring to the Negro all the oppression of the liberties that most of the workers and day laborers of the European nations now nominally enjoy; bring to him all the poverty and all the misfortunes that consume the life of the white slave, and then the Negro will indeed be the victim of the cruelest, most inhumane, and most unbearable of all slaveries. . . .

Without wishing to oppose modern currents of thinking, which defending the continuation of Negro slavery in white lands would certainly involve, we will say with all the sincerity of our convictions that that institution, though essential in the human family, must now change its name. For the time has come for it to take a new form, and the slave must become a worker, because those who have had to have a religion and to depend on a natural and social discipline that subjects them to the most powerful and the most intelligent must now pass into a state in which they have the nominal enjoyment of social rights and the patronage of those who wish to employ them, while watching out for themselves without the protection of any white owner, in a society in which there are many who may fool and take advantage of them, and certainly will do so. For the Negro must finally become a citizen and not a slave, now being considered a man and not a machine, as the neophilanthropists would have us believe that people of color have until now been considered in the civilized parts of the tropics. This will require regulating them, undoubtedly, and subjecting them to the penalties of a strict law code. . . .

But will Negroes given the artificial condition of citizens really be free in a society of whites? To those of us who have had a close look at those free men of color who are now rural and nonrural workers, it has not been possible to discern among them the clear signs that the true citizen shows, just as in states ruled by Negroes, where they try to base their social and political organization on constitutions thought up by white men, we have seen nothing but caricatures of the governments they intend to imitate. And so it is that in creation everything has its way of being, and its sphere of activity is circumscribed, and given that since the beginning of history [creation] has shown that among its immutable laws is the necessary and inevitable existence of races, those races will always tend to act and be distinguished by specific characteristics, including the tendency toward the unification of each race and hatred for other races, so they will never disappear without the destruction of one of the contending parties. . . .

Therefore we believe, now that the hour for the disappearance of slavery has arrived, that whatever arrangements may be made concerning the organization of the Negro race in our Antilles, they should not be permanent and definitive, but rather provisional, and only for such time as is necessary to replace Negro arms with white workers, while European settlement chases away the remains of the colored race. For only remains will still be present here shortly after they are declared free, given that when two races live together with equal rights, it is well known that one of them cannot help being subordinated to the other, and since the white race will never consent to being considered inferior, the other will have to disappear, either through extinction or emigration.

The former would be less humane than slavery itself, and the latter . . . could not happen without great injustice . . . if it were carried out following the practice of the Catholic kings with the Jews [in 1492] or that of Philip III with the Moriscos [in 1609]. Given the proportion in which Negroes and whites exist in our Antilles, Negroes will have no choice but to disappear once emancipation becomes a fact. Governments, anticipating the natural and inevitable course of events, should now try to see to it that gradually, and insofar as white immigration increases, the freed Negroes are transported to the zone that nature has indicated for them. Those who are taken there will reduce the barbarism of their ancestors, bringing tiny bits of the enlightenment and the religious principles learned from the whites, and they will contribute to carrying out the greatest and most genuine of human conquests, introducing civilizing notions among the hordes of those children of nature. There will undoubtedly be inconveniences in the implementation of these movements, and they will be felt particularly strongly by the small number of wealthy men in our Antilles, who now earn fabulous returns on their capital, and who will have to content themselves temporarily with an equitable and moderate income, but these rich men, faced with the obligatory realization of such a humane and beneficial idea, will perhaps not hesitate to lend their support and contribute to the general good with their generosity and self-sacrifice. They know, as all must know, that if our American possessions are to continue being Spanish while no longer relying on slavery, they must become whitened, just as the United States is whitening its territories in the West and the South, hoping to unify them and keep possession of them for a long time. We believe that the colored races cannot be free unless they live alone, even if they have written copies of the broadest liberal rights, for they will never avoid tacit or official tutelage as long as they remain together with white men. . . .

The most recent census of the population of Cuba, taken in 1867, showed 605,461 inhabitants of color, including 379,523 slaves; the population of color, after four years of war and without the introduction of [new] African [slaves], we can without exaggeration . . . estimate has been reduced to 290,000 slaves and approximately 190,000 freedmen, giving a total of 480,000 inhabitants threatened with becoming citizens as soon as the law of emancipation is passed. These people, out of custom and inferiority, will continue, in spite of everything, serving and obeying the roughly 700,000 whites who live on the island. And since the life of the freedmen following abolition will be like that of one condemned to extermination, by the tendencies we have been able to observe among the free Negroes in recent years . . . Christian charity, which is the real philanthropy, must, along with wise governmental policies, prevent this, removing from danger those beings who can still fulfill a purpose in the history of humanity as civilizing instruments.

We cannot think of any more efficient means to achieve this than the transfer to Africa of that sizable mass of human creatures, imitating the steps the North Americans took with their northern Negroes, forming the republic of Monrovia, or Liberia, in 1821. . . . Yet this transfer should not take place all at once, nor in a single year—for it would be practically impossible—but rather in a deliberate and gradual manner. Remove each year, for example, 15,000 individuals of color, 5,000 of whom are now free and 10,000 slaves, from the island of Cuba to the coasts of Africa, while taking great care that in each expedition one takes complete families and members of the same nation and origin, so that over there they will form centers of population that can develop and defend themselves from their savage ancestors, and in this way in ten years the Negro race will be extinguished in Cuba, keeping in mind the effects of the enormous natural population decline that they experience. Using the same system in the island of Puerto Rico, slavery will disappear completely from Spanish possessions. Landowners and industrialists who derive their wealth from Negro labor should not be alarmed at this proposal, for in order not to disturb things in the first stages of the reform, which are always the most difficult, authorization has already been granted allowing the introduction of 50,000 residents of the Canary Islands, now inhabitants of the American continent, and thus already acclimatized, and these people could easily replace as agricultural laborers the 10,000 slaves who would be removed in the first year.

For the second and following years there will undoubtedly be more than enough emigrants as long as the promises are kept regarding the first migrants. At the same time it will be possible to promote the emigration of sons of our land, who would volunteer to embark if they were exempted from military service where it is required, particularly in the provinces of the north and the Basque country, lands from which 20,000 to 30,000 per year have been going alone to Mexico, Venezuela, Buenos Aires, Montevideo, and other places in America; entire families would prefer to go to the Antilles, given the same advantages that are offered to those who go to the Canary

Islands. These emigrants would undoubtedly prevent the kind of great disruption of agriculture and industry that the powerful planters of Cuba fear; these planters, who might at first earn a slightly lower return on their agricultural capital than at present—though even that is doubtful—would soon see those returns increase with the use of modern machinery tried out in the fields of Europe, machinery that is so easy for intelligent white workers to operate.

And even if white immigration from the peninsula and the [Canary] islands were not sufficient to meet the planters' needs and to derive from the fields of the Spanish islands all the riches they contain, we see another means, which would be humane, civilizing, and easy to carry out as long as good-faith agreements are met and penal laws are applied with strict punctuality. This means is that of introducing Moroccans, fellahs, or Egyptian peasants, and inhabitants of Abyssinia or ancient Ethiopia and Nubia to our Antilles, as contract laborers; we know that the introduction of such people was considered not long ago with the aim of replacing slave laborers, whose numbers have been decreasing daily and very rapidly since the insurrection in Cuba began.

18. The Alcoy Federation, An Anarchist Manifesto (1873)

Anarchism was a workers' and peasants' movement largely formulated by the Russian political activist Mikhail Bakunin, but it quickly spread to many other countries, particularly Spain. Anarchism arrived in Spain in 1868 when an Italian associate of Bakunin, Giuseppe Fanelli, came to explain the movement's ideas to workers and others.

After the 1868 revolution that toppled Queen Isabella II, an Italian prince, Amadeo, was invited to become king of Spain. That experiment did not last long, and amid endless political plotting Amadeo fled Spain in 1873, at which point Spain became a republic for the first time. It was during that brief republican period in 1873 to 1874 that workers began forming their own local governments, including one in the Valencian town of Alcoy. The "Alcoy Federation" was anarchist, and its members did not trust any of the other groups on the left, including the moderate republicans and the more radical socialists; indeed, anarchists rejected the very existence of national governments. When the workers of the Alcoy Federation proclaimed a general strike, the Civil Guard was sent to crush it. The army overthrew the republic, restoring the monarchy in 1874, but anarchism continued to grow in Spain.

SOURCE: *El Mercantil Valenciano*, March 6, 1873; the text also appears in Fernando Díaz-Plaja, ed., *Historia de España en sus documentos: Siglo XIX* (Madrid: Cátedra, 1983), 348–50.

Compañeros,

An unexpected change in the politics of the middle class [the abdication of the king and the establishment of a republic] has produced a transformation in the name of the governmental organization of the present corrupt bourgeois society, as a consequence of the ruinous state of the economy and of the civil war provoked by the fanatic partisans of the Inquisition and of the absolutist king—criminal and absurd institutions that cannot and must not return.

The result of this change in bourgeois politics—which does indeed have great effects on the form of things but has almost no effects on the substance of the present authoritarian and centralizing organization [of power]—has been the fall of [King] Amadeo and the proclamation of a republic by the same monarchists who had so recently praised the virtues of monarchy.

We have viewed this change with satisfaction, not for the guarantees it could give to the working class, always hoodwinked and ridiculed in all bourgeois organizations, but rather because the republic is the last resort of the bourgeoisie, the final line of defense of the exploiters of the fruits of our labor, and the complete disillusionment for all those brothers of ours who have hoped for everything from governments, and continue to do so, not realizing that their political, religious, and economic emancipation must be the work of the laborers themselves. . . .

We must be on guard against all of those, whether they call themselves republicans or socialists, who, not wanting the complete and radical transformation of the present society, seek to delay the advent of justice, putting the working class to sleep with palliative measures so that it will not pursue its revolutionary march with vigor and energy. . . .

We, who love the complete liberty of the individual and the autonomy of all federations, want to be neither the directors nor the inspirers of our brothers, the workers, because the great work of the emancipation of the wage earners can be neither directed nor carried out by anyone or anything but the spontaneous action of the workers themselves, after having secured, through the identity of interests and aspirations, the unity of action that is necessary and indispensable to liberate us from the political, religious, and economic slavery that weighs upon us.

Therefore, we believe that for the emancipation of the workers themselves, during this period of relative freedom to exercise the natural rights of association and congregation, it is of the utmost importance that there be continuous assemblies of workers from all trades to discuss the line of conduct that should be followed in the present circumstances and during the inevitable political and social crises that will arise.

We believe that practice . . . in the free and truly federative form of organization is highly useful . . . so that we can put ourselves in a position to obtain a reduction in working hours very soon. And [we also] demand the freedom of natural groups—of the municipalities and free communes—to carry out the social revolution independently of any authoritarian power and against all authoritarian powers, creating as a logical consequence the complete social liquidation of the institutions of the present society, and then to continue from there to revolutionary agitation to reach the unlimited goal of the well-being and happiness of all humans.

We believe that the principal foundation of the revolution for which we yearn consists of the complete decentralization or, more precisely, the total destruction of authoritarian powers, eternal enemies of progress, liberty, and justice.

We believe that the time has come for all the international organizations to make a supreme effort, to be tireless and active in propaganda, to see to it that all the workers who have until now been apathetic begin to form new sections and to swell the ranks of those already formed, because in this way we will be more numerous and stronger, as well as invincible.

If we want the transformation of individual ownership of land and the great means of production into collective property, [the transformation] of the entire educational system, and the destruction of all privileges and monopolies, we must first be convinced that we deserve this. We must all conquer these things because everything is ours, and nothing will be given to us if we do not seize it from those who unfairly possess it.

It is necessary to proceed to the triumph of anarchy and collectivism, that is, to the destruction of all authoritarian powers and class monopolies, so that there are neither popes nor kings, nor bourgeois, nor priests, nor military men, nor lawyers, nor judges, nor scribes, nor politicians; but there should be a free, universal federation of free associations of agricultural and industrial workers.

We will only achieve this through the solidarity of the revolutionary action of all the workers of the world, and it will become a reality if we are tireless in the propagation of radical and revolutionary ideas, and in the organization of the powerful forces of the sons of labor.

Compañeros, with activity in propaganda and sincerely revolutionary organization, and without mystifications of any kind, victory is certain.

Long live the International Association of Workers!

Long live social liquidation, . . . anarchy, and collectivism!

19. Clarín, Hunger in Andalusia (1883)

This essay by the famous novelist Leopoldo Alas (1852–1901), known by his pen name Clarín, originally appeared as a series of newspaper articles dealing with Spain's most troublesome region. As Clarín points out, many theories purported to explain the persistence of poverty in Andalusia, but unequal land ownership patterns, which originated with land grants to knights who had fought in the Reconquest of Moorish Spain, certainly played a major part. Clarín refers to La Mano Negra ("the Black Hand"), a secret left-wing political organization that became the focus of almost hysterical fears and wildly exaggerated tales. He also refers to Jerez de la Frontera, an Andalusian town near Seville and a focal point of social unrest.

SOURCE: *El Día* (Madrid), March 4, 8, 13, 1883; the text also appears in Clara E. Lida, *Antecedentes y desarrollo del movimiento obrero español, 1835–1888: Textos y documentos* (Madrid: Siglo Veintiuno, 1973), 443ff; and in Fernando Díaz-Plaja, ed., *Historia de España en sus documentos: Siglo XIX* (Madrid: Cátedra, 1983), 391–98.

One must admit that when one considers the state of the economic life of a country, the multitude of factors on which it depends . . . introduces confusion in one's thinking, and it often happens that one confuses causes and effects. I have observed in Andalusia that one attributes the problems and the decline to various causes depending on one's political opinions, or culture, or profession, or even one's temperament. Some see all of the fault in the political system; some, being more specific, see it in the current government; some attribute it to the organization of property; some to the rivalry of classes; some to a specific class; some to defects of character; some to the influence of the climate; and some to the geological conditions of the terrain. One must note all of this and much more, without a doubt, but we must not accept simplistic explanations. . . .

There is good reason, for example, to blame the political and administrative organization of Spain. . . . Much would have to be said against the governing powers and the way they always and currently function. Yet it would be absurd, as well as unfair, to make this a weapon for the [parliamentary] opposition, and to reduce things to an attack on the government now in office, or even on governments in general. To fall into the pessimism into which some fall—freeing all the authorities from responsibility and saying that the problem cannot be solved because it is born from the inevitable defects of the [Andalusian] race, from the inevitable decline, or at least stagnation that is as inevitable as old age in physical organisms—is to forget the facts that are crying out that many of the errors spring from visible errors that have nothing to do with those sad ethnological considerations. If in a town such as Jerez there is such inequality in taxation that we see men who cannot even pay for their own burial high on the hierarchical list of taxpayers, while much lower than them on the list we see men who could pay to bury everyone in Jerez, can we attribute this to the physiological and moral defects of that race?

If there are mayors who put up insurmountable obstacles to the construction of a highway that would give work to many hungry locals and that is also necessary for the traffic of that district, and if they oppose it because it would cross the property of some magnate, of whom the mayor is a client and a kind of lackey; if this occurs—and it does indeed occur—can it be attributed to the influence of climate upon the muscular activity of the Andalusians?

I have observed, in traveling through various Andalusian districts, that in general those people are not sufficiently concerned about their social state; each one laments the problems that are weighing upon them or that are threatening them; but there are few who, showing a love for economic analysis, seek to acquire a broader awareness of the specific causes and effects of the crisis. . . .

While some workers insist on thinking that the whole problem consists in the lack or shortage of rain, . . . there is no shortage of people who attribute the miserable, and in some ways insufferable, state of those regions to the agitation they call socialist, which leads some to propose the Civil Guard as the supreme remedy. . . .

The approach of offering to use palliative measures to cure or reduce the acute pains that the evils cause is more simplistic than serious or fruitful. We now see that in Jerez the public order is endangered and unrest is growing . . . ; so it occurs to the government to send a special magistrate to Jerez; so be it, but if it is a question of judicial inquiries, why not send magistrates . . . to study the excesses of this or that cacique [political boss; see reading 20], who buys and sells justice, makes and unmakes mayors and other authorities, at his whim, and makes the free operation of public administration completely impossible in entire districts?

Will the government say that there is no way to combat these types, that their powers are untouchable, that everything is just a matter of vague accusations? But this is not true, and I believe that there is no shortage of people in Andalusia who would make concrete accusations before the tribunals if one could hope for justice in this matter.

And why send judges and Civil Guards only against armed bandits and the socialism of the poor, when the robbery that these strongmen carry out against the public treasury also cries out for swift and strong justice? . . . And isn't the scandalous concealment of [taxable] estates, which are so enormous in some Andalusian provinces, in fact robbery?

There are those who are accustomed to viewing the public treasury as a kind of private treasury . . . and [people] do not see that those who hide part of the territory they own are actually stealing land from the nation, which only benefits from that which is not its direct property through the indirect means of taxation. To hide territorial wealth is to steal from the nation, and it is to rob those citizens who have to pay more to make up for that part of the total that is hidden.

Yet the government does not think of punishing these crimes, nor does the opposition look upon them with all the hatred they deserve. I will point out that the facts that could illustrate this point were at the disposal of the treasury ministry for many years (and indeed still are)—facts that . . . include the names of those who are hiding real estate. And the treasury has done nothing because . . . the same ones whose interest it is that this kind of crime not be prosecuted are influential persons in the administration and in politics. There are [parliamentary] deputies, there are great dignitaries who would see their names on the list of the great concealers of wealth if that list were ever published. Where is the special magistrate who is going to investigate all of this? . . .

Many characteristics of the so-called socialist conspiracy of the poor against the rich in Jerez . . . indicate that it is not a passing aberration of a few people, nor . . . of banditry. . . . While I respect the opinion of the deputy who recently argued that La Mano Negra has its origins in banditry, and although I do not deny all such connections, I believe that its origins are different. . . .

People from Jerez who study these matters with intelligence and perseverance insist that the association has existed for at least five years, and that it is not a society with purely criminal aims and methods. . . . [Its statutes] describe the society in this way: "Association of the poor to make war on the rich." . . . It is clear that this is not pure banditry as it has classically been understood in Spain. . . .

It is also obvious that not all of the members understand all of the philosophy in these statutes. This society, like so many others of its kind, has as its leaders some of these half-educated men . . . who speak of the rights of labor but who do no other labor than hatching terrible conspiracies and propagating crazy doctrines, but doctrines that are attractive to those who really are poor workers, who are tired of suffering and correct in many of their claims. In Jerez, and even in other places, those who speak of general destruction, of great and even universal reprisals, of all that has to do with the metaphysical and transcendental elements of these barbarian utopias . . . are but a few people; they are the ones who have brought these statutes in from outside the province, people one only has to meet briefly to doubt that they are from this area. . . . They are the ones who have come to sow discord in a territory where, in effect, the existing conditions were already ripe, given the existing discontent.

The means of propaganda is the preaching, at times orally and at times through writing, as proven by the great number of copies of *La Revista Social* that are sold throughout Andalusia, and especially in Seville and Jerez—a newspaper devoted to attacking the rich and, in its own way, defending the poor. . . .

Unfortunately, the development of primary education is very backward in Andalusia, and especially in Jerez, but one may suspect that those peasants have on their own impulse studied the social problems that their statutes resolve, albeit in a bad way. They would not know about the universality of the complaints or the remedies unless someone came from the outside to open their eyes (or perhaps, better put, to close them). The rebellion, therefore, is not spontaneous among them, but there is spontaneity in their rallying to doctrines and procedures of those who promise them a solution. What has created this tendency? Why is it that the fire that does not catch in other places does damage here and spreads so quickly? . . .

It is now time to examine two elements that mainly account for the ease with which the most exaggerated communist doctrines spread throughout Andalusia, especially Jerez and other neighboring districts. . . . On the one hand, we must consider what there is in the customs of this people that makes them rally more readily than others to these tendencies, and on the other hand [we must consider] the problems that have come to place them in the desperate situation that inclines them toward extreme solutions. . . .

In much of Andalusia, an extreme kind of relationship between the landlords—the great landowners—and the poor workers who do not even own a speck of that land that they work on all of their lives is very ancient; a kind of relationship, I would say, that is contrary to sound economic principles. The land there belongs to very few people. The great domains that originated in historic causes still exist, [despite being] completely foreign to the technical requirements of cultivation as well as to a stable balance between the classes, which is impossible wherever only the privileged class has any guarantee of independent existence and assurance of being able to satisfy their needs; so an unstable balance was created long ago, an economic modus vivendi that is abnormal, but which has become a chronic problem, turning something that should have been temporary into something permanent. It is clear that the great landowners cannot do without the multitude of the dispossessed . . . ; they have needed them to work the land, and it would not be convenient for them if [the workers'] misery became so great that they died of hunger and disappeared. They thus allowed them nothing that would guarantee them a free existence, economically, permitting them nothing more than the minimum so that the population would not be annihilated. . . .

They did not give the class of day laborers enough because . . . the state of cultivation was so backward and imperfect that on many occasions there was no work for these day laborers (during droughts, for example, and throughout long seasons in some areas of cultivation); so at times capital had no demand for labor, and the only source of wealth, for those who depended on their wages each day, was lacking. What to do? That which the economy did not naturally supply . . . had to be sought through means of artificial assistance, outside the laws of the market. Hence that kind of socialism that is so deeply rooted in Andalusia arose, one that in urgent times consists of calming the misery of the day laborer with authoritarian measures, sometimes imposed, but always immediately accepted, which consists of having each landowner take on the responsibility of paying wages to a certain number of workers whether they need to hire them or not, simply so that they will survive the bad times.

Was this—or is this, since the phenomenon still exists—pure generosity? Was this simply a Christian act of protection that serves to alleviate poverty and give grounds for praising the good sentiments of the rich? No, certainly not; without denying the moral value of this aid in every particular case, one cannot call such a situation the normal state of affairs in a country, [as it is] a custom that points to a sick social organism. In Andalusia this custom of *alojamientos* is very ancient, because the problem it seeks to deal with temporarily is very ancient. It is not generosity; it is a custom that necessity has imposed. Yet it has not happened that the worker thus grows accustomed to asking for this assistance as a right, which is not even a right to employment, but simply to a day's wages, which is not the same thing. These *alojamientos*, these handouts of a day's wages, which so many municipalities have adopted, have recurred as the sole salvation, in the recent conflicts. . . .

Many false philanthropists, more inclined, strictly speaking, toward the traditions of domination than to charity, praise this kind of hidden assistance, which . . . place the worker under increasingly strong obligations toward the master; but remember that slavery and serfdom were defended in exactly the same way, by seeking to demonstrate that not only by the law was the slave tied to the land, but also by gratitude and affection. It is a dangerous philanthropy that always hides dependency in one way or another! . . . In Jerez, those who study these matters seriously know that there are memories of economic crises going back over a century, in which people have sought to use this system of public assistance; the workers have gathered around the doors of the officials or the religious houses, asking for assistance with the cry, classic in that region, of "Bread and beans!"

Also, many times, and even recently, the authorities have distributed the workers, we are told, among the richest people in the population, obliging them to pay the workers a day's wages, in the amount determined by the previous set of handouts. What is this, if not municipal socialism? . . . But a socialism for all, because it was imposed, and besides, without any other law than that of necessity, without regard to whether each one was working; it was not given to each one according to his labors. . . . Whether he worked or not, the obligation to pay him existed. . . .

Some say that [the two classes'] interests are the same, and that if the workers suffer from the . . . neglect, ignorance, etc. of the propertied classes, the latter also suffer from the workers' vices and flaws. This is obvious. But as a collectivist would say, the "means of resistance" are greater in the moneyed classes; . . . for them the problem a drought creates is purely economic, while for the worker it is a question of life or death. The landowner or entrepreneur may be ruined, but the worker may die. . . .

We can recognize that the worker always loses more in this kind of crisis, since he finds himself with reduced wages, because the paralysis of employment increases the supply of labor and reduces demand for it, while at the same time he finds himself facing higher prices for most essential items. Under these two tidal waves, those of falling wages and rising prices, the poor worker soon drowns. Go ahead and defend the threatened society all you want, but do not deny this. . . .

But unfortunately in Jerez everything contributes to poverty growing worse. To this compassion that the situation of the workers in that land inspires in me, many will reply that this is dangerous sentimentalism. There are those who say that there is not even so much hunger, and they cite various examples, true without a doubt, of bakeries assaulted by those who called themselves hungry, but who only wanted the bread of the upper classes, and who stole it while laughing. . . . Realize that there is much truth in what is said against the discontented Andalusian workers; but the error is in blaming them completely for their problems, whereas I believe that the upper classes, the administration, and, unfortunately, inevitable economic phenomena also deserve some of the blame.

20. Valentí Almirall, *Spain Such as It Is* (1887)

During the reign of Isabella II (1833–1868), voices on the left had called for an end to property-based qualifications for voting, and with the liberal revolution of 1868, those demands were finally satisfied. Yet the liberal elites who controlled Spain in the late nineteenth century were reluctant to give up their powers, so they devised a system to let them maintain their political power. That system, known as *caciquismo*, used local political bosses, or caciques, to implement orders sent from the central government in Madrid. (Spaniards had learned the term "cacique" in the New World, where it meant chief.) The Catalan political activist Valentí Almirall described the system in a book he published in French in Paris in 1887.

SOURCE: Valentín Almirall, *Espagne telle qu'elle est* (Paris: Albert Savine, 1887), 141–52.

In speaking of the electoral laws, we are referring to those that govern us at this moment, for it is well known that the laws change every time the government changes. . . .

In order to always maintain appearances, we also have a series of regulations that assure the liberty of the vote. The limitations imposed on the government and its agents are innumerable. . . . For anyone who would devote himself to studying our political and social situation in books, in the solitude of his office, we would certainly be one of the best-governed nations in Europe, in that which concerns the foundations of the representative system. But what a great difference there is between appearances and realities! What a contrast there is between that which the law prescribes and the facts! Were it not for the calamities that befall the country, our elections would be one of the most entertaining political spectacles one could see in Europe. For ours is, in fact, a bad parody of elections. Electoral lists, ballot boxes, tallying, everything is falsified. Elections in Spain turn out to be no more than a farce worthy of being put to music by Offenbach or Suppé. . . .

It does not matter if suffrage is universal or restricted, for there is never more than a single voter: the minister of government, who, aided by the provincial governors and by an army of bureaucrats of all kinds, not to mention the high dignitaries of the magistracy and the university, prepares, executes, and carries out elections of all kinds from his office located in the center of Madrid.

The lists of voters are made up by placing a few real names among a series of imaginary ones, above all deceased persons, who in the act of voting are represented by subordinate employees dressed as ordinary civilians. I have seen many times that my father, in spite of having died years ago, has gone to place his ballot in the box under the watchful eye of a city official or a policeman dressed in a borrowed suit. The individuals who make up the tables of the electoral college very often carry out similar transmigrations of the souls of their own fathers. There have been electoral lists in which [real voters] made up scarcely a tenth of the total of voters, with most of the names being imaginary or belonging to deceased persons.

This system of elections through the resurrection of the dead and policemen disguised as voters is not, however, the worst of the means that our supposed defenders of parliamentarianism and the representative system use to falsify elections. . . . What they do is purely and plainly to increase the number of votes cast until they have assured the election of the chosen candidate. In doing so they generally go beyond the limits of the grotesque and the absurd.

In order for foreign readers to get some idea of what happens, we will cite the case of a general of a brigade, a ministerial candidate for the district of Berga, who received more than a million and a half votes, even though the district only contained several thousand inhabitants. . . .

More than once, the police have absconded with the ballot boxes before the tallying of the votes, transporting them to the governor's office in order to obtain a favorable tally for the ministerial candidate, who is thus converted into a Lazarus candidate, a name used in political slang for those resurrected like the biblical Lazarus.

If we wanted to list all the forms of fraud used in Spain to overturn universal suffrage or limit it to the whims of the government, we would never finish. . . .

To summarize our elections, we will say that the deputies are manufactured purely and simply in the ministry of government, and that all the other acts of the electoral comedy only serve as a smokescreen to hide the truth from foreign countries or from some other Spaniard who is naive enough to take all this seriously.

We have already seen how ministerial deputies are made. But because a government cannot live without an opposition, he also chooses the opposition candidates to whom posts will be offered. . . . In the current Cortes, none of the opposition deputies . . . is a true representative of the voters, but they are instead creations of the minister, having been chosen by policemen and disguised public street-sweepers, who voted in the name of the transmogrified dead and of hundreds of thousands of imaginary voters. And one should not believe that all of these machinations are carried out in secret; far from it: our politicians are so lacking in prudence that, especially in the provinces, when the elections are about to happen, we already know beforehand who will be the deputies of the majority and the minority.

In almost all the districts, especially in the rural ones, the candidates are completely unknown to the voters and have no interests at all in the district. . . .

In sum, our electoral comedy respects nothing: electoral rosters, ballot boxes, tallying, everything is falsified by our politicians under the immediate direction of the civil governor in each province. Is the existence of a parliamentary regime or even a representative system possible upon such a basis?

21. Emilia Pardo Bazán, The Education of Men and Women (1892)

Emilia Pardo Bazán (1852–1921), a countess from Galicia in northwestern Spain, became one of Spain's most successful novelists and scholars of any period. Her achievements are all the more remarkable given the obstacles to women's education that existed at that time. Both of her parents, however, had encouraged her education, sending her to French schools and tutoring her in various subjects, and her husband also encouraged her studies, giving her access to the materials he was studying in law school. At twenty, she won a prize for her essay on Benito Feijóo, an early champion of women's rights, and she continued to publish throughout her life, in addition to raising three children. Over the years she won numerous honors—despite fierce resistance from Spanish men—and in 1916 Spain's education minister ignored virulent opposition and made her a professor at the University of Madrid. Although politically conservative, Pardo Bazán was also strongly feminist, and in 1892 she gave the following speech to a conference of Spanish educators.

SOURCE: *Nuevo Teatro Crítico*, year 2, no. 22 (October 1892): 14–82.

Concerning the similarities and differences that exist between the education of the man and that of the woman, one can note that the differences are much more serious and numerous than the similarities, being that we can affirm explicitly that at the present time the similarities between feminine and masculine education are merely superficial, while the differences . . . are rooted in the intimate and fundamental. The similarities are in the methods and programs of teaching and in inevitable parallels in the curriculum, while the oppositions consist in the diametrically opposed sense of the principles upon which the two forms of education are based. While masculine education is inspired by optimistic assumptions, that is, faith in the perfectibility of human nature, . . . feminine education rests on pessimistic assumptions, namely, the supposition that there is a conflict or clear contradiction between a woman's morality and intellectuality, with the moral aspect being damaged insofar as the intellectual aspect is developed. And to speak plainly and simply, the woman is [considered] so much more suited for her providential destiny when she is more ignorant and stationary. . . .

This dark and horrendous pessimism engulfs half the human race in the iron circle of immobility, prohibiting it from associating with the progress that the other half makes more or less slowly; this pessimism . . . is the offspring of another, no less transcendent error concerning the woman: the error of affirming that the role that belongs to the woman in the reproductive functions of the species determines and limits the remaining functions of her human activity, removing any individual significance from her destiny, and leaving her only that which she can have in relation to the destiny of the male. That is to say that the axis of the feminine life for those who think this way (and they are innumerable, I must point out) is not her own dignity and happiness but rather that of her spouse and children, and if there are no children or spouse, then that of her father or brother, and when even these are lacking, then that of the abstract masculine gender.

Many feel that . . . just as the individual is born savage, perhaps humanity was also born savage, and the male, with his bestial force, subjugated his companion there in the dark caves of the troglodytes. . . . There is no reason to wonder that those who, like [Jean-Jacques] Rousseau, want humanity to return to those caves, and who sing and mourn the passing of a primitive golden age . . . envision the woman's destiny in the same way that [Rousseau] understood that of his Sophie. The woman, in his view, has only been created for the man; she has neither individuality nor an existence of her own outside that of her husband and children. . . . Rousseau finds her so incapable of raising herself above a certain level that he believes one must not count on the natural process of time, as in the case of boys. . . . The sophists who derive laws from force were skilled in this case, basing a whole system of sexual metaphysics on the submission of women, for force alone secures only temporary submission, while perpetual consent is obtained by giving violence and servitude the color of duty and virtue; they thus base theories justifying accomplished facts upon brutal acts.

I do not wish to insinuate, gentlemen, that there has been a vast plot by one sex to dominate the other; the great phenomena of dominance and submission in history are not products of calculated efforts, but rather of unconscious impulses dictated by collective interest; simply notice the strange and poetic form of submission known as *monarchic loyalty*, a sentiment that has weakened but not been extinguished today. . . . The collective instinct of the male sufficed, then, to develop the concept of the woman's relative destiny and to give this gigantic error the very strong consistency that still sustains it, making it the final but formidable bulwark of inequality before the law in the heart of modern society, which has certainly proclaimed the rights of man, but which has yet to recognize those of humanity. . . .

According to James Mill, the purpose of education is to make the individual a proper instrument primarily of one's own happiness, and only secondarily of that of others; yet because the woman's education is carried out today with a relative and subordinate purpose, [French novelist] Stendhal was right that the woman's education seems deliberately designed to produce her unhappiness. A succinct sketch comparing that education with that of the man will demonstrate this.

Let us begin with a lower, but not unworthy, branch: physical education. No one doubts that muscular activity and the exercises that develop, invigorate, and beautify the human body must be an integral part of masculine education, and must continue to be practiced after childhood in order to prevent the damages of softness and the undesirable consequences of a sedentary life. On the other hand, when it comes to women, a concern and an atmosphere of vague and insulting suspicion surrounds physical education and the hygiene of exercise. "Why this singular difference?" asks the illustrious [British] philosopher Herbert Spencer, in a country where the woman is not as sedentary as she is here. "Can it be that the girl's constitution differs so fundamentally from that of the boy that she does not need active exercise? Without a doubt those who teach girls believe that extensive corporal development is improper and unseemly, and that a certain delicateness, an appetite of a bird, and timidity, the handmaiden of weakness, are more fitting to elegant young ladies." I do not know if the English people say the same things as those of Spain; I do know that if Spencer asked me these questions, I would remind him of the famous Spanish saying that imposes on the woman of honor "a broken leg," and I would read him a curious passage from a devout book I keep in my library, which praises certain Indians' custom of twisting and dislocating the ankles of the creatures of the feminine sex so that they will stay at home and not go out into the open air very often. I would teach him of works like *The Instruction of the Christian Woman* by Luis Vives—which was not retrograde, as it called for learned women—and *The Perfect Wife* by Fray Luis de León, which directs terrible diatribes against women who go out walking and lead what we would today call an active life. . . . I will answer that the type of *strong woman* who is often portrayed for us today differs little from that of the fifteenth and sixteenth centuries; that in certain matters related to the woman we have gone backward more than forward. . . . A woman who, after marrying, continues to cultivate her strength and muscular activity encounters hostility and surprise. . . . Physical exercise, recommended for the man, is tolerated for women during childhood and youth, and then reproached after marriage. Why? Out of tradition: in the name of the duty of watching over the house and of not placing herself in danger of seeing or being seen: the "broken leg" of our stale and distinctive teachers.

Let us move on to moral education, where, even more than in the case of physical education, we encounter these differences that are as illogical as they are universal. Female moral education combats, explicitly or implicitly, many of the moral qualities that the male displays; for example, courage; personal dignity; firmness of character; a strong sense of independence; the productive ambition to stand out among one's peers and to mark out one's path in the world; energy of thought, which seeks to assert itself by investigating the truth and recognizing it freely; amicable loyalty, frank truthfulness, initiative, noble pride, love of work. . . . [French writer Agénor de] Gasparin put his finger on the weak point of the moral education of the woman, describing it with diminutives and complaining that feminine education is saturated with that diminutive morality. . . . The woman chokes, caught up in the very fine links of a tiny, tiny net. *Debercitos* [little duties]: to please, to shine in a salon. *Instruccioncita* [little instruction]: music, a bit of dance, crumbs of history, superficial and truncated notions. *Devocioncilla* [little devoutness]: ritualized habits, genuflection, mechanical praying, everything in miniature, stunted, like miniature Chinese fruit trees. . . .

It is said that women's education's prime object is the teaching of good mothers. Isn't it strange to see people unaware how much the energy of an instinct—the strongest, blindest, most primal of all—impels the female to take care of and defend her little ones. . . . Education can help nature, but can never substitute for it. Realize that one cannot teach mothering; motherhood is the crowning piece of natural instinct, not only in the human species, but also among animals; the mother is nature itself. We have all seen the hen with a brood of chicks turn furious against a large and wild dog, as if the poor thing could hold up her end of such an unequal fight. . . .

Moving from moral to religious education, . . . I say that this teaching is carried out with considerable equality for the two sexes. . . . When I hear and read again and again that Christianity elevated and dignified women, I always think this common notion contains a shining truth. . . . Christianity dignified the woman, but not in the way most people think, because it is not true that before Christianity women lived in a general looseness of customs, nor that after Christianity and among Christian women themselves there have not been women as scandalous and depraved as the Agrippinas and Messalinas [ancient Roman women]; nor can one affirm, in the face of historical facts, that the woman . . . was any less valued in paganism than in Christianity, for it is certain that the Roman matron was in ancient times the archetype of dignity and of moral, social, and political influence, as well as of severe virtue. The great advance of Christianity in this area was to emancipate the woman's conscience, to affirm her personality and moral liberty, from which practical liberty necessarily derives. It was not in the family, but in the inner sanctuary of the conscience where Christianity emancipated the woman. . . .

The meaning of the teaching of Christianity's divine founder is this:

"From now on, among you, there will be neither master nor slave, man nor woman, but only children of my Father." But just as there continued to be masters and slaves as the long centuries have unfolded up to our own times, there are still ***men*** and ***women*** among Christians, with all the hierarchical meaning attributed to those two words in the family and in society. . . . The voice of the priest, which once taught the woman to affirm her spiritual independence ***usque ad efusionem sanguinis*** [to the point when blood flows], today inculcates marital docility and unexamined, routinized faith. Thus we must repeat that religious teaching [should be] the most egalitarian, that which distinguishes least between the sexes.

If one day the teaching of religion should fall into the hands of laymen, . . . I fear that they will . . . teach that there are two Gods, two sets of Ten Commandments, two heavens, two hells, and no more than one limbo, for women only; unless they wish to make things simple, like Rousseau, and say that the woman has no other religion than that of her husband, and leave it at that; by this thinking, women who never marry would be born predestined for atheism. . . .

In intellectual education, no one is unaware that the differences are enormous. At the very least, religious education is based on the supposition that souls are equal entities and of identical value in God's eyes; whereas intellectual education bases its anomalies and inequalities on the presumption of the congenital intellectual inferiority of the entire feminine sex. . . . I began by establishing that in the education of women and men today, the differences are greater and more serious than the similarities. . . . Nevertheless I will add that one notices in civilized society a tendency to . . . downplay the differences and highlight the similarities. . . . Today we could almost judge a state's level of culture by the breadth allowed to the intellectual education of the woman, not only in written laws but also in society, and by its correspondence with masculine education. Unfortunately, in Spain the legal disposition that authorizes women to receive an education equal to that of men remains, in practice, a dead letter in the public schools, and it will continue to be that way as long as one does not realize the inconceivable anomaly of opening up studies that women cannot use in the same way male students do. If the parents cannot hope to recoup the sacrifices a career requires, indeed if leading their daughters into studies that are useless among women will only leave them branded as eccentric and bold, few will choose to impose study for the sake of study on their daughters. Greater results and praise can be obtained by decking them out in finery, training them in the arts of flirtation, teaching them to stretch out their nets so that they may catch an unsuspecting fiancé, like a stunned fly. . . .

Morally, it would be . . . more noble and frank to close the classroom to women. There are people who believe that . . . all progress must be slow, gradual, and prepared in advance. I am more radical than those who think this way, but I will admit this for a moment and say: safely limit the woman's studies to certain professions, and open these to be exercised in the same conditions men enjoy. . . . These days . . . a woman can write a work of metaphysics but cannot be a veterinarian. A woman can occupy the throne but cannot elect city council members. Do you doubt her aptitude? You have—if you really believe in their effectiveness—exams, grades, . . . all the procedures by which one weighs and compares masculine acquisition of knowledge. There you would have, if you allowed it, . . . the slow and evident demonstration of aptitudes for the exercise of a profession or for the cultivation of knowledge as a social function. . . . Among men, many are called and few are chosen. That is to say, in both sexes the majority possesses inferior, or, in effect, average minds, endowed with normal intelligence. . . . Even when the right to a full education and its benefits is a universal human right that can be denied to no one without truly infringing upon the law of God, circumstances, independent of our good will, prevent millions of human beings from going beyond the limits of a rudimentary education. If I admit these limits for the education of the man, I admit them also for the woman. I say this because there is no lack of people who believe or claim to believe that those who think as I do want to make all women into scholars, writers, philosophers, astronomers, or professors. As if we kept bumping into philosophers and scholars on every street corner. Culture, these days, is limited to certain social classes, even if ideally we would extend and communicate it to the greatest number. All that . . . justice demands for the woman is the disappearance of the congenital incapacity with which society brands her. Equalize the conditions, and free evolution will do the rest.

Although it is not usually good strategy to reject allies, I must dissociate myself from . . . those who argue for the necessity of educating women intellectually so that they can transmit this teaching to their children. I reject this alliance because . . . I consider the concept of a relative destiny, one subordinated to that of another, very depressing for human dignity. The instruction and the rational culture that the woman acquires should be acquired in the first place for its own sake, for the development of her reason and the natural exercise of her understanding, because a rational being needs to exercise the intellectual faculties just as the other organs must not be allowed to atrophy. . . .

We must also calmly consider the question of maternity. Maternity is a temporary function: an entire lifetime cannot be submitted to it. The protection to which a child has a right must not be prolonged beyond childhood. In addition to being temporary, the function is secondary: all women conceive ideas, but not all conceive children. The human being is not a fruit tree, which is only cultivated for its fruits. . . .

I will not say that the teaching of men has reached a level of perfection, but ultimately certain general principles on which it is based today . . . are rational and productive. On the contrary, in the teaching of women it is the basic principles that must be uprooted, because of their lethal force. Feminine education is still in the midst of a stationary period; it must go through a revolutionary period if it is ever to enter into a peaceful, sane, and productive evolution. Strictly speaking, the current education of the woman cannot be called *education*, but rather *domestication*, since it has as its purpose obedience, passivity, and submission. . . .

The education of the woman is preventative and repressive to the point of shame; it starts from a supposition of evil, is born of suspicion, is nourished on jealousy, is inspired by mistrust, and tends to impede . . . transgressions of sexual morality by the same mechanical procedure in which bars are placed around a criminal so he cannot do harm. Positive education, providing instruction and direction, a true guide to human life, is prohibited to women. In the first phase of education, [German Enlightenment philosopher Immanuel] Kant teaches, passive obedience is the guiding rule; this period corresponds to tender infancy, to childhood. In the second phase, the student makes use of his liberty and [powers of] reflection. Who does not see that the woman has not left that first period? Like a child she is educated, and like a child she remains. . . .

For me it is obvious that the complete, rational, and totally human education of women will not harm true virtue but will instead promote it. . . . I will not say that the task will be easy. There is nothing more arduous or trickier . . . than education; and yet man needs it like bread and water, for we were made for it. All progress—I continue to be inspired by the venerable Kant—is only through pedagogy, through patient learning of the best; education must seek to break out of the prison of routine, making the children better than their parents were. Thus invoking tradition in matters of pedagogy, or fixing an educational method . . . for half of humanity . . . seems to me the greatest of absurdities. And if one indeed looks closely, one can see that it is on tradition and only tradition that the educational system for women is based. It will only be based on experience when this is verified, that is to say, when in some civilized nation one tries in due form and consistently to educate girls in the same way as boys, and to make the rights of both sexes equal under the common concept of humanity.

22. Pablo Iglesias, The Social Revolution (1892)

Anarchism appeared relatively early and grew quickly in Spain, but socialism in Spain lagged far behind movements in other European countries. A small socialist group was formed briefly in 1872, but it was only in 1879 that a Galician typesetter, Pablo Iglesias Posse (1850–1925) and a small group of his associates formed a lasting socialist organization in Madrid. In 1888, these socialists founded the Spanish Socialist Workers' Party (PSOE by its Spanish initials) and a socialist trade union, the General Union of Laborers (UGT). Throughout these years, the socialists competed with the anarchists for supporters, often disagreeing over tactics and doctrine, while agreeing on certain basic principles and goals. Here, in an article from the party newspaper, *El Socialista*, Iglesias comments on the anarchists' tactics and offers his views on how the workers' movement should proceed.

SOURCE: *El Socialista* (Madrid), November 25, 1892.

The social revolution, that is, the act of force that will allow the conscious working class to secure the elements needed to verify the transformation of property so that social classes are abolished and each individual becomes the owner of the product of his own efforts, constitutes the principal desire of those who yearn to see peace and harmony among all human beings.

Yet just as the bourgeoisie cannot prevent the revolution from breaking out . . . nor can those who favor it make it happen whenever they want. Events, which are superior to the will of man, are what must produce it. The most the bourgeoisie can do, by pursuing a skillful line of conduct, is to delay it. The most that militant proletarians can do, by acting with good judgment and determination, is to accelerate it. And that is what should be proposed.

But we do not work toward the social revolution, we do not get closer to it, by constantly speaking of murder and extermination. We do not get closer to the social revolution by urging the worker to kill the boss who exploits him. Nor by advising the workers to grab what they can from the shop windows and the stores. Nor by speaking to them of burning buildings and destroying other property. Nor by using explosive materials. Nor by recommending mutinies. All of these means, far from helping, harm the social revolution and the emancipation of the working class.

To preach murder and extermination is not only to show ignorance of what the triumph of the proletariat means, but also to make revolutionary ideas distasteful and repulsive to many individuals. The object of the social revolution is to socialize the means of production, so that each one may be the owner of the fruits of his labor and the social equal of all others, but it is not to take away life from these or those individuals. Men are not responsible for the form societies take, and by the same token it is not proper to impose any punishment on them. The only blood the proletariat should cause to flow when it comes to power should be that of those who stand in the way of their victory with weapons, or that of those who have committed atrocities with theirs. Moreover, that which must be awoken in the workers is not hatred for the bourgeois, which is already awake in them because of the way they treat them, but rather their energies, their activity, their consciousness, so that they may understand clearly what their interests are and what they have to do so that they may pass from being wage earners or slaves to being free men.

To recommend that they kill their bosses because they exploit workers is to lead them toward their downfall, not toward working to redeem their class. In killing his exploiter, does the exploited manage to make exploitation disappear or decrease? No, the dead bourgeois is replaced by another, the murderer goes to prison, and the misery of the working class does not decline at all. If these acts should be repeated with some frequency, the ruling class would punish those who committed them very cruelly. The result: the impoverishment of many proletarian families. Besides, is it by attacking persons that the Fourth Estate will be emancipated, or by changing the institutions that create the evils that we now experience? . . .

The same can be said of urging people to seize what is in the stores and the shop windows. One can defend those who, driven by hunger, grab this or that food, but . . . does this kind of act favor the proletarian revolution? No, since at the same time that it discredits it, it causes many who try to put such ideas into practice to go to jail or prison. Moreover, were we to accept such things, the craftiest, the shrewdest, or the most fortunate would change positions, ceasing to be proletarians only to become exploiters. And one must not think that if the workers used such means that the bourgeoisie would be frightened into treating them better, because what the moneyed class would really do would be to arm themselves to the teeth and to punish savagely those who laid a finger on any piece of their property.

The burning of buildings and the destruction of other property would be true foolishness, which would bear out the bourgeois and their defenders who call us barbarians and arsonists. Property being the fruit of labor, and the social interest demanding that property take the communistic form and belong to all, it is beyond explanation, it is absurd, that anyone who favors such a transformation should speak of burning or destroying it. Those who seek to enjoy that which they or their predecessors have produced cannot want the slightest part of the social wealth to be destroyed.

Does the use of explosives give the workers any benefit at this time or for the future? No one can answer affirmatively with any proof. The explosions so far carried out against the bourgeois, aside from the destruction of a few buildings, have produced no other consequences than the death of a few unlucky people or of the servants of a tiny portion of the ruling class, as well as an increase in the number of policemen and agents of public order . . . and the restriction of political liberties. . . . And no one can prove that in Paris, where explosions have been occurring recently, that the bourgeoisie now treats its workers any better, or that the bourgeois politicians have retreated in the defense of their privileges. . . . These explosions are counterproductive; instead of benefiting the working class, they harm it.

We have little to say about mutinies. . . . It is not in this way that the proletariat will take over political power, so mutinies can only induce the bourgeois authorities to limit political liberties even more, to close down workers' associations, to dissolve resistance organizations, to condemn some workers very harshly and to persecute others. . . .

No, we do not progress toward the social revolution by using any of these means to which we have just referred. Calling for murder, arson, looting, explosives, and mutinies will not accelerate economic evolution or make any new ideas penetrate the workers' minds, or make them acquire any greater activity, decision, or energy. All that is achieved is to create obstacles to the revolutionary education and organization of the working class and thus to retard its triumph.

One moves toward the social revolution, one works effectively toward making it happen sooner, by helping the workers to know the causes of their social inferiority; by making them notice the effects of economic phenomena and the foundations that these have, and [by showing them that] what is essential is the transformation of the means of production; by organizing them everywhere so that they can struggle against their bosses when they try to worsen their situation or when they oppose the improvements that are demanded; by organizing them equally so that they fight in the political terrain against all the parties that represent the ruling class; in a word, by giving them the necessary consciousness and vigor, so that when the opportune moment arrives, they have what it takes to defeat the bourgeoisie and to create the new social order that must replace the capitalist regime.

The privileged class, incapable of conjuring away the many conflicts that in the final phase of their development must necessarily be produced, will offer a propitious occasion for the active proletariat that knows its interests and its historic mission and can exercise its revolutionary action and put an end to the class that exploits productive humanity.

23. *La Epoca*, "Anarchist Attack in Barcelona" (1893)

Anarchists, as opponents of the very existence of national governments, refused to work within the parliamentary system, turning to "direct action" by the late nineteenth century and carrying out assassinations and other violent acts. The following report of one of the anarchists' more notorious actions appeared in the moderately conservative Madrid-based newspaper *La Epoca* on November 8, 1893.

SOURCE: *La Epoca* (Madrid), November 8, 1893; the text also appears in Fernando Díaz-Plaja, ed., *Historia de España en sus documentos: Siglo XIX* (Madrid: Cátedra, 1983), 436–38.

Bombs Exploded

The cultured Catalan capital last night witnessed a horrible attack, similar to the one that Pallás recently carried out on the Gran Vía.

The new season opened last night in the Teatro del Liceo, with the presentation of Verdi's opera, *William Tell*. The hall, our correspondent reports, looked magnificent: the boxes and orchestra seats were filled with the elite of Barcelona society, and the galleries were filled with people.

When the second act began, after the duet between the soprano and the tenor, a very loud sound was heard, similar to prolonged thunder. The public thought that a gas explosion had occurred, and screaming in terror, people rushed for the exits, trampling on each other. In the midst of the frightening confusion voices were heard saying, "It's a bomb! I saw it fall from above!" The singers fled from the stage in terror, and the spectators viewed with astonishment the central rows of the orchestra seats, where there were cadavers of various ladies and gentlemen, covered in blood.

From all directions one could hear cries of outrage and pain, while the police tried to calm the public in order to catch the criminals.

A Horrible Picture—What Happened Next

The people who were trying to leave the theater ran into a large group who were struggling to get in to find out about loved ones inside the theater.

The seats in rows 12, 13, and 14 were blown to bits, especially around the center aisle. Near the dead bodies were various injured people screaming in pain. Some ladies were suffering from fits; in the hallways the screaming was deafening, and some people were helping the police to move the injured.

From what I have heard from various spectators in the top balcony, this is what happened: an individual in the front rows threw an object to the main floor, and at that moment an explosion was heard. Some claim to have seen two objects. The explosion was immediate, causing the events described. . . .

The Bombs

A so-called Orsini bomb, which gave its inventor such notoriety, was found under a row of seats. It was unclear why it did not explode after falling from the fifth balcony, leading some to believe that someone left it there, hoping to set it off at the right moment. From fragments found, it has been learned that the bomb that exploded was the same kind as the one found under the seats. Both are also identical to the one that injured the illustrious General Martínez Campos and killed the Civil Guard Tous on the Gran Vía.

Anarchists Detained

Guards quickly gathered at the theater, investigating the bomb that did not explode. Accompanying them were three subjects known for their anarchist ideas: one of them, who was detained in the top balcony, seems to have been accused by some of the spectators of having thrown the bomb. . . .

A Conspiracy?

Different versions of the attack were circulating, which our correspondent reports with all due reserve.

Some believe that those responsible belong to an anarchist society of which Paulino Pallás was a member. The fact that the bombs were identical to those used at the Gran Vía is the basis of this view.

There are those who blame the civil governor, who was caught unaware by the events. . . .

Opinion in Barcelona

In the plazas, cafés, and streets people were discussing the events at the theater until late into the night. People were unanimous in calling on the government to take extraordinary measures to finish off the anarchists. People feel that violent propaganda should be outlawed, as it leads to crimes such as the one Barcelona is lamenting. . . .

The press is unanimous in demanding strong measures to punish the authors of this savage attack. *La Epoca* has expressed its opinion on various occasions, asking the public powers for special laws to punish, with the necessary energy and severity, those who, on the pretext of defending ideas of social equality, commit crimes worthy of monsters and bring destruction and terror to so many homes.

24. Enric Prat de la Riba, *Compendium of Catalanist Doctrine* (1894)

Those Catalans who sought to advance the region's fortunes and powers within the framework of a Spanish state faced several obstacles, not the least of which was trying to spread their message to a broader public. Borrowing the form of the catechism, which the Catholic Church had developed for instructing those with limited education and literacy, a leading Catalan activist, Enric Prat de la Riba, published the following pamphlet in 1894 (with assistance from a colleague, Pere Muntanyola). Prat de la Riba (1870–1917) was born near Barcelona in a family of rural landowners; after earning a law degree, he began a remarkable career of promoting Catalan consciousness and rights, founding various political organizations and newspapers, most notably *La Veu de Catalunya.* For the last three years of his life, he headed the Mancomunitat, a federation of governments of the four Catalan provinces.

SOURCE: Enric Prat de la Riba with Pere Muntanyola, *Compendi de la doctrina catalanista, premiat en lo concurs regionalista del Centre Catala de Sabadell* (Sabadell: Impremta de lo Catalanista, 1894).

I. The Fatherland

Q: What is the most fundamental political duty?

A: To love the fatherland.

Q: What is the Catalans' fatherland?

A: Catalonia.

Q: Is there some basis for the distinction between the lesser fatherland and the greater fatherland?

A: None; man has only one fatherland, just as he has only one father and one family. What is generally called the greater fatherland is nothing but the state made up of various social groups that are true fatherlands.

Q: So Spain, therefore, is not the Catalans' fatherland?

A: It is no more than a state, or a political organization to which they belong.

Q: What difference is there between the state and the fatherland?

A: The state is a voluntary, artificial, political entity. The fatherland is a necessary, natural, historical community. The former is the work of men; the latter is the fruit of the laws to which God has subjected the life of human generations.

Q: What example from contemporary history makes these differences clear?

A: That of Poland. The Polish state died when the Prussian, Russian, and Austrian armies divided it up; but Poland continues to be the only fatherland of the unfortunate Polish.

Q: So what is the fatherland?

A: The community of people who speak the same language, have a common history, and live as brothers in a single spirit that imprints with something original and characteristic all the manifestations of its life.

II. Catalonia

Q: How should we regard Catalonia?

A: As a long chain of generations united by the Catalan language and tradition, which follow one another in the land we have occupied.

Q: Is the Catalan tongue a language or a dialect?

A: It is a language. People call it a dialect, some out of ignorance, others out of ill will, considering it a corruption of the official language, Castilian [Spanish].

Q: So it's not a corruption of Castilian?

A: Quite the contrary; the Catalan language is older than Castilian, and it had already acquired a certain splendor when Castilian had just begun to show signs of existence.

Q: But is it true that Castilian is a prettier language?

A: On the contrary; Catalan is prettier, because while our language has eight vowel sounds of many gradations, much like French, Castilian only has five vowel sounds, all open, and it is full of guttural sounds such as the j and the light a, which resemble Semitic languages.

Q: Then how can you explain the error being so common among Catalans?

. . .

A: It comes from . . . being seduced by the attraction of novelty . . . and from the imperfection with which many Catalans speak our language, a result of it not being taught in the schools.

Q: What elements make up the Catalan character?

A: A practical, utilitarian spirit, a commercial spirit, and an open and decidedly liberal and traditionalist temperament as well.

Q: How can this commercial spirit be demonstrated?

A: It has been demonstrated by the growth of Catalan commerce despite the obstacles placed by Spanish governments, and by the fact that Catalonia was, when it governed itself, one of the leading commercial and maritime powers in Europe.

Q: But didn't Catalan industry have the Spanish market available?

A: Yes, but the Spanish market is quite inferior to that which Catalonia had been able to conquer in the period of its autonomy. So Castilian policy, working toward Spanish uniformity, has hampered the expansion of Catalan trade and industry, limiting it to Spain and its colonies, and thus tying together the different nations of the [Spanish] state by their interests

Q: And how is Catalonia's love for liberty demonstrated?

A: In the truly democratic institutions that Catalonia has had in past centuries; in the determined and heroic struggles with which it resisted absolutism. . . .

VI. Catalonia's Demands

Q: What famous phrase summarizes our aspirations and constitutes the slogan on our flag?

A: Catalonia for the Catalans!

Q: What does that phrase mean?

A: That Catalans have to govern Catalonia, and not, as they have, Castilians, or Castilian-style politicians . . . [as if] we were children or did not know how.

Q: How must we put an end to that insulting imposition?

A: By decreeing that all public offices in Catalonia must be occupied by Catalans.

Q: What else must we demand?

A: Catalonia's indisputable right to constitute and organize itself according to its needs and character and to give itself laws of any kind that are most suitable to its way of life.

Q: What other rights must be recognized?

A: That of using the Catalan language as the only official language in all public and private acts.

Q: How can those extremely just demands be harmonized with the political unity of Spain?

A: Through a regionalist organization that consists of a federative union of the ancient Spanish nationalities.

Q: What attributes would the central or federal power have in that organization?

A: All those related to Spain's relations with other states and, in general, to interests that are common to all Spanish regions, with the army, the customs service, the railroads, etc.

Q: And the Catalan national government?

A: It would have all the rest.

Q: How would the Catalan Cortes [parliament] be formed?

A: By means of universal suffrage of heads of households, by unions and professions, in order to put an end to the kind of parliamentarianism that turns the governing of the states over to professional speechmakers. . . .

Q: Won't the establishment of the regionalist system cause major disturbances to Catalan commerce and industry?

A: No, because the economic system will be the same throughout all of Spain . . . and our producers will be able to conquer the most important markets for us.

Q: And yet, in retaliation for our breaking their monopoly on the government, won't the Castilian people reject our products?

A: Private interest is the motive behind commerce, and so all such attempts motivated by rivalries between peoples have always failed.

Q: Are there any countries in which an organization like the one just described has been established?

A: Switzerland, the United States, Germany, the United Kingdom, the Austro-Hungarian Empire, etc.

Will We Triumph?

Q: Being fewer in number as we are, is it possible that we will win?

A: It is certain, because we are not the only ones to strive for this, and besides, the trends of the current period are favorable to us.

Q: Whose help can Catalonia count on?

A: On that of Navarre, the Basque country, and Galicia, and, in short, on that of the other states of the old Crown of Aragon. All of those regions desire for themselves what we want for Catalonia. . . .

Q: What will replace the current regime?

A: Regionalism, because all the other systems of government are discredited by the disastrous results they have produced.

25. Sabino de Arana, "What Are We?" (1895)

Sabino de Arana y Goiri (1865–1903) was the son of a shipbuilder who supported the Carlists. As a young man he embraced his father's conservative Catholicism, but he rejected the Carlists and began to develop a keen sense of Basque nationalism. Eventually, Arana became a founding father of the modern Basque nation, coining the term "Euskadi" to give the country the name it had lacked, as well as writing the words to a national anthem, designing a flag, and founding the Basque National Party. His harshly polemic style and combative personality alienated many, and his views embarrassed even many Basque nationalists, but his role in founding Basque nationalism is undeniable. The following article, published in Spanish and entitled "What Are We?" appeared in a Basque newspaper. Although he refers here to Vizcaya, a province within the Basque country, his ideas obviously applied to the entire Basque territory.

SOURCE: *Bizkaitarra* (Bilbao), June 16, 30 and July 7, 1895; the text also appears in Sabino de Arana, *Antología de Sabino Arana: Textos escogidos del fundador del nacionalismo vasco* (Donostia-San Sebastián: Roger, 1999), 264–76.

We Vizcayans, are we Russians? Such a question would occur to no one.

Are we Austrians? Nor would anyone ask that.

Are we Spaniards? Here is the crux of the problem, and all of our misfortunes lie in the affirmative answer to that question.

Let us then give a brief answer to such a significant question. . . .

Nationality can be determined or classified using five characteristics or elements. But to begin, let us establish some basic assumptions. Let us start from the point of view of the law, not actual fact. In other words, though we Vizcayans may seem Spanish, in that we are ruled by Spanish laws governed by the Spanish government, this means nothing if, looking squarely at history, it turns out that things are contrary to their true nature. In a word, we are going to demonstrate that the Vizcayans are not Spanish by their nature, although they may be in fact, and by force; our demonstration thus has no other object than to serve as a foundation for the definition of the rights of Vizcaya.

We have said, then, that the elements or characteristics of nationality are five in number. They are (1) race; (2) language; (3) government and laws; (4) character and customs; (5) historical personality.

Is the Vizcayan a Spaniard by race?

Let us see what race the Spaniard is.

Some twenty-odd centuries before the birth of Jesus Christ the Celts arrived in Spain, and they mixed with the people who already lived in most of the territory. It seems certain that the race that already populated the area was that which now speaks Basque. . . . After the Celts, the Phoenicians invaded many parts of Spain; then, the Greeks. Later, the Romans completely conquered it, mixing with the natives to the point that the native race disappeared, with Latin replacing the older language. For this reason, Spain is now one of the Latin nations. . . . The Spanish race is a product of all the invasions that have taken place over more than forty centuries: the Celts, Phoenicians, Greeks, Romans, Germans, and Arabs, with the Latin element predominating.

Now let us see what the Vizcayan race is. This race is part of that which speaks the language called Basque. This very original race is neither Celtic, nor Phoenician, nor Greek, nor Latin, nor Germanic, nor Arab. . . . It is distinct to the point that there is no evidence that would serve to categorize it among the other races of the earth. The Vizcayan is thus not a Spaniard by race. . . .

Is the Vizcayan a Spaniard by language?

Which is the Spanish language? There is one official language, Castilian, but the native languages are many: Catalan, Valencian, Galician, Asturian, Portuguese, etc. Portuguese now belongs to a portion of the territory of Spain that is set apart from the whole and stands as an independent kingdom. Some believe that Catalan, Galician, etc. are derivations from Castilian, being mixed with French, but this is a popular misconception: Castilian, Catalan, Galician, and all the Spanish languages are direct descendants of Latin . . . with touches of Arabic and Gothic.

And what is the Vizcayan language? It is a dialect of Basque; more precisely, one of the various forms in which that language now appears. Now then, before the Spanish languages began to be formed, before Latin originated, even before Sanskrit existed, this mother tongue of the Indo-European languages that is now spoken only in a small territory in India existed, as fully developed as now. Philologists keep discovering more or less close relations among the languages spoken throughout the far corners of the world. Only Basque remains isolated among all the other languages, as the race that speaks it is among the races of the world. . . . The most one can deduce is that it had a close relationship with the mother tongue or tongues of all known languages. Thus Vizcayans are no more Spaniards by language than are the Chinese, the Zulus, the Greenlanders, the Lapps, the English, the Turks, or any other nationality.

Is the Vizcayan a Spaniard by government and laws?

Spain, in the second century before Christ, passed from the rule of the Carthaginians (who were of the Phoenician race and had dominated for some time) to that of the Romans, who divided it into provinces, governing them with praetors. Roman domination lasted until the fifth century A.D., so consequently Spain obeyed Roman power for those six centuries, and the laws by which it was ruled were Roman.

From the fifth through the eighth century, the Latin nation was subjected to Visigothic kings, so the laws were then Gothic-Roman. When Spain, in the eighth century, was invaded by the Arabs, and its various regions could no longer communicate with each other, a movement of reaction began independently in each of them, producing the development and formation of various other kingdoms and counties, and each one obeyed its particular sovereign and was ruled by distinct laws (derived primarily from those of Rome), while that abnormal state of Muslim domination persisted.

Once that yoke was shaken off, those small states naturally began slowly uniting, reconstituting the national whole that had been fragmented, with all coming together under a common government. Nevertheless, amid this fusion of regions, some regions and cities preserved certain special laws and privileges (*fueros*) obtained from those who had been their individual kings and feudal lords. In the modern era, however, to the unity of the government was added the unity of the laws, and Spain came to be a unified state, as it had been before the Arab invasion. Thus the Spanish legal code is a combination of Roman, Gothic, indigenous, and French laws, just as the Spanish people are a combination of those races. Let us see whether the government and laws of Vizcaya have been distinct.

The history of Vizcaya before the ninth century is almost completely unknown. It is only known that Vizcaya was never subjugated by any nation in any previous time.

In the ninth century, our fatherland appears to have been divided into various confederations of republics. The family was a real state within the republic or the ecclesiastical district, the republic within the federation, and the confederation within Vizcaya, if all did not govern themselves in common.

The government of Vizcaya resided, then, in the people, gathered in a general assembly. The laws were simply customs of that same people, that is, resolutions passed following the public sense in the practice of social life. Toward the end of the ninth century Vizcaya instituted the seigneurial form, that is to say, it freely named the first *jaun* (lord). The latter had no role in the legislative authority, as kings do. It was the assembly or Junta General that continued to legislate.

In 1379, the then-lord of Vizcaya inherited the Crown of Castile-León, and given that the latter was hereditary and the position of lord of Vizcaya was also normally conferred in the same form, from that time on one single person was simultaneously lord of Vizcaya and king of Castile-León, titles whose functions could not be blended together. . . . The Junta General retained legislative authority, so the laws either originated from Vizcayan customs or they were laid down and authorized by the Vizcayans themselves. This is how the government and legislation of Vizcaya worked until Spain enslaved it in this century. Thus the Vizcayan is not a Spaniard by his government and laws.

Is the Vizcayan a Spaniard by his type, his character, and customs?

The face of the Vizcayan is intelligent and noble; that of the Spaniard is inexpressive and passive. The walk of the Vizcayan is manly and stylish; the Spaniard either does not know how to walk stylishly, . . . or, if he does, [his walk] is feminine (for example, the bullfighter). The Vizcayan is tough and agile; the Spaniard is weak and languid. The Vizcayan is intelligent and skilled in all kinds of labors; the Spaniard is short on intelligence and lacks the aptitude for even the plainest of labors. Ask any contractor and you will see that a Vizcayan can do in a given amount of time what it would take three *maketos* [a derogatory term for Spaniards] to do. The Vizcayan is hard-working (see how his hillsides are cultivated all the way to the summit); the Spaniard, lazy and aimless (notice his immense plains completely lacking in vegetation). The Vizcayan is entrepreneurial (look at history, and also see him now occupying lofty and respected positions everywhere—except in his own country); the Spaniard undertakes nothing, dares to do nothing, and is good for nothing (look at the state of his colonies).

The Vizcayan is not well suited to serve, having been born to be a lord . . . [while] the Spaniard was only born to be a vassal and a servant. . . . The Vizcayan's character degenerates through contact with foreign lands; the Spaniard occasionally needs a foreign invasion to civilize him. . . .

The Vizcayan family shows more concern for food than clothing, which although it is clean, is modest; go to Spain and you will see families whose daughters eat nothing but onions, peppers, and raw tomatoes, but out in the streets they dress extravagantly, even if their underclothing is of poor quality.

The Vizcayan who lives in the mountains, which is the true Vizcayan, is naturally religious (go to a mass in an outlying village and you will learn what I mean); the Spaniard who lives far from population centers, which is the true Spaniard, either does not know a word of religion, or is a fanatic, or is impious. . . . Hear a Vizcayan speak, and you will hear the most melodious, moral, and cultured of tongues; hear a Spaniard, and if you only hear him braying like a donkey, you can be satisfied, for the donkey does not pronounce indecent words and blasphemies.

The Vizcayan loves his family and home (as for the former, it is well known that adultery is very rare in families not infected by *maketo* influence, that is, in truly Vizcayan families; as for the latter, if the Vizcayan, out of his entrepreneurial character, has to go away from his home, he does not go a single day without longing for home); among the Spaniards, adultery is common in both the upper and lower classes, and affection for the home is nonexistent, since they do not have a home.

Finally, according to statistics, 95 percent of the crimes committed in Vizcaya are committed by Spaniards, and four out of the remaining five are committed by Hispanicized Vizcayans.

You tell me, then, whether the Vizcayan is a Spaniard by type, character, and customs.

26. Francisco Silvela, "Without a Pulse" (1898)

In 1895, rebellion broke out again in Spain's main colony, Cuba, and over the next three years American newspapers carried tales of Spanish atrocities in the war against the rebels. In 1898, the USS *Maine* blew up and sank in Havana harbor under circumstances that were unclear at the time, but which American newspapers—amid a furious circulation battle—blamed on Spain. After Washington demanded that Spain grant Cuba independence, Spain chose to declare war. The war known to North Americans as the Spanish-American War lasted only a few months, as American ships proved far superior to Spain's outdated fleet. In the peace treaty, Spain agreed to give up Cuba, Puerto Rico, the Philippines, and Guam (all of which then came under U.S. influence).

The defeat humiliated Spanish nationalists, and it touched off a wave of accusations and recriminations, as well as countless essays analyzing Spain's ills. Among those taking part in this collective introspection was Francisco Silvela (1845–1905), leader of the Conservative Union Party, writing in the Madrid-based daily newspaper *El Tiempo.*

SOURCE: *El Tiempo* (Madrid), August 16, 1898; the text also appears in Francisco Silvela, *Artículos, discursos, conferencias y cartas* (Madrid: Mateu Artes Gráficas, 1922–23), 2: 493–98.

"Illustrious men, how long will you harden your hearts? Why do you love vanity, and why do you seek out lies?" [Psalm 4: 2].

We would like to hear these words or similar ones springing from the lips of the people, but we hear nothing. We perceive neither agitation of minds nor movement among people. Those with doctorates in politics and the analysts of minds will study the evil, no doubt, and they will orate about its origins, its qualities, and its solutions; but ordinary people who pay any attention to public affairs will note this strange state Spain is in: wherever you may put your fingers, you will not find a pulse.

Monarchists, republicans, conservatives, liberals, all those who have any interest in the survival of this national body must be alarmed and worried about such a fact. . . . The war with the ungrateful sons of Cuba did not move a single fiber of the national sentiment. The orators in the chambers spoke with eloquence of sacrificing the last peseta and spilling the final drop of blood . . . of other people; the municipalities praised the soldiers who saluted and marched in rank . . . ; the "Marcha de Cádiz" was played; the press applauded, and the inert country let all of this be done for it. . . .

Then peace was made, as reason demanded, which men of sound judgment do not dispute. But it means our defeat, the expulsion of our flag from lands we discovered and conquered. . . . Everyone expected and feared some agitation in the popular conscience, but one only saw a vague cloud of silent sadness that acted like a gray background of a picture, and there was no alteration of customs or diversions. . . .

It is that materialism has taken us over, some said. It is that selfishness is killing us, that the ideas of duty, glory, and national honor have passed away, that martial passions have died out, that no one any longer thinks about anything but his own personal benefit.

This is a profound error. This combination of good and bad passions that constitute the soul of a people . . . are an expression of man's essential nature. What is happening is that when a people is weakened and dies, their passions are weakened and die; it is not that their instincts or their ideas, or their affections and ways of feeling, are transformed and modified, it is that they are finished off by an even more serious cause: by the extinction of life. . . .

Those who have as their job and their responsibility the direction of the state will not be fulfilling their most basic duties if they do not quickly and energetically seek a solution to this problem, seeking to limit the damage through a total change of the system that has brought the public spirit to such a point.

We must set aside lies and seek the truth; we must abandon vanities and subject ourselves to reality, reconstituting all the organisms of the national life on modest but firm foundations that our means will allow us, not on the empty forms of a conventionalism that fools no one and mocks and discourages everyone.

We must not pretend we have arsenals and shipyards where we have only buildings and installations that guard nothing and build nothing. We must not consider as a fleet that which does not maneuver and does not fire its guns, nor count as armies mere collections of young men eligible for the draft, nor strive to keep more than that which we can administer without disastrous fictions. . . . We must raise at any cost, and without pausing for bitterness and sacrifices and risks of partial objections and rebellions, the moral concept of central governments, because if this . . . does not take place, the disintegration of the national body is sure to happen.

The inevitable effect of a country's disrespect for its central government is the same as that produced in living bodies by anemia and the decline of its central force. . . . If we do not change course soon, the risk will be infinitely greater, being deeper, and the solution will be impossible if we are too late, producing the risk of a total breakdown of national bonds and our own condemnation of our destiny as a European people.

27. Pablo Iglesias, "Our Bourgeoisie" (1898)

As opinions about what was wrong with Spain poured forth in the aftermath of Spain's humiliating military defeat in 1898, the Socialist Party leader Pablo Iglesias offered his own diagnosis in the party newspaper, *El Socialista*.

SOURCE: *El Socialista* (Madrid), August 17, 1898.

We have said it many times. No country has as inept a bourgeoisie as Spain. Neither the bourgeoisie of the colonies nor that of the privileged soil of the [Iberian] peninsula has been able to obtain the immense benefits that another, less stupid, could have gotten.

Lacking in education, dominated by routine, without even the gift of being able to imitate good things done in other nations, it has scarcely entered in the sphere of modern production, as its industry and agriculture remain very backward.

Instead of covering the country with railroads, multiplying the telegraph lines, digging canals to connect the rivers, repopulating the countryside, and promoting general education (especially primary education), it is lazy and careless, contenting itself to tell tales from our history, many of which are nothing to be proud of, and it only aspires to live on the interest it earns from buying government bonds.

As one might expect, its political leaders are at the same level. They have neither foresight, nor knowledge, nor initiative. Substituting for these good qualities pointless jabbering and a cynical idleness, they care least about developing the country's wealth—which is where the country's regeneration must occur—and they pay most of their attention to securing positions in the government and seeking their own personal gain.

Look at most of the bourgeois politicians; compare their modest origins with the luxurious positions they now occupy in society, and you will find the proof for what we are saying. Hard work, basic hard work, being so poorly paid, allows no one to become a millionaire in the present social system.

With such a bourgeoisie and such politicians it will surprise no one that Spain has gotten caught up in a war with the United States; that is to say, with the most powerful country in the world.

What would we have said about a three-year-old child who would have challenged or accepted the challenge of a man six feet tall, young and strong? That it was foolishness. But our bourgeois and their political representatives have committed this foolishness by not avoiding—which was possible—the conflict with the North American republic.

They did not take into account the immense economic power of that nation; they did not realize that wealth is today what gives a nation strength and energy, and they now confront, and make us confront, all the consequences of such tremendous stupidity.

Is it that bourgeoisie and those politicians who call the socialists senseless, utopian dreamers because of the ideas we support, for the reforms we seek, and the tactics we use? They are the ones who are senseless and dreaming!

To live in reality, we socialists, instead of declaring war, propose solutions that could avoid it.

To live in reality, we socialists, when the conflict was about to break out, argued that it must be avoided at all costs.

To live in reality, and to see our predictions confirmed almost at the very beginning of the war, we socialists called strongly for peace.

To live in reality, and being strongly convinced of the great damage the war had to produce, we socialists have not stopped calling on the fools of all classes to seek peace.

And peace we now have; and peace the bourgeoisie and all the politicians now want, with only a few exceptions.

Who was in the right? Who demonstrated more reflection, more judgment, better calculation? It was not the bourgeois, nor the governors chosen by them; it was the socialists.

The socialists, opposing the war before it was declared and defending peace from the instant the conflict broke out, looked out for the interests of the working class but, at the same time, for the interests of the bourgeoisie as well.

Yes, the rare case has occurred when the socialists have had to defend, against the actions of the ruling class, not only the proletarians' interests, but also those of the ruling class itself.

Such is the mental state of our bourgeoisie, a mental state that, if it is not modified, will make our country suffer new calamities and will hamper the economic evolution whose outcome will be the triumph of revolutionary socialism.

28. The Army and the Catalans (1905)

In the early twentieth century, relations between the military and civilians were in a poor state for various reasons, including Spain's humiliating defeat in the 1898 war with the United States. In that war many officers felt that civilians and politicians had not supported them adequately, while many civilians called into question the military's competence and bravery. Moreover, the loss of Cuba, where Catalan investors and industrialists had extensive interests, fueled the growth of regional movements that questioned close ties with Castile and Spain's central government, while the continuing growth of those regional movements (in the Basque country as well as Catalonia) in turn led Spanish nationalists in the military to see those movements as a real threat to Spain's integrity and existence.

In 1905, as these tensions were building, a Catalan organization decided to hold a political banquet in Barcelona; at the same time, a Catalan newspaper, *Cu-cut*, published a cartoon that many officers found insulting. The following article reporting on the reaction of the Cortes to these events appeared in the army newspaper *El Ejército Español.*

SOURCE: *El Ejército Español* (Madrid), November 23, 1905; the text also appears in Fernando Díaz-Plaja, ed., *Historia de España en sus documentos (nueva serie): El siglo XX*, vol. 1, *1900–1923* (Madrid: Instituto de Estudios Políticos, 1960), 97–99.

The session held yesterday in the Congress, dealing with the shameful events provoked by the Catalan separatists, did not live up to expectations, nor was it equal to the task at hand. A republican deputy, Mr. Junoy, and a Carlist deputy, Mr. Lloréns, spoke, placing in their speeches all the indignation that the sight of the fatherland being wounded in its most sacred dignity and threatened in its untouchable integrity produces in all good Spaniards. The government minister was in a poor way, weak, as if he did not feel any patriotism. Two Catalan regionalist deputies, without going to the extremes of the separatists, also failed to find the phrases called for at that moment to place our mother Spain above their passions, above their ideas, above their interests. Mr. Junoy and Mr. Lloréns, they and they alone in the Congress yesterday, were the defenders of the prestige of the fatherland.

And when the incident was declared over, the impression could not have been more disastrous. Those who consider themselves patriots were hoping for more, much more. They hoped to hear . . . virile tones proclaiming punishments for those who would dare to insult Spain; they hoped that in this session the mayor of Barcelona would be removed from office for having committed the criminal imprudence of having attended the [Catalan nationalist] banquet on Sunday, whose antipatriotic meaning was well known. They also hoped to hear from the lips of the regionalist deputies an energetic protest condemning the shameful events, anathema launched against the spurious sons of Spain who renounce their mother amid the echoes of this hymn of impotent hatred called "Los Segadores" [a Catalan anthem]. And since they did not see any of these things, they wondered upon leaving the session what interests the governmental parties of the monarchy could have, in that when it is a question of defending the insulted and ridiculed fatherland, there are only republicans in the streets of Barcelona, and a republican and a Carlist in the hall of the Congress.

Beyond this, our opinion is already known. Our hopes have not been betrayed, because we never hope for anything from the Cortes. The answer to the separatist rabble is in the army. To the weakness of the governments that equivocate with them, one must oppose the extremely firm will of the soldiers, who cannot and must not consent to these outrages against Spain.

All opinions are legitimate, even the most absurd ones, even those that appear to be most disturbing, but not those that go against the fatherland. The fatherland cannot be attacked. The fatherland is untouchable, for the fatherland is everything: the air that we breathe, the cradle of our children, the tomb of our forefathers. To offend the fatherland is to offend our own mother. Anyone who would allow Spain to be insulted would allow his own mother, who carried him inside of her, to be insulted, and the soldiers, who because of their career are more obliged than others to have sentiments for the fatherland, cannot and must not tolerate its being insulted. Against the foreigner who would dare to attack it, there is war; against the unworthy Spaniard who commits this crime, there is the law. If the law, for not having made provisions for this case, does not punish the crime, then individual initiative must.

Will the Cortes make up for the deficiencies of the laws? Then let it pass these reforms, but immediately, in a single session, by acclamation and without debate. It is not a matter of political ideas or of individual opinions, but rather of something that is common to all, that is the patrimony of all, that is under the safeguard of all.

The Cortes will not do this? Then may the soldiers do it alone.

May all be filled with a sense of the duty that is facing them, and either in isolation, without working together, or in a group, wherever they may be found, and wherever they hear the cry "Death to Spain," may they smother the criminal cry in the throats that pronounce it without even thinking of the consequences that this act of theirs might have. And if they die? Well, then they will have died for the fatherland, fulfilling the oath they swore upon entering the service. And if a weak government should punish them? Well, then the punishment, in this case suffered for the fatherland, will be an honor for them and a laurel for their banners. Anything, anything but tolerating what is now being tolerated. Anything, anything except permitting the dirty hordes of sons without mothers to bellow against that which is the mother of all the Spaniards.

A handful of soldiers from the garrison at Bilbao [in the Basque country] understood things this way a few years ago. The fact cannot be forgotten, because we recall it frequently.

The civic parade of May 2 was being celebrated in that town, and the "Bizcaitarras" [Basque activists] had partly unfurled their banner in the circle they have in that city. As the procession passed in front of the circle, a very worthy colonel, who is now a general, saw the insulting banner flying and felt it like a slap in the face. "Arriba," he said, and all the chiefs and officials at his side understood him. Seized by the same feeling, they broke ranks, went up to the "Bizcaitarra" circle, trampled on the members who wished to block their way, took hold of the banner, tore it into pieces, which they threw from the balcony, and, going back down calmly after having avenged the insult to Spain, went back to join the cortege, and the parade continued on its route. There lay the shreds of the banner and the "Bizcaitarras" on the ground. They did not even dare to complain, out of fear that the soldiers might return.

Ever since then, there have been no more separatist demonstrations in Bilbao.

The liberal Madrid-based newspaper *El Imparcial* published the following report in November 1905.

SOURCE: *El Imparcial,* November 27, 1905; the text also appears in Fernando Díaz-Plaja, ed., *Historia de España en sus documento (nueva serie): El siglo XX,* vol. 1, *1900–1923* (Madrid: Instituto de Estudios Políticos, 1960), 100.

Last night, at the beginning of the evening, more than two hundred army officers, bothered by the cartoons and articles that the Catalan press was publishing, gathered in the Plaza Real. They began to shout "Long live Spain!" and from there they marched to the presses of the Catalanist weekly *Cu-cut*. They smashed all the tools and equipment they found, and they took a large number of newspapers and set fire to them, creating a huge bonfire.

From there they marched to Cardenal Casañas Street, where the editorial offices of the same newspaper are located, and they repeated the scene, smashing the furniture and setting it on fire, beating those they found inside and forcing them to shout "Long live Spain!"

The officers then marched to the Ramblas de las Flores, where the newspaper *La Veu* is located. They once again entered the editorial offices, smashed a great amount of furniture and presses, and once again set them on fire. They struck those who were there with their swords and forced them to shout "Long live Spain!" They destroyed everything, respecting only the Catalan coat of arms, saying that Catalonia was a Spanish province.

Several people were injured as a result of the blows from the swords, one of them seriously. The military governor, the acting captain general, went to the editorial offices of *La Veu*, found the officers, and forced them to go to the headquarters of the military government. Summary proceedings have been ordered, with a special judge having been named by Commander Gotarredona.

29. Alejandro Lerroux, "Rebels, Rebels!" (1906)

Amid the growing political tensions of the time, a lawyer and journalist named Alejandro Lerroux y García (1864–1949) made a name for himself by issuing fiery, often anticlerical, messages to the lower classes. Elected to the Cortes from a working-class district in Barcelona in 1901, he became the leader of the Radical Republican Party, which enjoyed considerable support from the lower middle classes, particularly in Catalonia (though he was a rival of the Catalan movement and did not support its aims). Although Lerroux was known as one of Spain's more inflammatory political figures, the following article, which appeared in the Barcelona newspaper *La Rebeldía* on September 1, 1906, exemplified the rhetorical violence and excess that marked Spanish political culture in those years. Lerroux's activities and writings often earned him time in jail and exile, but he later became increasingly moderate, ending up cooperating with the right while serving as prime minister during the Second Republic in the 1930s.

SOURCE: *La Rebeldía* (Barcelona), September 1, 1906; the text also appears in Alejandro Lerroux, *De la lucha: Páginas de Alejandro Lerroux* (Barcelona: F. Granada, 1909), 119–20.

Rebels, rebels!

Fight, fine legion of rebels, for the sacred destinies, for the noble destinies of a great race, of a great people now perishing, of a great fatherland that is sinking.

Rise up so that you will join a humanity from which you have been excluded for four hundred years.

Young barbarians of today, go in and sack the decadent and miserable civilization of this unfortunate country, destroy its temples, finish off its gods, tear the veils from its nuns and turn them into mothers to invigorate the species, go into the property registers and make bonfires of their papers so that the flames will purify the infamous social organization, go into the humble homes and assemble legions of proletarians, so that the world will tremble in fear of their awakened judgment.

Everything must be made anew, with the dusty stones, with the smoking rafters of the old toppled edifices, but first we need the catapult that brings down the walls and the battering ram that levels the mansions.

Discover the new moral world and go in search of it with all your youthful energy, with all your apocalyptic boldness.

Push on, push on, . . . and do not even stop before the tombs or the altars.

There is nothing sacred on the earth other than the land, and you will make it fertile with your knowledge, with your labor, with your love. . . .

"The school and the pantry," said the greatest of Spanish patriots, Joaquín Costa.

In order to create the school we must topple the church or at least close it or reduce it to a subordinate position.

In order to fill the pantry we must create the worker and organize labor.

This whole gigantic project is opposed by tradition, routine, entrenched privileges, conservative interests, caciquismo, clericalism, entailed estates, centralism, and the stupid collection of parties and programs made up by empty heads in the machines that fabricate religious dogma and political despotism.

Young people, make all of this crumble, as you can, as in France, as in Russia. Create an atmosphere of self-sacrifice. Spread the contagion of heroism. Fight, kill, die . . .

And if those who come after do not organize a more just society and more honorable powers, the fault will not be theirs, but rather yours.

Yours, because at the moment of action, you will have been cowardly or timid.

30. The Tarrasa Manifesto (1909)

In Catalonia in July 1909, social and political tensions were escalating when the army, which was fighting a colonial war in Morocco, issued a new call for reservists to report for combat duty. Many workers from Barcelona objected to fighting in a war they felt served only the interests of a few capitalists, and they also resented their having to fight while sons of the bourgeoisie could buy their way out of military service. As one contingent of soldiers was preparing to depart, a group of conservative Catholic women handed the departing troops religious medals to thank them for their military service, but some of the resentful soldiers (who undoubtedly held anticlerical, if not atheistic, views) began tossing their medals into the water, and that action helped touch off a broader revolt in Catalonia. As calls for a general strike and rebellion proliferated, a group of workers and labor organizers met at the town of Tarrasa, near Barcelona, and drafted the following statement. The ensuing events, which included a massive general strike, burnings of churches, and a particularly bloody government crackdown in which troops shot over one hundred workers, later came to be known as "the Tragic Week."

SOURCE: Luis Simarro Lacabra, *El proceso Ferrer y la opinión europea*, vol. 1 (Madrid: Eduardo Arias, 1910), 47–48.

Considering that the war is a fatal consequence of the regime of capitalist production; considering, moreover, that given the Spanish system of military recruitment, the workers alone fight the wars that the bourgeois declare; the assembly protests energetically:

1. Against the actions of the Spanish government in Morocco.

2. Against the endeavors of certain ladies of the aristocracy, who insult the pain of the reservists, their wives, and their children, giving them medals and decorations instead of supplying them with the means of subsistence, which are taken away from them with the departure of the heads of families.

3. Against the sending to war of citizens who are useful to production and, in general, indifferent to the triumph of the cross over the crescent, when one could instead form regiments of priests and monks who, aside from being directly interested in the success of the Catholic religion, do not have families or homes, nor are they of any use to the country, and

4. Against the attitude of the republican deputies who, despite boasting of their mandate from the people, have not taken advantage of their parliamentary immunity to place themselves at the head of the masses protesting the war. And it calls upon the working class to concentrate all its forces, for it is necessary to declare a general strike to force the government to respect the Moroccans' rights to keep their country's independence intact.

31. Spanish Bishops, Against the Existence of the Secular Schools (1909)

Historically, the Catholic Church had controlled education in Spain, but with the rise of liberalism in the nineteenth century, education became a major battleground, as both conservative Catholics and their liberal opponents viewed the schools as the key to shaping minds and promoting their vision of society. By the late 1800s, liberals had made significant inroads into the Church's previous hold on Spanish education, opening new schools such as Francisco Giner's Institution of Free Education, but the growing social and political turmoil of the early twentieth century led many Catholics to see these secular schools as the cause of Spain's ills. That conservatives felt that way became even clearer in the aftermath of the Tragic Week in Barcelona (see reading 30), for the main figure singled out and prosecuted for the uprising was Francisco Ferrer, an anarchist who had played no significant role in the events, but who had founded a school known as the Escuela Moderna. On November 26, 1909, Spain's bishops issued the following declaration

SOURCE: Jesús Iribarren, ed., *Documentos colectivos del episcopado español, 1870–1974* (Madrid: Biblioteca de Autores Cristianos, 1974), 89–93.

A Letter from the Spanish Prelates to the Prime Minister

Most Excellent Sir: We Spanish prelates believe we are fulfilling a duty of conscience and giving proof of our patriotism in calling your attention and that of the government . . . to the damage that allowing secular, or so-called neutral, schools to function may cause, and in asking that you somehow consent to the opening of those [church schools] that were closed by the authorities because of the horrible events in Barcelona, which still have not been sufficiently denounced, and which constitute a stain on the history of the country and a cause for shame for all of humanity.

Although such schools proclaim themselves neutral toward religion, they are actually and necessarily irreligious. It is in education that one can most easily observe this truth of Christ: "He who is not with me is against me." Never speaking of religion in school leads the students to conclude either that the religious ideas their parents and priests inculcated in them are antiscientific, and consequently false, or that they are not worth the citizen fighting for outside the home. Even in the most basic notions of teaching it is essential to touch upon matters that are religious in nature and that must be resolved either against or in conformity with religion. An antireligious teacher, even while wishing to remain neutral before the students, will not be successful for long; and the students, who see in him a superior figure whose authority merits full respect, do not take long to begin imitating his disdain for religion. But the neutrality of the secular schools is a vain notion, a pretext for not alarming people, and a lure offered to heads of families so that they do not remove their children from those schools. In all places, things happen as they did in France, where an inspector of public education wrote to the secular teachers: "The secular school is a war machine against Catholicism. The secular school's object is to train freethinkers. We would be disappointed if a respectful neutrality were maintained in it. . . . The secular school is a mold into which one places a child of a Christian and out of which one removes a renegade."

Even if they are not contrary to religion, such centers of teaching cannot be moral if they lack religion. Teaching morality while omitting religion is like trying to build a building without a foundation. Man being inclined to evil, he needs the belief in eternal rewards and punishments to contain himself within the narrow limits of duty and to walk along the demanding paths of virtue. If he is not taught to respect God's authority, it will be pointless to hope that he will respect any kind of authority, for respect requires corresponding sacrifices and deprivations. Public force and self-interest will be the only restraints that guide his passions; but when his interest is in conflict, in his view, with that of society, he will seek to escape the action of [public] force. . . . Even thinkers who cannot be suspected of bias, having had the misfortune of losing their faith, have deplored the pointlessness of efforts to teach morality to the young while disdaining the doctrines and methods of this great educator that is called the Church. . . . Merely to instruct is not to educate and giving knowledge to intelligent minds without taking care to strengthen and guide the will is like putting in the hands of a madman a sword, which is all the more dangerous the sharper it is.

Statistics show that the idea that "for each school that opens a prison closes" is absolutely false if it refers to teaching without God. In France, while the number of crimes by adults is staying about the same, it is rising at an alarming rate among children and youths, coinciding with the increase in secular education, to which conscientious and objective observers attribute the rapid increase in criminality. In Italy, the criminologist Garofalo has proved that the criminality that is spreading among the youth there owes a great deal to the fact that, unlike the educational systems in the nations of the Anglo-Saxon race, the curriculum in Italian schools contains no religious content. In Japan, where even more than in Spain there could seem to be good reason for neutral teaching because children belong to families of different religions, they have followed the European way of doing away with the teaching of any religion, substituting the teaching of universal morality for it; but experience has demonstrated what unfortunate results have come from this, and the government has hurried to strike at the root of the problem, returning to the obligatory teaching of religion, whether Buddhist or Christian. If that can happen in Japan, where the teachers were not hostile to the divine cult and struggled to find the purest morality through the path of reason, what can we hope for from secular schools like the Spanish ones to which we refer, where notions of law, authority, conscience, virtue, and obligation are attacked and ridiculed?

Just as the neutrality of the schools quickly leads to atheism, from atheism to socialism is only a short step. Bebel proclaimed in the German parliament that those who are socialist in economics are republican in politics and atheistic in religion. Those parts of Germany where religious teaching is least emphasized are those where socialism has had its greatest triumphs. . . .

If any doubt could remain over the extremely unfortunate effects of the schools we have been talking about, they would be dissipated in a very sad and painful way by the alarming scenes that Barcelona was the victim of in the last week of July. . . . One would have to be blind not to see, by the light of the flames of those fires, the effects of the dissolving ideas and the influx of pernicious doctrines, which are never more so than when they work on the tender minds and weak wills of children. To the applause of impartial opinion, schools have been closed which, although they were not called anarchist, were in reality and which posed a grave threat to public order, and had a large role in the savage scenes that bathed the streets of the most populous city in Spain in blood. . . .

A tremendous responsibility falls on those who . . . allow the enemies of property, the family, and all established order to have open centers where, abusing the docility of young people, they take advantage of them and prepare them for a new attempt at a revolution that will attack more than just religious establishments, now that they have seen that they are not where the money is. . . .

On the basis of these arguments, being a matter of justice, and asking the legitimate authorities not to let these schools that go by the name of modern or secular to reopen, we place our hope in your justice and the righteousness of Your Eminence, whose life God has guarded for many years.

32. Miryam, "Anticlerical Women: What We Want" (1910)

The opinion that women were more religious than men in Spain (as in other countries) was widely shared, but as one can see in this article by an anonymous woman writing in the republican Valencian newspaper *El Pueblo,* at least some women saw the Catholic Church in a very different light.

SOURCE: *El Pueblo* (Valencia), April 3, 1910; the text also appears in Ana María Aguado et al., eds., *Textos para la historia de las mujeres en España* (Madrid: Cátedra, 1994), 418.

The confessional, a place infected with corruption and vice, where women are taught all the nonsense they do not already know, is, has been, and will be, as long as it exists, a constant cause of women's moral degradation, . . . and a factor retarding their development. . . . The Church, which with its unmarried priests brings unrest to families and societies; the Church, which places celibates in the confessional, introduces spurious ideas into the family; the Church, which in its own homeland has given the shameful spectacle of an increase of illegitimate births reaching unprecedented levels; that Church should not speak at all about wives and households, because it neither knows nor understands them. It must not claim to have dignified women because one does not give women dignity by keeping them in ignorance, teaching them to love the convent and to reject men as husbands, abusing their weakness (in favor of the priest) and using them as instruments to govern from the confessional. . . .

We anticlerical women . . . , convinced that our greatest enemy is the Catholic Church, given that it is the cause of disrespect for us and of the backwardness in which we live, have taken on the honorable task of using clear proof to convince other women that, being ignorant and fanatically religious, they have allowed the priest to be the owner of their minds, making them beings lacking awareness, slaves without any will, attentive only to the commands of the papacy. . . .

Radical men of all kinds should keep in mind that we anticlerical women place our confidence in them. . . . All of them should understand that by separating their wives from the Church, they are watching out for the fate of their children. . . . Here is one of the primary duties of any liberal man: to share with his wife the sacrosanct ideals of his creed. Only in this way can a man fulfill his duties as a republican, as a freethinker, as a radical. To preach liberty outside the house, to combat clericalism in the streets, while taking a young lady, one's daughter, to take her first communion in church is not to be a republican, is not to be a liberal, is not to de-Catholicize Spain; it is to send commissions in the name of the Vatican, which ask governments for the destruction of radical men and even their disappearance from Spain.

33. Julián Juderías, *The Black Legend* (1914)

By the late nineteenth century, nationalism had become a remarkably strong force throughout Europe and much of the rest of the world. In Spain, of course, this trend had taken the form of the growth of regional nationalisms, such as those of the Basques and Catalans, and for Castilians and others, those movements merely demonstrated the need for a new articulation and assertion of Spanish national identity and pride. At the same time, Europe had recently completed a new wave of colonial expansion that fed off nationalist impulses, and Spain had largely been left out of the spoils of that wave of colonization while also losing its principal remaining colonies in the 1898 war with the United States. For Spanish nationalists such as Julián Juderías y Loyot (1877–1918), an eminent and well-traveled sociologist, linguist, and historian from Madrid, this bleak situation called for a reassessment of images of Spain that were widely held both inside and outside the country. The following passages are from the introduction and conclusion of his book *La leyenda negra*.

SOURCE: Julián Juderías y Loyot, *La leyenda negra y la verdad histórica* (Madrid: Revista de Archivos, Bibliotecas y Museos, 1914).

What is . . . the black legend? . . . By the black legend, we mean the atmosphere created by the fantastic tales about our country that have seen the light in almost all countries; the grotesque descriptions that have always been given of the character of the Spaniards as individuals and as a collectivity; the denial, or, at least, the systematic ignorance of everything that is positive and honorable about us in the various manifestations of our culture and art; the accusations that in all periods have been leveled against Spain, being based in exaggerated events that are either misinterpreted or totally false; and, finally, assertions contained in books that seem respectable and true, assertions that are often reproduced, commented upon, and elaborated upon in the foreign press, stating that our country, in terms of its tolerance, culture, and political progress, constitutes a lamentable aberration within the community of European nations.

In a word, we mean by the black legend the legend of a Spain that is inquisitorial, ignorant, fanatical, incapable of belonging among the civilized peoples today as in the past, and always inclined toward violent repression; an enemy of progress and innovation; or, in other words, the legend that, having started in the sixteenth century, with the [Protestant] Reformation, has not stopped being used against us ever since then, and especially at critical moments of our national life. . . .

In most foreign books about literature, art, philosophy, economics, legislation, or any other subject, rarely is Spain mentioned or its activities described, unless it is to hold it up as an example of backwardness, in order to say that its religious fanaticism prevented it from thinking, or to allude to its love for cruel spectacles, which is not surprising, they assure, for people who in other times found enjoyment in watching the bonfires of the Inquisition. It is thus quite clear that in the most famous books published in Europe concerning art, literature, and science—encyclopedic and magisterial works—Spain's efforts are sketched hastily, and whereas individual chapters are devoted to art, literature, and science in Germany, England, France, and Italy, Spain is usually included in a chapter entitled "Other Countries." In the brief paragraphs dedicated to its writers and artists, if they are not denounced as intolerant, then it is asserted that Spaniards have done nothing in the world other than impose their beliefs by force and exploit those they had subjugated by force. . . .

Although it is sad to admit it, we ourselves have the greatest share of responsibility for the formation of the black legend. We have it for two reasons: first, because we have not studied our own matters with the interest, attention, and care as foreigners have done with theirs, and lacking this highly essential foundation, we have had to learn about ourselves in books written by foreigners and inspired, as a general rule, by disdain for Spain; second, because we have always overflowed with unfavorable information about Spain and severe critiques.

We cannot therefore complain about the anti-Spanish legend. That will not disappear as long as we do not correct these defects we have. It will only be erased from the memory of nations when we see the rebirth of hopes for a better future—a hope founded on the study of our own matters and on an awareness of our own strength and not on foreign books or servile imitations of all that is foreign, but rather on ourselves, on the treasure of traditions and energies that our ancestors bequeathed us—and when, believing that we *were*, we also believe we can once again be. Nevertheless, in the hopes that we may correct these faults, it is appropriate to study the anti-Spanish legend and to confront the appearances of truth with real historical truth. . . .

Let us not go on at length, then, about the popular misconceptions that circulate elsewhere and are considered solid fact. Let us not say, as they say in Europe and as some Spaniards repeat, that we were and continue to be the country of the Inquisition and intolerance; let us not repeat that our repression was more cruel and heartless than that of other peoples in similar cases; let us not copy the idea that our colonization was a series of cruelties and acts of greed.

These and other similar assertions are not based in historical truth. Let us say it: yes, we were an intolerant and fanatical country in a time when all the peoples of Europe were intolerant and fanatical; we burned witches when they also burned them in France, when one group in Germany persecuted another in the name of religious freedom, when [Martin] Luther incited the nobles against the peasants who had risen in rebellion, when [John] Calvin denounced [Spanish theologian Michael] Servetus to the Catholic Inquisition. . . . We burned witches when all others, without exception, believed in sorcery and witchcraft, from Luther to Philip II. We prohibited the reading of certain books when the Sorbonne [the University of Paris] and the Parlement of Paris gave us the example by solemnly burning, by the hand of the executioner, the works of Luther and the books of [Father Juan de] Mariana. We imposed our beliefs by blood and fire when no other means of domination were known, and we colonized our possessions showing more respect [for the inhabitants] than the foreigners showed for theirs. To the sad and legendary figure of Philip II, the "demon of southern Europe," let us respond by pointing to the truly repulsive figures of Henry VIII, executioner of his wives; of Elizabeth, who ordered the execution of Mary Stuart and persecuted her adversaries viciously. . . .

For we may have been intransigent and fanatical, but at least we did not impose our beliefs in the name of a freedom of thought that was purely hypocritical; nor did we slaughter each other [in wars of religion], as happened in the countries where this liberty existed; nor did we pursue, in our wars, ideals other than those that really were ideals, being that they referred not to material matters but to matters of the spirit, and which led us to decline and ruin; the true cause of that decline and ruin should not be sought in religious intolerance, nor in that inability to be civilized that is so generously imputed to us, but rather in an extraordinary lack of practical sense and in a consequent ignorance of the reality of things. . . .

Let us recall the fine words of a foreigner [Alfred Morel Fatio, in *Etudes sur l'Espagne*], and say, with him: "The nation that blocked the way to the Arab invasions; that saved Christianity at Lepanto [a victory over the Turks in 1571]; that discovered a New World and brought our civilization to it; that formed and organized the fine infantry units that could only be beaten by imitating their methods; that created, in the arts, a style of painting of the most powerful realism; in theology, a mysticism that elevated souls to prodigious heights; in letters, a social novel, the *Quixote*, whose philosophical significance equals, if it does not surpass, its achievements in creativity and style; the nation that managed to give the sense of honor its most refined and sublime expression; that nation, without a doubt, should be held in a certain esteem and should be studied seriously, without foolish enthusiasm but also without unfair prejudices."

Without foolish enthusiasm and without unfair prejudices. . . . Can we Spaniards who subscribe to the words of Morel Fatio have any more modest intentions? Can we ask for any less than an equitable interpretation of our history and a fair appreciation of our conduct? We can ask for no less in these times, when even the smallest of nations dream of grandeur and triumph, and when unbridled passions and the cruelty so long repressed by a purely external civilization outline the dignified and serene attitude of the people who did so much in the world, and who only seek the consideration and respect of others.

34. Program of the National Association of Spanish Women (1918)

The immediate aftermath of World War I was a crucial period for women's movements throughout the West, as women gained the vote in many countries (though not in Spain, where feminist movements were still much smaller than in Britain, the United States, and other countries). Reflecting the strength of at least some Spanish women's desire for greater equality between the sexes is this program drawn up by a leading Spanish feminist organization. The Asociación Nacional de Mujeres Españolas (ANME) was founded in October 1918 and soon became the country's leading women's organization. Despite its feminist views, the group supported Spain's Conservative Party, and its founders came mostly from the upper classes.

SOURCE: María Espinosa, *Influencia del feminismo en la legislación contemporánea* (Madrid: Talleres de la Editorial Reus, 1920), 23–29; the text also appears in María Angeles Duran, ed., *Mujeres y hombres: La formación del pensamiento igualitaria* (Madrid: Editorial Castalia, 1993), 121–27.

Politico-Social Part

1. To oppose, by any means the Association may have, any proposal, act, or manifestation that harms the integrity of the national territory.

2. To try to see that every Spanish mother, in perfect parallel with the schoolteacher, inculcates in the child, from the earliest childhood, love for our one and indivisible mother the fatherland [*la madre patria*].

3. Scrupulous examination and revision of the existing laws for the protection and defense of women. . . .

4. To consider women eligible for public popular positions.

5. To give women access to the exercise of all those public positions involving the governing and administration of the moral and material interests of their sex.

6. Extensive study of the rights that belong to women under the existing Civil Code to demonstrate her precarious condition and to solicit from the Codes Committee the reform of those articles of the Civil Code that very specifically refer to marriage, to the powers of the father, and to the administration of conjugal property.

7. To obtain for women the right to take part in juries, especially in crimes committed by their sex, or in which women are victims.

8. Joint matrimonial administration, that is to say, the signature of both should be needed for any public document related to this matter. . . .

10. The same rights over the children as the father has in a legal marriage.

11. The legal right of the wife to the salary or wages of the husband, like that of the husband to those of the wife.

12. Complete legal personality for women, with the husband being able to represent her only by her delegating that power.

13. The right to keep the natural daughters recognized by the father.

14. Equality in legislation on adultery.

15. Punishment for the spouse for abandoning the home without the other's consent. . . .

17. Punishment of habitual drunkenness and making it grounds for marital separation.

18. Punishment for abuse of the wife, even if it does not threaten her life.

19. Greater punishment for crimes against decency. . . .

21. Suspension of the regulation of prostitution.

22. Enforcement of the White Slave Act.

23. To seek the creation of public schools in sufficient number that one can demand the observance of the legal principle that makes schooling obligatory, and to establish this same legal principle for the creation of schools for the mentally abnormal.

24. That pedagogical licenses be required of professors in private educational establishments.

25. Support and assistance for the study of medicine by women.

26. Support for the studies of physicians and dentists.

27. The right to rise in the professions that are already exercised, in the same conditions as men, and with the same pay.

28. The right to other new ones in these conditions.

29. To grant representation to women in the chambers of commerce, industry, and property.

30. To see to it that women participate in the syndicates and trade unions for the classification of the industries specific to their sex. . . .

32. To establish educational centers for domestic service and schools for women working in cooking, ironing, etc.

33. To found hospitals for domestic service.

34. To declare the elementary education of maids obligatory, asking the ladies who employ them that on the days of the week of their choice . . . they allow their female servants who do not know how to read or write to spend one hour attending classes that will be established, pursuing the goal that . . . there should be no maid who does not know how to read or write, thus carrying out one of the finest works of Christianity, that of "teaching those who do not know." The same can be extended to those [male] workers who find themselves in the same situation. . . .

Economic Part

1. To do away with the capitalist intermediary in the manual labor of women, seeking by all possible means for the female worker to receive the maximum pay for her work. . . .

In this broad field there is so much labor that the true emancipation of the working classes can be achieved as much by this means as by establishing feminine industries, workshops, factories, and other such things; so, with the Association acting as representative, contractor, or boss, one can manage to avoid the great exploitation of which they are the object by persons or entities which, not knowing anything about the work that is done, reserve for themselves or for great beneficiaries enormous and disproportionate profits.

Any capital invested has the right to remunerative, but limited, interest, so that it allows the female worker to receive the due benefits. The regulation of women's work to obtain an equal economic result will be in the hands of the National Association of Spanish Women, once producers and consumers have given their allegiance to its constitution and program.

We must do away with the traditional commercial custom of excessively exploiting the work of the producing woman, paying a pittance for rich embroidery, valuable lace, and elegant products, for those who charge and receive from the consuming women extremely high prices and exorbitant profits.

2. The creation of establishments for the children of female workers, offering . . . excellent food and childcare from the youngest infancy to those who are old enough to have to go to work in workshops or public schools. . . .

3. A duly authorized body of feminine vigilance will be created, chosen by the Association among its associates, to put an end to the abuses and pernicious habits of many [female] schoolteachers, mistresses, and nannies who abandon or mistreat the children in the streets, boulevards, and parks. . . .

In some ways, the childhood of the upper classes of society is just as deprived of protection and external oversight as that of the poorest; everything primarily comes down to mothers being more assured of believing their children to be free from all danger while in the care of a well-paid person. . . .

4. The intellectual classes will also benefit greatly from this Association, which proposes to publish on its own those literary works of true merit whose female authors do not have the economic wherewithal to do so, thus making it possible to avoid losing their property, through usury, of so many works that now enrich certain industrialists. . . .

5. In this way, . . . one will seek to sustain and elevate the social situation of women who because of their exceptional qualifications for the arts, sciences, education, etc., deserve it, thus putting an end to the exploitation and neglect of women of merit who can be useful to the fatherland.

35. José Ortega y Gasset, *Invertebrate Spain* (1922)

The leading Spanish philosopher of the twentieth century, José Ortega y Gasset was also noted for his involvement in the country's current affairs and political life. Born in Madrid in 1883, Ortega was the son of a noted journalist and novelist, and he received an extensive university education before going on to teach philosophy and other subjects in various Spanish universities. In addition to being a respected academic, Ortega was a prominent public intellectual, and he founded several important journals and newspapers, including *El Sol* and *Revista de Occidente.* Ortega also had a brief political career, serving as a deputy in the Constituent Cortes from 1931 to 1932, but he soon tired of the endeavor. The philosopher spent much of the post-Civil War years in exile, but he did return to Spain before his death in 1955. In this work, which first appeared in 1920 as a series of newspaper articles in *El Sol,* Ortega offers his views on the vexing problems of Spanish nationhood and regionalism.

SOURCE: José Ortega y Gasset, *España invertebrada* (Madrid: La Lectura, 1922).

In [Theodor] Mommsen's *History of Rome*, . . . the author . . . writes these words: "The history of every nation, and above all the Latin nation, is a vast system of incorporation.". . . If processes of incorporation play the same role in history that movement plays in physics, everything will depend on our having a clear notion of incorporation. . . . An erroneous tendency . . . tends to represent the formation of a people as the growth through expansion from an initial nucleus. . . . No, historical incorporation is not expansion from an initial nucleus. . . . The common identity of a race does not necessarily imply incorporation in a national organization, though it sometimes favors and facilitates that process. The Romans had to subject the Latin communities, their sister race, by the same processes they had to use, centuries later, to integrate into the empire peoples as ethnically distinct from them as the Celtiberians and Gauls, Germans and Greeks, Scythians and Syrians. It is wrong to assume that national unity is based on unity of blood, and vice versa. Racial difference, far from excluding historical incorporation, simply points to what is specific in the genesis of any great state.

Rome forced its Latin sisters to form a social body, a unitary entity, . . . the Latin Federation. . . . The next step was to dominate the Etruscans and the Samnites. . . . Once this was achieved, the Italian world was already a historically organic unit. Soon after, . . . all the other known peoples from the Caucasus to the Atlantic were added to the Italian torso. . . . Thus the stages of the incorporative process form an admirable ascending trajectory: initial Rome, . . . Latin Federation, Italian unity, colonial empire. This scheme suffices to show us that historical incorporation is not a matter of expansion from an initial nucleus, but rather the organization of many preexisting social units in a new structure. The initial nucleus neither swallows up the peoples it brings under its control nor annihilates their character as vital units. Rome conquered the Gauls, but this does not mean the Gauls ceased to see themselves as a social entity distinct from Rome. . . . Rome itself, the initial nucleus of incorporation, is nothing but another part of the colossal organism, which enjoys a privileged rank for being the agent of the "totalization."

It would be misreading the genius of history to assume that when a greater national unit is formed out of smaller nuclei, the latter cease to exist as actively differentiated elements. This erroneous idea would lead one to assume, for example, that when Castile forced Aragon, Catalonia, and the Basque country into Spanish unity, those peoples lost their character as distinct peoples. . . . No; subjection, unification, and incorporation do not mean the death of groups as groups; the independent force that exists in them endures, even if under control. That is, their centrifugal force is held in check by a centripetal force that impels them to live as parts of a whole. . . . All it takes is for the centripetal force, the sculptor of the nation—Rome in the empire, Castile in Spain, the Ile-de-France [the Paris region] in France—to weaken, and one sees the secessionist energy of the incorporated groups reappear automatically.

Nations' creative powers are a *quid divinium*, a genius or a talent as variable as that for poetry, music, and religious innovation. Some extremely intelligent peoples have lacked this gift, while, on the other hand, some peoples who have been poorly suited for scientific and artistic tasks have possessed it in large amounts. Athens, despite its unlimited powers of understanding, could not figure out how to incorporate the eastern Mediterranean into a single nation, while Rome and Castile, which were poorly endowed intellectually, forged the two largest national structures ever. . . .

This talent for nation-building . . . is a talent for leading, not a theoretical kind of knowledge or a rich imagination. . . . It is about knowing how to want and knowing how to command. Now commanding is neither a matter of simply convincing or of obliging, but rather an exquisite mixture of the two. Moral persuasion and material force go together intimately in any act of commanding. I am very sorry that I cannot go along with contemporary pacifism in its dislike for force; without it there would not have been any of the things that are most important to us, and if we rule it out in the future, we will only be able to imagine a chaotic world. Yet it is also true that nothing worth doing has ever been accomplished through force alone.

By using force alone, one creates pseudoincorporations that do not last long and disappear without leaving any appreciable historical traces.

In any true incorporation, force has the character of an adjective. The truly sustainable power that spurs and cultivates the process is always a national dogma, *a suggestive project for a life in common*. Let us repudiate any static interpretation of a common national life and instead understand it as something dynamic. People do not live together for any other reason; this a priori cohesion only exists in a family. The groups that make up a state live together for some purpose; they form a community of proposals, of desires, of great practical utility. They do not live together *to be* together, but *to do* something together. . . . It is not yesterday, the past, and tradition that determine whether a nation exists. . . . Nations are formed and live by having a program for the future.

As for force, it is not hard to determine its mission. However profound the need for a historical union between two peoples may be, it is opposed by private interests, whims, low motives, passions, and above all, collective prejudices found on the surface of the popular soul. . . . It is pointless to try to overcome these things through persuasion based on reasoning. Only force, the great historical surgeon, is effective against those things. . . .

Over the past century, Europe has been burdened with harmful propaganda disparaging force. . . . Think for a moment about all the fervor, the lofty virtues, the genius, and the vital energy that must be accumulated to put together a good army. How can one deny that it is one of the most impressive creations of the human spirit? The force of arms is not brute force, but a moral force. . . . Certainly, the force of arms is not the force of reason, but reason does not determine moral force. . . . To be precise, it is not the physical violence by which an army defeats its enemy in battle that produces historical effects. Rarely does a defeated people use up all its powers of resistance in combat. Victory is more exemplary than material, making clear the superior quality of the conquering army, while also demonstrating the superior historical quality of the people that created this army. . . .

The respect earned in a battle helps avoid many others, and not so much because of fear of physical oppression, but because of respect for the vital superiority of the victor. . . . So although force plays only a secondary and auxiliary role in the great processes of national incorporation, it is inseparable from that other, divine force that, as I have said, creative and imperial peoples possess. . . .

One of the most characteristic phenomena of the last twenty years has been separatism; that is, movements of ethnic and territorial secession. Are there many Spaniards who have managed to perceive the true historical reality of such movements? I am afraid not.

For most people, Catalan and Basque "nationalism" is an artificial movement that, out of nothing and without profound causes or motives, suddenly began a few years ago. According to this way of thinking, before these movements began, Catalonia and the Basque country were not social units that were distinct from Castile and Andalusia. Spain was a homogeneous mass . . . and to speak of regions now, of different peoples, of Catalonia, of Euskadi, is to cut with a knife into a homogeneous mass and to form distinct bodies out of what was a compact volume.

[In most people's view] a few men, moved by economic desires, by personal pride, by more or less private envies, are deliberately carrying out this task of taking apart the nation, which would not be taking place if not for them and their capricious labors. Those who hold such ideas . . . logically conclude that the only way to combat them is to smother them by direct strangulation—by persecuting their ideas, their organizations, and their members. . . . In Barcelona and Bilbao, "nationalists" and "unitarists" are fighting each other . . . [and] the central government should lend the unparalleled force it has as a central government to one of the parties: naturally the unitary one. This is, at least, what centralist Basques and Catalans ask for. . . .

I cannot tell you how far this thinking is from my opinions on the origins, character, transcendence, and treatment of these secessionist concerns. I have the impression that the "unitarism" that has so far opposed the Catalan and Basque movements is the product of Catalan and Basque minds inherently incapable . . . of understanding Spain's history. Do not invert the process: Spain is a thing created by Castile, and . . . in general, only Castilian minds are capable of perceiving the great problem of Spanish unity. . . .

For anyone born on the rough high plains stretching from the Ebro to the Tagus, there is nothing quite as impressive as reconstructing the process of incorporation that Castile imposed on the periphery of the peninsula. From the outset one can see that Castile knew how to lead. One has only to see the energy with which it commanded itself. To be in control of oneself is the first requirement for ruling over others. Castile struggled to overcome its own tendencies toward the hermetism of the villager, toward the narrow vision of one's local interests that reigned in the other Iberian peoples. From that foundation, it oriented its spirit toward great enterprises that required broad cooperation. It was the first to initiate broad, complex projects of international policy, another indicator of the genius for nation-building. . . . The ongoing frontier battle that the Castilians waged against the crescent, against another civilization, allowed them to discover their historical similarities with the other Iberian monarchies, despite the outward differences of appearance, speech, temperament, and physical environment. A "unified Spain" was thus born from the mind of Castile not as a premonition of anything real—Spain was not, in reality, one—but as an ideal scheme for something *realizable*, a project capable of inciting wills, an imaginary future capable of disciplining and orienting the present, in the same way that the target attracts the arrow and stretches the bowstring. . . .

When Castile's traditional policy succeeded in winning over the clear and penetrating mind of Ferdinand the Catholic, everything became possible. The clever Aragonese fox understood that Castile was right, that it was necessary to tame the wildness of his rural people and incorporate his kingdom into a greater Spain. His ambitious plans could only be executed from Castile. . . . So Spanish unity was achieved, but for what, for what end, and under what ideas displayed as inspiring banners? . . . The union was formed to cast Spanish energies to the four winds, to inundate the planet, to create an even greater empire. Spanish unity was made for this and through this. . . . There is no doubt that *Spanish unity was, first of all and above all, the unification of the two great international policies that existed in the peninsula at that time:* that of Castile, facing Africa and the heart of Europe, and that of Aragon, facing the Mediterranean. The result was that for the first time in history, a *Weltpolitik* [world policy] was conceived: Spanish unity was created to attempt that. . . .

From 1580 to the present, Spain has experienced decline and disintegration. The incorporative process continued growing up until Philip II [reigned 1556–1598]. The twentieth year of his reign can be considered the dividing line of the peninsula's destinies. Until its peak, Spain's history was ascending and cumulative; from that point on, Spain's history has been declining and dispersing. The process of disintegration has advanced in a strict order from the periphery to the center. First, the Low Countries and Milan, then Naples; at the beginning of the nineteenth century, the great overseas provinces were lost, and at the end of that century, the smaller colonies in America and the Far East. In 1900, the Spanish body returned to its original peninsular nakedness. Will the disintegration stop there? Perhaps it is coincidence, but the loss of the last overseas possessions seemed to be the signal for the beginnings of intrapeninsular disintegration. In 1900 one began to hear the rumbling of regionalisms, nationalisms, separatisms. . . . It was the sad spectacle of a very broad and long-term autumn, periodically carried out by adverse gusts of wind blowing piles of dead leaves off of the sickly branches.

The incorporative process consisted in a task of *totalization*. . . . Disintegration is the reverse: the parts of the whole all begin to live separately. I call this phenomenon of historical life *particularism*, and were someone to ask me what is the most profound and serious character of Spain today, I would answer with that word.

Thinking in this way, it clearly seems frivolous to me to consider the Catalan and Basque movements as artificial products of certain individuals' private whims. Far from this, both are nothing but the clearest manifestation of the state of decomposition into which our people have fallen, and they merely perpetuate that work of dispersion that began three centuries ago. . . .

The essence of particularism is that each group ceases to feel that it is a part, and consequently it ceases to share the others' feelings. The others' hopes and needs do not matter to them, and they feel no solidarity with them to help them with their concerns. An ailment that one neighbor suffers does not irritate other national nuclei through sympathetic transmission, but the former remains alone in its suffering. Indeed, hypersensitivity to one's own ills is typical of this social state. . . .

In this essential sense we can say that particularism now exists throughout all of Spain, although taking different forms according to each region's conditions. In Bilbao and Barcelona, which perceive themselves as the peninsula's greatest economic powers, particularism has taken an aggressive and expressive tone, with ample rhetorical musculature. In Galicia, a poor land inhabited by resigned and suspicious souls lacking confidence in themselves, particularism has returned as a force that cannot bloom, and it takes the form of a silent and humiliated resentment, of an inert obedience to the will of another, in which it delivers itself physically without protesting in order to withhold its internal willingness all the more. . . .

The purpose of this essay is to correct the errors of current political thought, which seeks the root of the evils of the Catalan and Basque movements in Catalonia and the Basque country, when that is not where those roots are to be found. Where, then? For me there is no doubt: when a society consumes itself as a victim of particularism, one can always affirm that the first to show itself to be particularist is precisely the central power. And this is what has happened in Spain. Castile made Spain, and Castile has unmade it.

The initial nucleus of Iberian incorporation, Castile managed to overcome its own particularism and invite the other peninsular peoples to collaborate in a gigantic project of common life. Castile invented great inspiring enterprises, offered high legal, moral, and religious ideas; sketched out a suggestive plan for a social order; imposed the norm that every better man should be preferred over his inferiors, the active over the inert, the bright over the dull, the noble over the lowly. All these aspirations, norms, habits, and ideas remained alive for some time. Men were indeed influenced by them, believed in them, respected them, or feared them. But if we look at the Spain of Philip III [1598–1621], we notice a terrible change. . . . The lively words of yesteryear were still repeated, but they no longer influenced people's hearts. . . . Nothing new was undertaken. . . .

Beginning with the monarchy and continuing with the Church, no national power thought of anything but itself. When did the heart of a Spanish monarch or the Spanish Church—both ultimately foreign—beat over profoundly national destinies? Apparently never. . . .

Instead of periodically renewing the treasury of vital ideas, modes of coexistence, unifying enterprises, the government has undermined national coexistence and used its powers almost exclusively for private ends. So is it strange that after all this time most Spaniards, and of course the best of them, should wonder: why are we living together? . . . The resonance of the past is not enough for living, much less for living together. This is why [Ernest] Renan said that a nation is a daily plebiscite. In the inexpressible secret of people's hearts, a fateful vote is taken every day, deciding whether a nation can really continue to exist.

36. Miguel Primo de Rivera, The Barcelona Manifesto (1923)

Translated from Spanish by Dillwyn F. Ratcliff

Social and political unrest, which had been growing for years in Spain, reached a new peak after World War I. In 1923, at a time when the Russian Revolution (1917) and the Italian Fascists' seizure of power (1922) were on many Spaniards' minds, Spain experienced yet another military coup. The chronic political violence of the post-World War I years had much to do with the coup, but so did events in Morocco, where Spain was waging a colonial war. In 1921, Spain had suffered a serious defeat at Anual, leading civilians and politicians to question the military's judgment and to launch an investigation into "responsibilities" for the defeat. The results of that investigation were due to be delivered to the Cortes in September 1923.

Just before the report was delivered, General Miguel Primo de Rivera (1870–1930), captain general of Catalonia, issued a "pronouncement" against the government. Primo de Rivera had considerable support within the military, and with the existing political system having lost much of its popular support in recent years, few were willing to oppose the military. At that point the government resigned, and the king named Primo de Rivera prime minister, and he quickly declared martial law and consolidated his power. Primo de Rivera's seizure of power met substantial support, and he remained the head of Spain's government until 1930.

SOURCE: Dillwyn F. Ratcliff, *Prelude to Franco: Political Aspects of the Dictatorship of General Miguel Primo de Rivera* (New York: Las Américas, 1957), 89–93. The original text appears in *La Vanguardia*, September 13, 1923, and in Genoveva García Queipo, "Primo de Rivera," *Cuadernos de Historia* 16, no. 269 (1985).

To the Country and to the Army,

Spaniards, for us arrived the moment more feared than hoped for (because we should have desired that . . . legality should without interruption rule over Spanish life); the time has come to give heed to the anxiety, to respond to the urgent demands of all those who, loving the mother country, see for her no other salvation than deliverance from the professional politicians, from the men who . . . offer us the spectacle of the misfortunes and corruption which began in the year 1898 and which threaten Spain with an early end. . . . The thick net of politics of greed has caught [Spain] in its meshes and has misdirected even the will of the monarch. . . .

Well, then, we shall now assume entire responsibility and the nation shall be governed by us or by civilians who represent our morality and our principles. Enough, now, of gentle rebellions which, without remedying anything, damage as much or more than that strong and virile discipline to which we ardently devote ourselves for Spain and for the king. This is a movement of men; let him who is not entirely sure of his complete masculinity await, quietly and in a corner, the good days which we are preparing for the fatherland. Spaniards! Long live Spain and long live the king!

We do not have to justify our act, which the uncorrupted people demand and require. The murder of prelates, ex-governors, civil officials, employers, foremen, and workmen; bold and unpunished holdups; depreciation of currency, the squandering of millions from special funds, . . . base political intrigues having as their pretext the tragedy of Morocco, indecisiveness in confronting this most serious national problem, social indiscipline . . . ; unpunished communist propaganda, impiety and misbehavior, justice influenced by politics, shameless propaganda in favor of regional separatism, tendentious passions relative to the problem of responsibilities for the disaster in Morocco, and finally—let us be just—one single count in favor of the government, . . . a feeble and incomplete campaign against the vice of gambling.

We have not come to bewail shame and disgrace, but to apply a prompt and radical remedy, for which we demand the support of all good citizens. To this end, and by virtue of the confidence and mandate given me, there will be constituted in Madrid a military Directorate of Supervision and Inspection, of a temporary character, charged with maintaining public order and insuring the working of the ministries and official bodies, requiring of the country that, in a short time, it offer us men upright, wise, industrious, and honorable who can constitute a ministry under our auspices, but with complete independence of action, in order that we may offer them to the king. . . .

We propose to avoid the shedding of blood and although, logically, no clean, pure, patriotic person will oppose us, we declare that faith in our ideals and the instinct of preservation of our regime will lead us to proceed with the greatest rigor against those who oppose it.

We wish to live in peace with all peoples. . . . We are not imperialists, nor do we hold that upon a stubborn insistence in Morocco depends the honor of the army, for that honor is vindicated daily by valorous conduct. To this end, then, . . . shall we seek for the Moroccan problem a solution that will be prompt, worthy, and reasonable.

The country does not want to hear more talk about responsibilities, but does want to know them and demand for them a prompt and just accounting, and this we shall entrust . . . to tribunals of moral authority which are impartial. . . . The collective responsibility of the political parties we shall punish by this total interdiction from public life to which we condemn them. . . . We do want to do this because we think it our duty and, on receipt of any duly substantiated accusation of collusion, bribery, or immorality, we shall prosecute and punish implacably those who have offended against the mother country by corrupting and dishonoring her. We guarantee that accusations will be received in absolute confidence, although they be against persons of our profession and class, although they be against ourselves. . . .

A manifesto does not admit of further details. Our work will very soon be known, and the nation and history will judge it, for our conscience is at rest as regards our purpose and intent.

Directives

When military law is declared in each military region, the captain general or his substitute will expel from office all civil governors and will entrust their functions to the military governors and commandants. They will take possession of all telephone exchanges and means of communication and, except for personal and business messages, they will not permit communication by any official who does not serve the new regime. . . .

Appropriate places will be occupied, such as communist or revolutionary centers, railway stations, banks, electric power stations, and reservoirs, and persons suspect and of ill-repute will be placed under arrest. Otherwise, an impression of normal, tranquil life is to be created. . . .

We have not conspired. We have, in broad daylight, championed the aspirations of the people and we have given them something in the way of organization, in order to direct them toward a patriotic end devoid of ambitions. . . . In this holy undertaking are associated, in the first place, industrious and upright people of all classes, the army and our glorious navy, both of these down to their lowest ranks, which we could not have consulted previously without relaxing the bond of discipline, but who assure us of their valued and efficacious support because of their well-known loyalty to their officers and their sensitivity to patriotic aspirations.

Although we may come into being through an act of technical indiscipline, we do represent that true discipline which is due our principles and love of country, and so we shall conceive, practice, and require discipline, not forgetting that, since we are not moved by ambition but . . . by the spirit of sacrifice, ours is the highest authority.

And now, again, long live Spain and long live the king! And receive, all of you, the cordial greeting of an old soldier who asks of you discipline and fraternal union, in the name of the days he shared military life with you in peace and in war, and who asks of the Spanish people trust and order, in the name of his efforts devoted to its prosperity, especially in the name of this undertaking in which he offers and risks all in order to serve the people.

37. Platform of the Patriotic Union (1928)

Translated from Spanish by Dillwyn F. Ratcliff

Like the other European dictatorships of the interwar period, General Miguel Primo de Rivera's regime allowed the existence of only one political party: his own. Five years into that regime, his Patriotic Union issued the following platform, which reflects the regime's structure and ideology (as well as the influence of Benito Mussolini's Fascist Party in Italy).

SOURCE: Dillwyn F. Ratcliff, *Prelude to Franco: Political Aspects of the Dictatorship of General Miguel Primo de Rivera* (New York: Las Américas, 1957), 95–98.

Fatherland, Religion, Monarchy

If the significance of these three words should be considered excessively ample or diffuse, and if we should be accused of lack of concreteness with regard to doctrine, aspirations, and commitments, I am going to specify . . . the chief points to which our league devotes special attention. . . .

1. The promulgation of a new constitutional law [that] . . . will assert the concept of national unity, sovereignty of the state, and the organization of a parliamentary regime based upon a single chamber legislature, in which shall have voice, vote, and joint representation people, Crown, state, and government-sponsored guilds, with abolition of any electoral system by districts, which is the base and proven source of demoralizing boss rule.

2. That for the approval of the new fundamental code of the state, the plebiscite be employed as a representation of the direct vote of the citizenry. . . .

3. To maintain at all cost, as [the] fixed and permanent basis of the national economy, the balanced budget and the commitments of amortization of public debts as provided by law.

4. To set up a system of renting and acquisition of rural property, which, without injury or damage to the primary rights of the landowners, will permit the gradual grant to individuals or groups of demonstrated capacity for it the ownership or maintenance of the lease in form such that it will assure them just participation in the improvements due to their efforts. All delay in setting up and perfecting . . . such system, in addition to being a flagrant injustice, will contribute to the incubation of germs of revolution in the countryside, which can only be avoided, to the benefit of all, by a forward-looking agrarian law. . . .

5. To foster through thrift and cooperatives, together with the aid and sponsorship which the state should lend to work of such indisputable importance, the increase in the amount of cheap and moderately priced housing

and the acquisition of farms, since this, aside from furthering the periodic and indispensable renovation of the great cities and intensifying country life, will keep forming, in the quiet of the home and amid the security of property and shelter, feelings of brotherhood and social relationship. . . .

6. To organize, with the required cooperation of the worker, the employer, and the state, insurance against unemployment, old age, and being incapacitated, so that no citizen who has expended his strength in labor may ever be found in the sad and embarrassing situation of having to beg for his daily bread.

7. To encourage and favor vertical guild organization to the end that all activities may be grouped in accordance with that system, not only for the purpose of appropriate, defined, and clear representation at specified times, but as a means of settling harmoniously the differences and disagreements which arise in social life.

8. Elementary schooling with complete religious and patriotic instruction, obligatory and organized on such a scope that it may be received without exception by all minors of both sexes before the age of eleven years; such instruction to be entrusted, without undue influence of special doctrines or organizations, to the personnel most adequate for its diffusion, according to the capacity of each, undertaking to put an end to illiteracy with such energy and example that each Spaniard will consider as the highest and most meritorious achievement the fact of having himself taught a fellow citizen to read and write.

9. Military organization which will permit, within the shortest possible period of instruction, adequate individual training of recruits and the creation of district schools for specialist, cadre, and command practice, so that the system remains associated with that of national physical education and premilitary training. . . .

11. Vigilant attention and spiritual, civic, and economic aid to the organizations of colonies of Spaniards abroad.

12. Ever closer spiritual, intellectual, and mercantile relations with the countries of Iberian origin, so that, while the nations preserve the characteristics of their independence, they consider themselves included, especially during difficult moments in world affairs, in a great league which is to be a sort of comprehensive expression of the genius and the duties of the [Hispanic] race and is to tend primarily to the maintenance of peace and justice.

13. Intervention in national production and in the sale of its products, in order to avoid usury or ruinous domestic competition, undertaking to guarantee the quality of the articles and products exported, in order that the

reputation of Spanish business for integrity may not decline and that the national prestige may not suffer. . . .

18. Persistent propaganda, everywhere and at all times, until a change in habits is achieved, inspired in the most healthful ethical principles and in the precepts of hygiene, which, without depriving our country of its unique aspect of joy and optimism, will convert it into an insuperable example of industry and orderly life.

19. To surround [the] woman with ever greater manifestations of respect, by granting her the participation which she deserves in social life; to give more tender care to children and more positive and efficacious protection to the humble, not only by means of institutions devoted to such high objectives, but also by taking advantage of all circumstances to preserve in the people their fine sensibility.

And the last point to be stated concretely, which should have been the first: To proceed tenaciously and inflexibly with the cleansing of the august functions entrusted to justice at all its levels, undertaking the radical reform of the laws of procedures, and giving to the citizens, more than the sensation, the absolute guarantee that justice in Spain has come to be upright, prompt, understanding, cheap, and invulnerable to all influences.

38. Alfonso XIII, Message of Renunciation (1931)

Those Spaniards who wanted to replace the monarchy with a republic had been growing in number ever since the second half of the nineteenth century, as many associated the monarchy with the forces opposing social justice and modernization in Spain. Anger at the monarchy only increased when King Alfonso XIII (reigned 1886–1931) endorsed the dictatorship of Miguel Primo de Rivera, and when that dictatorship fell in 1930, republicans intensified their efforts to end monarchy.

When municipal elections were held on April 12, 1931, monarchist parties generally did well in rural areas, but those parties' defeat in many of Spain's largest cities—and the enormous republican demonstrations that filled the plazas of many Spanish cities—led Alfonso to make the following announcement. The king fled Spain, never to return, and republican political leaders formed a provisional government while preparing for the election of a Constituent Cortes to write a new constitution for Spain.

SOURCE: *El Sol*, April 17, 1931.

The elections held on Sunday show me clearly that today I do not have the love of my people. My conscience tells me that this divergence will not be permanent, for I will always try to serve Spain, placing my only concern in the public interest, even in the most critical circumstances.

A king can make mistakes, and I have undoubtedly erred at times; but I know well that our fatherland has always shown itself to be generous concerning faults committed without ill will.

I am the king of all the Spaniards, and I am also a Spaniard myself. I could find more means than necessary to maintain my regal prerogatives, effective for resisting those who would combat them. But without any doubt, I wish to distance myself from any act that would pit one of my compatriots against another, in a fratricidal civil war. I do not renounce any of my rights, because they are not simply mine, but rather are accumulated by history, which will one day ask for a strict accounting of how I have used them.

I hope to know the authentic and proper expression of the collective consciousness, and while the nation speaks, I deliberately suspend the exercise of the royal power, and I am leaving Spain, thus recognizing it as the only master of its destinies.

I also now believe that I am fulfilling that which my love for the fatherland dictates. I ask God that the other Spaniards feel this love as profoundly as I do, acting accordingly.

39. Spanish Bishops, On the Proposed Constitution (1931)

Even before King Alfonso XIII's departure from Spain in April 1931, republican political leaders across a fairly broad spectrum of the political left and center had been conferring about how to take power. In August 1930, a group of republican, socialist, and Catalanist leaders signed a pact in the town of San Sebastián, pledging to work together to establish a republic, to secure the election of a new Cortes to write a new constitution, and to promote religious and political liberty in their new regime. The Pact of San Sebastián thus established the blueprint for the changes that began taking place with the king's departure in April 1931.

Over the previous decades, the Vatican had shown ambivalence toward liberal regimes, at times urging compromise with regimes such as France's Third Republic, and at other times taking a harder line. The leaders of the Church in Spain, however, tended to be even more intransigent than the Vatican, and not long after the proclamation of the Republic in April 1931, Cardinal Pedro Segura issued a pastoral letter that was hostile to the Republic; angry crowds then rioted and burned churches and convents, worsening relations even further. On July 25, while the Constituent Cortes was just beginning its task of writing a new constitution, Spain's bishops issued the following statement.

SOURCE: Jesús Iribarren, ed., *Documentos colectivos del episcopado español, 1870–1974* (Madrid: Biblioteca de Autores Cristianos, 1974), 136–49.

Venerable brothers and beloved children,

Having indicated the imperative norms of respect and obedience toward official powers that the Church has always recommended for the very preservation of human society, and having pointed out the duties incumbent upon Catholics regarding the election of deputies to the Constituent Cortes, we now believe it opportune to hope that with spirits being calmed we can begin to establish the guiding principles of national life. . . .

With an advisory committee having now submitted for the examination, discussion, and approval of the Constituent Cortes a proposed constitution under which Spain will be governed in the new regime, it is our duty to instruct you, with apostolic liberty and clarity, regarding the points of that proposal that directly or indirectly refer to our holy religion, explaining to you very faithfully the infallible doctrine of our holy mother the Catholic Church, which none of its children, under any pretext whatsoever, can fail to obey without suffering a disaster in their beliefs and without endangering their eternal salvation.

Because, to state this at the outset, the constitutional project has such serious problems that if it were to come out as it now stands, it would create a very grave situation in Spain that we must guard against at any cost if we wish to avoid extremely negative consequences, primarily in religious and moral matters, but also in social and even material matters.

The Secularity of the State

In the first place, the proposed constitution establishes the absolute secularity of the state, with all its consequences. . . . Regarding secularity, see how our Holy Father Pius XI [1922–1939] condemned it:. . . calling it "the plague of our times," he wrote that "they started out by denying the sovereignty of Christ over the nations; they denied the right of the Church to teach the human race, to give laws, to govern peoples in accord with their eternal blessedness. Then, little by little, they equated the Christian religion with the false religions, and with utter shamelessness they placed it on the same level. Then they subjected it to civil authority and turned it over, so to speak, to the arbitrary whim of princes and governors. . . ."

How rightly the Holy Father affirms that this social crime, that this deadly plague, did not mature in a day, but rather appeared cursedly in our days after having hidden in the entrails of society. . . .

The proposed constitution assumes that authority comes only from the people; from this postulate of official atheism, incarnated in the godless democracies of our times, come terrible consequences for the social order. . . . The sovereign pontiff Pius IX [1846–1878] expressly condemned the doctrine that teaches that "the Church must be separate from the state and the state from the Church" and that "in our times it is not proper for the Catholic religion to be considered the state's only religion to the exclusion of all others." . . .

On this point it is useful to recall what Leo XIII wrote to French Catholics in 1892: "Catholics must be very careful not to defend the separation of Church and state. To want the state to be separate from the Church is to want, as a logical consequence, the Church to remain reduced to living by the laws that apply to all the citizens." . . .

Modern Liberties

Very brief comments will suffice to guide you regarding the so-called "modern" liberties, which are considered the most precious conquest of the French Revolution and held to be the intangible patrimony of the democracies that are enemies of the Church. . . . The very names that the Roman pontiffs have given these liberties are an eloquent condemnation of them: "Insanity," Gregory XVI [1831–1846] called them; "liberties of damnation,"

Pius IX denoted them, using a phrase of Saint Augustine; and Leo XIII [1878–1903] said of them that "rather than liberties, they are license."

These modern liberties are discussed at length . . . by Leo XIII: "In no way is it allowed to ask for, defend, or grant liberty of thought, of education, of the press, and of religion, as if these were a right granted to man by nature. For if nature had granted man these liberties, there would be a right to remove oneself from the sovereignty of God, and then there could be no law capable of regulating human liberty."

Present Duties

Grave are the dangers that surround you at the present time. "Do not let yourselves be seduced," we say, with the apostle Saint Paul. "Bad conversations corrupt good customs." . . .

Avoid, as much as possible, contact with enemies of the Church, and above all, flee, as you would from a snake, from the evil press, from that impious and blasphemous press that is the demolishing battering ram of faith, good customs, and even of the order and prosperity of peoples. . . . All the children of the Catholic Church in Spain, facing the risks to their faith and their holy traditions, must act with prudence and energy in the public arena, struggling relentlessly "for their altars and their homes."

40. Manuel Azaña, "Spain Has Ceased to Be Catholic" (1931)

No subject was more divisive in the 1930s than the Church's role in Spain, and as the Constituent Cortes (the body elected to write a new constitution) drafted the articles on the Church, Catholics protested loudly. Just before Manuel Azaña y Díaz (1880–1940) gave this speech in the Constituent Cortes on October 13, another Republican, Fernando de los Ríos, had made a speech seeking to mollify Catholics, but many Republicans found his words too conciliatory. War Minister Azaña was highly influential within the Cortes, and the final text adopted generally reflected his outlook. Largely because of the passage of the articles concerning the Church (especially article 3, which separated Church and state, and article 26, which called for an end to state funding of the clergy and created strict restrictions on the religious orders), Prime Minister Niceto Alcalá Zamora resigned, to be replaced by Azaña on October 16. Azaña remained prime minister until September 1933.

SOURCE: *El Sol*, October 14, 1931. The text also appears in Fernando Díaz-Plaja, ed., *Historia de España en sus documentos (nueva serie): El siglo XX*, vol. 2, *Dictadura . . . República (1923–1936)* (Madrid: Instituto de Estudios Políticos, 1965), 299–312.

Right now . . . principles considered invulnerable, inspirations that have been in place for centuries . . . are losing force. . . . [We are seeing] a revolution, which is not illegal so much as essentially antilegal, for it is . . . destroying the laws that do not correspond to the new state of legal thinking. If this revolution were merely superficial, if it were nothing more than a mutiny, it would only conflict with ordinary laws or with this or that constitutional law, but if it is to be a profound, tenacious, lasting, and thorough one, then a radical transformation of the state is necessary, corresponding to the divergence that has arisen between the law and the state of the public mind. . . . The political revolution, that is, the expulsion of the dynasty and the restoration of public liberties, has resolved a specific problem of great importance . . . but it has done little more than point to and indicate those other problems that must transform the state and Spanish society to their roots. These problems . . . are basically three: the problem of local autonomies, the social problem in its most urgent and acute form, which is the reform of property ownership, and this thing called the religious problem, which is, strictly speaking, the implantation of the secularity of the state with all its inevitable and rigorous consequences. . . .

I will not refer to the first two problems, but only to the one known as the religious problem. The premise of this problem, which is now a political one, I will put this way: Spain has ceased to be Catholic. The consequent political problem is to organize the state so that the Spanish people will be up to this new and historic phase.

I do not accept . . . this being called a religious problem. A true religious problem cannot exceed the limits of personal conscience, for it is within the personal conscience that the question of the mystery of our destiny is addressed and answered. The one at hand is a political problem, one of the constitution of the state, and right now this problem loses any connection with religion, with religiousness, because our state—unlike the old state, which took upon itself the monitoring of consciences and offered means to push people toward their salvation, even against their will—rejects any otherworldly concerns and any regulation of faith, removing from the Church that famous secular arm that offered it so many great services. . . .

In affirming that Spain has ceased to be Catholic, we have reasons similar to those for affirming that Spain was Catholic in the sixteenth and seventeenth centuries. It would be pointless now to examine what Spain owes Catholicism, which is usually the favorite subject of pro-Church historians. I am more inclined to believe that it is Catholicism that owes Spain, for a religion does not exist in the texts written by councils or in the writings of its theologians, but rather in the spirit and in the works of the people who embrace it. . . .

Spain, at the moment of the ascent of its genius, when Spain was a creative and inventive nation, created a Catholicism in its own image and likeness. . . . And so there was then a Spanish Catholicism, for the same psychological reasons that produced Spanish novels and paintings and theater and morality, in which the influence of religious faith was palpable. And in the same way it is true that the Company of Jesus was a Spanish creation, the work of a great member of our race, which demonstrates the extent to which the Spanish spirit has influenced the orientation of the historical and political government of the Roman Church.

But now . . . the situation is exactly the opposite. For many centuries, the speculations of European thought were carried out within Christianity, which took for itself the thought of the ancient world and adapted it more or less faithfully to the Christian creed. But by the same token, European speculative thought and activity have for several centuries ceased . . . to be Catholic. All the superior movement of civilization goes against it, and in Spain, despite our lesser mental activity, Catholicism has for the past century ceased to be the expression and guide of Spanish thought. That there are millions of believers in Spain I do not deny, but that which gives a country and a society its religious character is not the numeric sum of beliefs or believers, but rather the creative force of its mind and the direction its culture pursues. [Comment from the other deputies:] (*"Very good."*)

Consequently, I have the same grounds for saying that Spain has ceased to be Catholic as I do for saying that the opposite was true of the old Spain. Spain was Catholic in the sixteenth century even though there were many very important dissidents, some of whom are the glory and splendor of Castilian literature, and Spain has ceased to be Catholic even though there are today many millions of Spanish Catholics, believers. . . . Christians took over the imperial Roman state when, with the original spirit of the ancient world having grown weak, the Roman state had no other spiritual basis than that of Christian faith and the disputes of its philosophers and theologians. And this was done without hoping that the millions of pagans, who took centuries to convert, would embrace the new faith. The Roman Empire was Christian, and the modest Hispano-Roman farmer still sacrificed to the Latin gods in the same places that now have statues of Virgins and Christs. This means that the layers of sediment overlay each other throughout history and that a layer may take some time to disappear and be covered when the religious spirit that created it has already evaporated at the higher levels. . . .

We have said: separation of Church and state. The immense majority within this Cortes would not even subject this to discussion. And yet, what kind of separation? Are we going to make a break in relations between the state and the Church, remaining on our side of the line while paying no attention to what happens on the other side? Are we going to ignore the fact that in Spain there is the Catholic Church, with its faithful, with its hierarchy, and with its supreme powers outside the borders? . . .

In the minister of justice's speech . . . I noticed vagueness, indecision, almost a void concerning the future; and this vagueness, this void, this indecision filled me with fear and apprehension, for I can see this void being filled with a concordat. It is not that His Honor wants a concordat; none of us wants one; but this void, this line beyond which one does not venture, places a republican government . . . in the absolute necessity of dealing with the Church of Rome . . . under conditions of inferiority. . . . (*"Very good."*) And this, gentlemen, we must oppose, seeking a solution that, based on the principle of the separation, leaves the Republican state, the secular state, the unilaterally legislating state, the means of not being ignorant of either the actions or the purposes or the government or the policies of the Church of Rome. For me this is fundamental.

Other aspects of the question are less important. The budget for the clergy will obviously be abolished. . . . The question of the Church's property is more important. [Azaña calls for its nationalization without compensation.] In reality, the pressing question . . . is that of the religious orders. . . .

On the one hand, we have the obligation to respect freedom of conscience, naturally, without making an exception of Christian liberty. But we also have, on the other hand, the duty to keep the Republic and the state safe. These two principles clash, . . . so what shall we do? Shall we . . . continue the old system, which consisted of suppressing . . . the security and independence of the state, leaving the way open for the multitude of religious orders to invade Spanish society? No. But I ask, is it legitimate, is it intelligent, is it useful to suppress . . . all the other obligations we have toward this freedom of conscience? I say clearly not. (*"Very good, very good."*) What must be done . . . is to take the better of the options among the conflicting principles, which for us, as secular servants of the state and political leaders of the republican state, can be nothing other than the principle of the good of the state. (*"Very good."*) . . . .

In my modest judgment, the way to resolve this question is . . . to treat unequals unequally. In the face of religious orders we cannot reply with an eternal principle of justice, but rather with a principle of social utility and defense of the Republic. . . . We have to prohibit the religious orders because of their attitude toward the Republic. . . . I believe that this dissolution must be decreed in the constitution (*"Very good."*) not only because it is honest, frank, and noble to state it, since we intend to do it, but also because if we do not do it, we may not be able to do it later. . . .

[As for] the benevolent actions of the religious orders, . . . those who have experience with these things, the doctors who run hospitals, and the people who visit the charitable houses, and even the ailing poor themselves who take refuge in these hospitals and establishments, know that behind the charitable impulse, which is doctrinally irreproachable and admirable, there is above all a means of proselytizing, which we cannot tolerate. (*"Very good."*) . . . .

At no time, under no condition, in no way, will either my party or I accept . . . that the function of teaching be turned over to the religious orders. This, never. I am very sorry, but this is truly defending the Republic. The more or less clandestine agitation of the Company of Jesus . . . [and] this continuous action of the religious orders on the minds of young people . . . must be prevented at any cost. (*"Very good."*) Do not tell me that this is contrary to liberty, because this is a question of public safety. Those of you who call yourselves liberals, . . . would you allow a university professor to teach Aristotelian astronomy and to say that the heavens are composed of various spheres to which the stars are attached? Would you allow the medical beliefs of the sixteenth century to be taught in Spanish universities? . . . In the matter of the moral and political sciences, the obligation of the Catholic religious orders, given their dogma, is to teach all that is contrary to the principles upon which the modern state is based. . . .

This is my point of view, gentlemen; more precisely, this is the point of view of Acción Republicana, which has no reason to hide its secularism or its constructive radicalism or the modern conception it has of Spanish life. . . . It is determined to contribute to its renovation from the roots to the branches. . . . (*Great and prolonged applause.*)

41. Parliamentary Debate on Women's Suffrage (1931)

The provisional government that took over after the king's departure in April 1931 called for the writing of a new constitution by an assembly known as the Constituent Cortes. In drawing up regulations for the election of that Cortes, the provisional government denied women the right to vote but allowed them to be elected, and three women were elected. Victoria Kent Siano was a lawyer and member of the Radical Socialist Party; Clara Campoamor Rodríguez, also a lawyer, was a member of the Radical Party; both were elected in Madrid.

When the Constituent Cortes took up the issue of allowing women to vote there was already ample precedent for the idea; women in Britain, the United States, and other countries had recently received that right, and even General Primo de Rivera had granted women the right to vote in certain elections (though he never held such elections). Most leaders accepted the common belief that women were more religious than men and would thus follow the clergy's instructions and vote for parties seeking to restore the monarchy; consequently the deputies' positions on women's suffrage were somewhat unpredictable. The complexities of the issue are apparent from the following excerpts from an October 1 debate in the Cortes, which ultimately did grant women the right to vote.

SOURCE: María Angeles Duran, ed., *Mujeres y hombres: La formación del pensamiento igualitaria* (Madrid: Editorial Castalia, 1993), 161–71.

MR. PRESIDENT: Miss Kent, if you wish to explain your vote, you may do so now.

MISS KENT: Mr. Deputies, at this time I ask the chamber for its respectful attention to the problem that is being debated here, because I believe it is neither a problem of mine nor a problem we should take lightly. At this time, we are discussing women voting, and it is significant that a woman such as me, who does nothing but devote herself fervently to labor, should rise this afternoon to tell the chamber, frankly, that I believe that the vote for women should be postponed. (*"Very good!" Applause.*) That I believe that it is not the moment to grant the vote to the Spanish woman. (*"Very good!"*) . . .

At this moment we are going to give or deny the vote to more than half of all Spanish individuals, and it is essential that those of us who feel the Republican fervor (*"Very good!"*), the democratic, liberal, and Republican fervor, stand up here to say: the vote for women must be postponed. (*"Very good!"*) And it is necessary, Mr. Deputies, to postpone the vote for women because I would need to see . . . mothers in the street asking for schools for their children; I would need to have seen mothers in the street preventing their sons from going to Morocco [to fight a colonial war]; I would need to see Spanish women all united, asking for what is essential for the health and upbringing of their children. For this reason, Mr. Deputies, because I believe that in this way I am serving the Republic, as I believe I have served it with my modest abilities and have committed to serving it as long as I live, it is because of this state of consciousness that I rise this afternoon to ask the chamber to awaken Republican consciousness, to intensify liberal and democratic faith and to postpone the vote for women. . . .

It is not true that by doing so I am denying women's abilities in the slightest way; no, Mr. Deputies, it is not a question of abilities; it is a question of how opportune this is for the Republic. This is why I ask for the postponement or the placement of conditions on it. But if we place conditions on the vote for women, perhaps we would be committing some injustice. If we postpone women's suffrage no injustice of any kind is being committed, in my view. I believe that the woman, to become attached to an ideal, needs some time to live with that very ideal. The woman does not apply herself to matters she does not see clearly, and for this reason I believe that a few years of living under a republic are necessary; women need to see that the Republic has brought Spain something the monarchy never brought: these twenty thousand schools of which the minister of education was speaking to us this morning, these laboratories, these popular universities, these cultural centers where a woman can take her children to make them into real citizens.

When a few years have passed and women have seen the fruits of the Republic, when women have reaped the benefits of the Republic in the education and life of their children, the fruit of this Republic in which one is working with this zeal and generosity, when the Spanish woman realizes that only in the Republic are her children's rights of citizenship guaranteed, that only the Republic has brought to her household the bread that the monarchy did not bring, then, Mr. Deputies, women will be the most fervent, the most ardent defenders of the Republic. But at this moment, when our president has just received a petition from Spanish women who, in all good faith, believe at the present time that the ideals of Spain should be pursued in a different way, when I desired fervently to see thousands of Spanish women signing petitions of support for the Republic (MISS CAMPOAMOR: *"They have!"*), when I wished to see thousands of signatures and thousands of women in the streets crying out, "Long live the Republic!" and "Long live the government of the Republic!" and when I had been hoping that that parade of Spanish women who went to pay tribute to Primo de Rivera would be offset by another of Spanish women favorable to the Republic, I must humbly confess that I have not seen it, and that I cannot judge all Spanish women by these college girls who went to jail, to the honor of young women in schools, because they were only four young ladies. Nor can I judge the Spanish woman by these working women who leave their jobs each day to support their households along with their husbands. If Spanish women were all workers, if Spanish women had spent some time in college and were mentally liberated, I would rise today before the entire chamber and ask for the vote for women. (*"Very good!" Applause.*)

But at this time I rise precisely to say the opposite and to say it with all the conviction of my spirit, confronting the judgment that women who do not have this fervor and these Republican sentiments . . . may form of me. This is why I clearly rise to say to the chamber: either conditions on the vote or its postponement; I believe its postponement would be more beneficial, because I consider it more just, so that, after a few years of being in a Republic, of living under a Republic, of struggling for the Republic and appreciating the benefits of the Republic, you would have, in women, the Republic's most enthusiastic defenders. But today, Mr. Deputies, it is dangerous to grant the vote to women. I cannot be seated without my thoughts and feelings being clear, and without thus absolutely clearing my conscience. This is what I wished to explain to the chamber. (*Great applause.*)

MISS CAMPOAMOR: I would like the floor.

MR. PRESIDENT: The floor is yours.

MISS CAMPOAMOR: Mr. Deputies, far be it from me to censure or to attack the expressions of my colleague, Miss Kent. Understanding, on the contrary, the tortures of her spirit in having been seen today in the difficult situation of denying the initial capacities of women (*noise*); in finding herself in the difficult situation of denying, as she did deny, the initial capacity of women. (*The noise continues.*) I believe that, by her thinking she has lived up to the bitter phrase of Anatole France, when he spoke to us of those socialists who, forced by necessity, went to parliament to legislate against their own. (*New noise.*)

With respect to the series of claims that have been made this afternoon against the vote for women I must say, with all due respect, with all the necessary consideration, that they are not based in reality. Let us take one of them at random. This "when have women risen up to protest the war in Morocco?" first of all, why haven't men done so? Second, who protested and rose up in Zaragoza during the war in Cuba more than women did? Who filled the ranks of the demonstrators in favor of the responsibility of the Atheneum, as a result of the disaster at Anual [a military defeat in Morocco in 1921], more than women did, who went in greater numbers than men did? (*Noise.*)

Women! How can one say that when women give signs of life for the Republic, we will concede them the right to vote as a prize? Haven't women struggled for the Republic? In praising women workers and women in the universities, isn't she attesting to their capacities? Besides, in speaking of women workers and women in the universities, will she ignore all those who do not belong to one class or the other? Don't both suffer the consequences of the situation? Don't they pay taxes to support the state in the same way that others do and that men do? Aren't they all affected by the consequences of the legislation that is passed here for the two sexes, though only created and developed by one? How can it be said that women have not struggled, and that they need a long time, many years under a republic, to demonstrate their abilities? And why not men? Why should men, at the advent of the Republic, have their rights while tying down those of women?

And besides, Mr. Deputies, those of you who voted for the Republic, and for whom Republicans voted, think for a moment and say whether you voted alone, if only men voted for you. (*Various deputies: "Yes!" Other deputies: "No!"*) Has the woman's vote been absent? . . . Do you have the right to do all this? No, you have the right that the law gives you, the law that you yourselves passed, but you do not have natural rights, the fundamental rights that are based on respect for every human being, so what you are doing is to exercise a power; let women express themselves and you will see that you cannot continue to exercise this power. . . .

But let us not speak of these things, because what matters here is the principle. (MR. PÉREZ MADRIGAL: *"What matters is the Republic."*) This is the principle. To me, Mr. Pérez Madrigal, the Republic is so important . . . [that] I believe that it would be a very grave political error to deny women the right to vote. (MR. PÉREZ MADRIGAL: *"Granting the vote to women amounts to restoring the monarchy."*) Your lordship is mistaken; what you claim is only a hypothesis. (MR. PÉREZ MADRIGAL: *"One as respectable as yours."*) and against that hypothesis I have my own: that of my conscience, that of my faith, that of my fervor. You do not have the right, by reason of your hypothesis, to close the door to more than half of the Spanish race. (MR. PÉREZ MADRIGAL: *"We are not closing the door; it is a matter of time; it is a commitment for next year."*)

MR. PRESIDENT: I ask the chamber to remain silent.

MISS CAMPOAMOR: I ask the chamber to listen to me in silence. It is not with attacks or irony that you will overcome my determination; the only thing that I have here as I stand before you, Mr. Deputies, . . . is precisely my defense of a right that my nature and my faith compel me to defend with firmness and determination. (*"Very good!" Applause.*) I would not like to acknowledge interruptions, so as not to prolong the discussion, but since I heard someone say "within a year," do you believe that in that period of time women are going to acquire these abilities? Do you believe that in that period of time you will shape their ideology? Then why do you not begin the crusade immediately, to shape it sooner? Can it be that to take control of this nature you need one year? . . .

This question is not being dealt with here today from the point of view of principles, . . . and it is an ethical question, a purely ethical question, whether to recognize all of the rights of a woman, who is a human being, because ever since [Johann] Fichte, in 1796, the postulate has been accepted, also in principle, that only one who does not consider a woman a human being can claim that all of the rights of man and the citizen must not be the same for women as for men. And in the French parliament, in 1848, Victor Considérant rose to say that a constitution that grants the vote to beggars, domestic servants, and illiterates . . . cannot deny it to women. . . .

And from the practical and utilitarian point of view, of what are you accusing women? Is it of ignorance? Well I cannot resist referring to a study, no matter how annoying statistics may be, by Mr. Luzurriaga, regarding illiteracy in Spain. He made a study of the years from 1868 to 1910 . . . and observed that while the number of illiterate men, far from decreasing, increased by 73,082, the number of illiterate women declined by 48,098. . . . This basically means, the author adds, that the decrease in illiteracy is more rapid among women than among men, and [he adds] that if this trend continues, not only will women reach the educational level of men, but they will even surpass it. That was in 1910. And since 1910, the curve has continued rising, so that today women are less illiterate than men. So it is not on the grounds of ignorance that women can be denied access to the securing of this right. (*"Very good!"*) . . .

I, Mr. Deputies, consider myself a citizen first and a woman second, and I believe it would be a profound political error to leave women on the margin of this right, the women who hope and trust in you. . . . Do not let the woman, if she is backward-thinking, think that her hope lies in dictatorship; do not let the woman, if she has advanced ideas, think that her hope of equality lies in communism. Do not, Mr. Deputies, commit the political error of grave consequences. Save the Republic, help the Republic, attracting to us and adding to us this force that anxiously awaits the moment of redemption.

Each one of us speaks from experience, and I am speaking from my own. I am a deputy from the province of Madrid; I have traveled throughout it, not only to fulfill my duty, but also out of affection for it, and many times, indeed always, I have seen that at public events there was a larger female turnout than a male turnout, and I have seen the hope of redemption in the eyes of these women, I have seen the desire to help the Republic, I have seen the passion and the emotion that they hold for their ideals. The Spanish woman today places her hopes of redemption, and her children's redemption, in the Republic. Do not commit a historic error that you will not have time to regret (*noise*); that you will not have enough time to regret in leaving women on the margins of the Republic, women, who represent a new force, a young force; who have provided sympathy and support for the men who were in the jails; who have suffered in many cases as you have, and who are diligently applying themselves to [Alexander] Humboldt's idea that the only way to gain maturity in the exercise of a liberty and to make it accessible to all is to practice it.

Mr. Deputies, I have spoken my final words in this debate. Pardon me if I have bothered you, and consider that it is my conviction that is speaking; that I speak as a Republican, but as a Republican who would defend an ideal to the death; who would place . . . her head and heart in the balance . . . to persuade you in favor of the vote for women. I continue to think, and not out of vanity, but rather out of intimate conviction, that no one is serving the Spanish Republic any more than I am at this moment. (*"Very good!" Applause.*)

42. The 1931 Constitution

Having lived through seven years of dictatorship and then seen the monarchy collapse in April 1931, Spain's republicans and working-class parties felt that the time had finally come to create their desired regime. Elections produced a Constituent Cortes dominated by the Socialists, anticlerical Radicals, liberal Republicans, and regionalist parties, and that body, which first met on July 14, 1931, completed its constitution on December 9 of that year. The constitution expressed the victorious coalition's outlook, but it also reflected basic disagreements among the parties of the left and center.

SOURCE: *El Sol*, December 5, 1931.

Spain, using its sovereignty, and represented by the Constituent Cortes, decrees and sanctions this constitution:

General Dispositions

Article 1. Spain is a democratic Republic of workers of all classes, organized in a regime of liberty and justice.

The powers of all its organs emanate from the people.

The Republic constitutes an integral state compatible with the autonomy of the municipalities and regions. . . .

Article 2. All Spaniards are equal before the law.

Article 3. The Spanish state has no official religion.

Article 4. Castilian is the official language of the Republic. Every Spaniard has the obligation to know it and the right to use it, without detriment to the rights that the laws of the state recognize for languages of the provinces or regions. Except for what special laws may call for, no one can be required to know or use any regional language.

Article 5. The capital of the Republic is established in Madrid.

Article 6. Spain renounces war as an instrument of national policy. . . .

Title I: National Organization

Article 8. The Spanish state, within the irreducible limits of its current territory, will be made up of municipalities combined into provinces and of regions under a system of autonomy. . . .

Article 9. All the Republic's municipalities will be autonomous in matters of their competence, and they will elect their municipal councils by equal, direct, and secret universal suffrage. . . . Mayors will always be chosen by direct election by the people or by the municipal council. . . .

Article 11. If one or more adjoining provinces with common historical, cultural, and economic characteristics agree to organize themselves as an autonomous region in order to form a political-administrative nucleus within the Spanish state, they shall present their statute in accordance with the content of article 12. . . .

Article 12. The following conditions are required for the approval of the statute for an autonomous region:

1. That it be proposed by the majority of its municipal councils, or at least those whose municipalities include two-thirds of the registered voters of the region.

2. That it be accepted by . . . at least two-thirds of the registered voters in the region. If the plebiscite turns out negative, the proposal for autonomy cannot be renewed for five years.

3. That the Cortes approve it.

The regional statutes shall be approved by the parliament whenever they correspond to this title and do not contain any kind of clauses contrary to the constitution or the organic laws of the state. . . .

Article 13. Under no circumstances shall the federation of autonomous regions be permitted.

Article 14. Legislation and the direct execution of the following matters are under the competence of the Spanish state:

1. Acquisition and loss of nationality and the regulation of constitutional rights and duties.

2. The relationship between churches and the state, and the regime concerning forms of worship.

3. Diplomatic and consular representation, and in general, that of the state abroad; the declaration of war; peace treaties; the governance of colonies and protectorates and all kinds of international relations.

4. The defense of public security. . . .

5. Ocean fisheries.

6. The debts of the state.

7. The army, the navy, and national defense.

8. The system of tariffs. Commercial treaties. Customs and the free circulation of merchandise. . . .

10. Matters of extradition.

11. Jurisdiction of the Supreme Court, except for powers recognized for the regional authorities.

12. The monetary system . . . and general regulation of banking.

13. The general regulation of communications, airlines, mail, telegraphs, submarine cables, and radio broadcasting. . . .

16. Policing of foreign borders, emigration, and immigration.

17. The general treasury of the state.

18. Regulation of the production and sale of arms. . . .

Article 15. On the following matters, legislation is a matter for the Spanish state, but its execution can be delegated to the autonomous regions. . . .

1. Penal, social, commercial, and judicial legislation; and in regard to civil legislation, the form of matrimony, the ordering of property registers and mortgages. . . .

2. Legislation on intellectual and industrial property. . . .

10. Regulation of the press, associations, and public meetings and shows.

11. The right of expropriation. . . .

12. The socialization of natural resources and economic enterprises. . . .

Article 16. In matters not included in the two previous articles, exclusive powers of legislation and direct execution may be under the competence of the autonomous regions. . . .

Article 17. In the autonomous regions, there can be no discrimination between natives of that territory and the rest of the Spaniards.

Article 18. All matters not explicitly recognized in the autonomous region's statute will be considered to be under the competence of the state. . . .

Title II: Nationality

Article 23: Spaniards are:

1. Those born to Spanish fathers or mothers inside or outside of Spain.

2. Those born in Spanish territory of foreign parents, as long as they opt for Spanish nationality in the form that the laws require.

3. Those born in Spanish territory of unknown parents.

4. Foreigners who obtain naturalization papers. . . .

Title III: Rights and Duties of the Spaniards

Article 25. Birth, relationship, sex, social class, wealth, political ideas, and religious beliefs cannot be the basis of any legal privilege. The Spanish state does not recognize noble titles or distinctions.

Article 26. All religious persuasions shall be considered associations subject to a special law. The state, the regions, the provinces, and the municipalities may not support, favor, or economically assist churches or religious associations or institutions.

A special law will regulate the complete abolition of the budget for the clergy within a maximum of two years.

Those religious orders that by statute include, in addition to the three canonical vows, any other vow of special obedience to any authority other than the legitimate authority of the state are dissolved.

The other religious orders will be subject to a special law voted by this Constituent Cortes, in accord with the following requirements:

1. The dissolution of those which by their activities constitute a danger to the security of the state. . . .

3. The inability to acquire and keep, either directly or through others, more property than that . . . needed for their own sustenance or the direct fulfillment of their particular duties.

4. The prohibition on engaging in industry, commerce, or teaching.

5. Subjection to all of the country's tax laws.

6. The obligation to render an annual accounting to the state on the investment of their holdings. . . .

7. The property of religious orders may be nationalized.

Article 27. Freedom of conscience and the right to profess and practice any religion freely are guaranteed in Spanish territory, except for the respect owed to the demands of public morality.

Cemeteries shall be subject to exclusive civil jurisdiction. They may not contain any separate sections based on religious motives. . . .

Public demonstrations of religion must be authorized by the government in each and every case.

No one can be forced to officially declare religious beliefs. . . .

Article 34. Everyone has the right to the free expression of ideas and opinions, using any means of expression, without prior censorship. . . .

Article 36. Citizens of both sexes over 23 years of age shall have the same electoral rights. . . .

Article 38. The right to meet peacefully and without arms is recognized. . . .

Article 40. All Spaniards, without distinctions by sex, are eligible for public jobs and positions according to their merit and qualifications. . . .

Article 43. The family is under the special protection of the state. Marriage is based on the equality of rights for the two sexes, and can be dissolved by mutual consent or by petition of either spouse given allegations of just cause. . . . Parents have the same duties toward children born out of wedlock as toward those born within it. . . .

Article 44. All the country's resources, whoever owns them, are subject to the national economy's interests. . . . Property of any kind may be the object of forcible expropriation for reasons of social utility, in exchange for adequate compensation. . . . Public services and enterprises that affect the common interest may be nationalized in those cases in which social necessity demands it. . . .

Article 46. Work, in all its various forms, is a social obligation and will enjoy the protection of the laws. The Republic will assure every worker the necessary conditions for a worthy existence. Its social legislation will regulate: cases of insurance against illness, accident, involuntary unemployment, old age, disability, and death; the labor of women and children, and especially the protection of maternity; the workday and the minimum wage . . . ; annual paid vacations; . . . the participation of workers in the management, administration, and benefits of the enterprises, and all that affects the defense of workers.

Article 47. The Republic shall protect the peasant, and toward this end it will legislate . . . on family properties . . . exempt from all kinds of taxes; agricultural credit; indemnities for the loss of harvests; producers' and consumers' cooperatives; insurance funds; practical schools of agriculture, and experimental farms, irrigation works, and rural roads. . . .

Article 48. The promotion of education is an essential responsibility of the state, and it will be carried out through educational institutions linked in a unified school system. Primary education will be free and obligatory. Teachers and professors . . . are public employees. Freedom of teaching will be recognized and guaranteed.

The Republic will legislate in the sense of helping needy Spaniards to gain access to all levels of education. . . . Teaching will be secular, and it will make labor the axis of its methods, being inspired by the ideals of human solidarity.

The right of churches to teach their respective doctrines in their own establishments is recognized. . . .

Article 50. The autonomous regions shall be able to organize education in their respective languages, in accordance with the powers granted to them in their statutes. The study of the Castilian language is obligatory, and it shall also be used as an instrument of teaching in all the primary and secondary schools in the autonomous regions.

43. Fernando de los Ríos, The Republican Education Program (1937)

For many years, Republicans and others on the left had understood that their hopes for significant social and political change in Spain depended on mobilizing the country's urban and rural working classes, but they also knew that any such mobilization would have to overcome the ignorance and poverty that kept the poor from playing much of a role in politics. Consequently, when the Republic was finally declared in 1931, its leaders made mass education one of their highest priorities. The existing educational system, however, was in the hands of the Church, whose approach to education seemed to the Republicans designed to keep the lower classes ignorant and obedient.

Overseeing the Republic's efforts to create a secular educational system was Education Minister Fernando de los Ríos (1879–1949), a socialist who was appointed to that position in October 1931. In 1937, while serving as ambassador to the United States, he gave the following speech at Sarah Lawrence College in New York, explaining the Republic's educational policies as part of his efforts to seek American support for the Republican side in the Civil War.

SOURCE: Spanish Embassy, Washington, D.C., Bureau of Information, *Excerpts from a Speech Delivered at Sarah Lawrence College . . . on April 7, 1937, by Professor Fernando de los Ríos, Ambassador of Spain, Former Minister of Education* (Washington, D.C.: Spanish Embassy, Bureau of Information, 1937). This document can be found in the Blodgett Collection, Harvard University.

We thought it was urgently necessary to put all the resources and the efforts of the State at the service of the education of the people. That is why, when, at the end of 1931, the Spanish Republic entrusted me with the responsibilities of the Ministry of Education, I put into this cause all the enthusiasm and the devotion of a man for whom popular education had been for many decades the most cherished dream of his life. I shall attempt to sketch . . . the work that was carried out during the two years in which I was the head of the Department of Education. . . .

What was the hope of our program of popular education? First, the creation of elementary schools; second, the organization of state-maintained school lunchrooms; third, the education of adults, liquidating illiteracy; fourth, the artistic education of the people.

When the Republic was established, Spain needed no less than 40,000 new schools. There were cities, like Madrid itself, where thousands and thousands of children were lacking the opportunities of getting the most elementary education. One month before the new institutions were inaugurated, the mothers of Madrid were standing in queues at the doorsteps of the schools, fearing that overcrowding might lessen the chances of securing admission for their children. . . . Thus, our first and most urgent task was that of opening new schools, and within the period of two years, 10,500 new institutions were founded in both urban and rural Spain.

Nevertheless, the children of small villages—the children of the agricultural regions, where life is so shockingly miserable—found it impossible to attend these schools, because their parents had to send them to take care of the flocks, or to pick olives in the fields . . . so that they might earn a few cents. . . . How were we going to rescue these children, and bring them under the influence of the school? The only way of accomplishing that was to organize the *cantinas* (school lunchrooms) and the *roperos* (clothing storerooms) in the schools . . . [and] to give them food and clothing, so that the parents might release them from their work. To this effect the republic increased its budget for *cantinas* and *roperos* 800 percent. As a result of this, there was such a run of children to the rural schools that it was practically impossible . . . to accommodate them all.

This situation compelled me to introduce a bill in parliament proposing a loan of 400,000,000 pesetas, for the exclusive use of school construction. Parliament granted me that money, and in eight years we planned to build a minimum of 20,000 new buildings. This was begun on a great scale in 1932.

My next project was to make similar provisions for adult education. . . . I wanted to organize . . . community suppers at the schools, for the peasants, during the course of which they could be taught to read and write. This plan did not materialize, because the time factor did not enable me to carry out the idea. . . . The education of the adult was accomplished, however, through another method, namely, the "pedagogical missions," the theater, and the traveling museum.

The Spanish Republic attacked with enormous enthusiasm this enterprise. The Pedagogical Mission was composed of a group of true missionaries of culture: boys and girls, teachers of both sexes, university students, and youngsters from the workshops, who would go, with the traveling theater or library, the radio, the movie, etc., to the village, to spend a few days with the peasants, putting within their reach some of the cultural facilities which they were lacking. Sometimes young medical students and nurses would also teach the peasant mother how to take care of her children, how to keep them clean, to prevent infectious diseases, etc. Students in agriculture would teach those peasants who owned some land how to cultivate it more efficiently, how to prevent or check tree diseases, how to take care of the domestic animals, etc. Thus, we were trying to enrich not only the intellectual world of the peasant, but also to improve the economic means at his command.

All this required, however, an essential supplement . . . found in the *escuelas de trabajo* (Schools of Workers), the aim of which was to convert the untrained workers into skilled workers. Through establishment of horticultural and agricultural schools we found an effective medium for changing the ignorant peasant into a farmer knowing the economic possibilities of his land.

This necessitated a special type of teacher, and with this purpose in mind we reformed the curriculum of the Normal School in such a way that a completed program of secondary education universal in character, was a prerequisite for the specialized course for those teachers who were to teach workers. Furthermore, we organized . . . intensive courses for the teachers themselves. Under this system the teachers took turns in giving demonstration lessons before the Provincial Congress of Teachers, which were followed by discussions on the ways and means of improving the teachers' techniques.

We also fostered field trips from one province to another, and during the summer we used . . . palaces . . . for summer schools. Here thousands of children lived in the invigorating air of the mountains, or else we would send thousands of children to the seashore. . . . We took great pains to do away with the overacademic atmosphere in the secondary schools; instead of a university in miniature we made of it an integrated educational institution, in which the emphasis was less on indoctrination and more on the give-and-take relationship between teacher and student and, above all, on the development of a spirit of social responsibility in both teacher and student.

A cultural work of this kind, however, is incomplete if it has no repercussion on the institutions of higher learning, such as universities, research bodies, museums, etc. With this last purpose in mind, we founded on a similar basis . . . the Centros de Investigación, the Centro de Estudios Históricos, and the Sección de Monumentos Hispánicos, to bring to light unexamined documents of historical importance, of medieval Spain, and to reinterpret on their basis those which had already been uncovered. . . . We also founded centers of research in economics, physical science, international politics, etc., to which large sums were allotted in the federal budget. There never was before in Spain a greater interest for cultural problems than that witnessed between 1931 and 1932.

Finally, we conceived the project, which fortunately I was able to put into effect, of creating the International University of Santander. In the magnificent Palacio de la Magdalena . . . thousands of students and professors from all over Europe and America gathered . . . to discuss and analyze cultural problems of international character. . . .

This is in brief the educational program brought into effect by the Spanish Republic during the last six years, especially in 1931 to 1933 and 1936.

44. La Pasionaria, "From Childhood to Maturity" (1966)

Translated from Spanish by Dolores Ibarruri

One of the most remarkable Spanish women of the twentieth century was Dolores Ibarruri, better known as La Pasionaria. Born in a family of miners in the Basque province of Vizcaya in 1895, she eventually became one of the major figures on the left in Spain in the 1930s, and she was elected a parliamentary deputy for the Communist Party during the Second Republic. She also became famous for her fiery speeches, including many on the radio. In this excerpt from her autobiography, entitled *El único camino*, she describes her early years and the beginnings of her political consciousness.

SOURCE: Dolores Ibarruri, *They Shall Not Pass: The Autobiography of La Pasionaria*, trans. Dolores Ibarruri (New York: International Publishers, 1966), 59–62. Reprinted by permission of International Publishers Co., Inc.

At 15 I finished school. I was in poor health and not able to go to work. This meant an added burden for my family, which I was reluctant to impose on them. Since my good grades qualified me for further academic training, I decided to take the one-year preparatory course for the Teachers' Normal School and then the two-year teacher-training course. After completing the first two years, my adolescent dreams faded, in the face of hard economic realities; books, food, clothes were all expenses my parents simply could not continue to meet. So I transferred to a dressmaking academy for two years. After this apprenticeship, I worked as a domestic for three years in the homes of local businessmen. At 20, seeking liberation from drudgery in other people's homes, I married a miner . . . I had met during my first job as a domestic.

My mission in life was "fulfilled." I could not, ought not, aspire to more. Woman's goal, her only aspiration, had to be matrimony and the continuation of the joyless, dismal, pain-ridden thralldom that was our mothers' lot; we were supposed to dedicate ourselves wholly to giving birth, to raising our children, and to serving our husbands who, for the most part, treated us with complete disregard.

My mother used to say, "She who hits the bull's-eye in her choice of a husband cannot err in anything." To hit the bull's-eye was as difficult as finding a pea that weighed a pound. I did not find such a pea. May the happy wives forgive me; but each of us judges the market by the good values we find there.

Although I had no tendency to be nostalgic about the past, I used to long for the time when women worked in the mines. However brutish the work, it offered an outlet no longer available to women in the mining valley; in addition to wages, it had added a social dimension to women.

When the demand for ore fell off and there was an excess of manpower, women workers were no longer hired. This discriminatory act was carried out under the hypocritical cloak of solicitude for the mother, the woman, the family, and the home. Women were freed from brutalizing mine work only to be converted into domestic slaves, deprived of all rights. In the mine, the woman was a worker and, as such, she could protest exploitation together with other workers. In the home, she was stripped of her social identity; she was committed to sacrifice, to privation, to all manner of service by which her husband's and her children's lives were made more bearable. Thus her own needs were negligible; her own personality was nullified; in time she became "the old lady" who "doesn't understand," who was in the way, whose role eventually became that of a servant to her household and a nursemaid to her grandchildren. This was the tradition of generations.

When my first child (a girl) was born, I had already suffered a year of such bitterness that only love for my baby kept me alive. I was terrified, not only by the odious present but also by the dismal, pain-filled future that loomed before me, as day by day I observed the lives of the miners' wives. Nevertheless, like other young people, I built castles in the air. And, full of illusions, I closed my eyes to my surroundings and built my dream house on the shifting sand of "contigo pan y cebolla" ("with you, bread and an onion"), believing that mutual attraction and fondness would compensate for and surmount the difficulties of privation. I forgot that where bread is lacking, mutual recrimination is more likely to enter; and sometimes, even *with* bread, it still creeps in.

Raw, stark reality struck at me, as at other women, with merciless fists. A few fleeting days of illusion and then. . . . Afterward, the icy, wounding, pitiless prose of existence. Out of my own experience I learned the hard truth of the popular saying, "Madre, que cosa es casar? Hija, hilar, parir y llorar." ("Mother, what is marriage? Daughter, marriage is weaving, giving birth, weeping.") Weeping, weeping over our hurts and our impotence; weeping for our innocent children, to whom we could offer nothing but tear-stained caresses; weeping for our dismal lives, without horizons, without hope; bitter weeping, with a curse in our hearts and on our lips. A woman's curse? A mother's curse? What is so surprising about that, since our lives were worse than that of the most accursed?

Was life worth living? My companions in misery and I often asked this question as we discussed our situation, our wretchedness. They spoke with resignation; after all, what could we women do? I rebelled against the idea of the inevitability of such lives as ours; I rebelled against the idea that we were condemned to drag the shackles of poverty and submission through the centuries like beasts of burden—slapped, beaten, ground down by the men chosen to be our life companions.

I was then 21 and my daughter Esther was still an infant. When my husband's wretched wages were not enough to pay the rent; when, instead of meat we ate a few potatoes cooked with red peppers to give them color; when we had to mend our *alpargatas* (rope-soled canvas shoes) with wire; when I had to patch the patches on my husband's work clothes; when, for lack of food, I hadn't enough milk to nurse my baby, I confronted my husband with a desperate question: "Do you think we can go on living like this?"

The answer was disheartening: "How do you think the others live?"

"The same as we. But I can't resign myself to living worse than animals. Let's go away; let's go somewhere else where life isn't so hard, where we can at least feed our children."

"Somewhere else? Wherever the ox goes he will be harnessed to the plow."

It was true. Where could the worker go where he would not be cruelly exploited?

The intimate daily contact with harsh reality began to fray the fabric of my religious convictions. And every day I moved a little further from religious superstitions, prejudices, and traditional fears of the supernatural. I was beginning to learn that our poverty—the lack of the most basic human necessities—was not caused or altered by the will of any deity. The source of our misery was not in heaven but on earth. It arose from institutions established by men which could be altered or destroyed by other men.

I began to read Marxist literature and for me it was a window opening on life. My ideas and sentiments began to change and take concrete form, although there was much I did not yet understand. My former Catholic beliefs began to dwindle, although not without resistance, as if they were determined to leave a shadow, a fear, a doubt in the depths of my consciousness. The struggle for a Socialist society—even though it was clearly not imminent—began to give content and substance to my life; it was the force that sustained me under the oppressive conditions of our pariah-like existence. The more I learned about Socialism, the more reconciled I was to life, which I no longer saw as a swamp but as a battlefield on which an immense army of workers was gaining daily victories, advancing even through its defeats.

My new faith was more and more solid than my religious faith had been. Now I expected nothing from the mercy of an unknown and unknowable god; my expectations were anchored in the strength of mankind—our own strength, our own struggle. I was not willing to leave the world as we had inherited it. I would struggle to change it, to make it a better world, to open a path for our children that would lead to a society without oppression and without poverty.

45. Artists' Statements (1931–1934)

Among those who felt that the advent of the Republic meant a social revolution were many of the country's artists and intellectuals. The interwar period saw a great deal of highly politicized art in Europe, and with a government perceived as favorable to their aims now having come to power in Spain, many artists looked forward to great changes in their society and their cultural environment. *Arte* magazine was founded by a diverse group of artists, the Sociedad de Artistas Ibéricos; both *Nuestro Cinema* and *Octubre* were politically close to the Communist Party.

SOURCES: *Arte* (Madrid), no. 1, September 1932; *Adelanto de la revista Octubre* (Madrid), May 1, 1933; *Nuestro Cinema* (Madrid), October 1933; and *Octubre,* April 1934. These articles also appear in Jaime Brihuega, ed., *La vanguardia y la república* (Madrid: Ediciones Cátedra, 1982), 71–75, 76–78, 83–86, 250–52.

"Our Greetings and Our Proposals," *Arte*, September 1932

We wish, in writing and in publishing this magazine, to address ourselves to all; but before we speak to all, we wish to address ourselves to the government. . . . We must speak to the authorities first of all because they are the patrons of all in matters of art. There is, in Spain today, no public artistic consciousness. . . . Who should be blamed? We do not know. In part [we blame] the apathy of the entire citizenry; in part [we blame] our governments, which in all official areas have been maintaining a certain mixture of neglect and favoritism, which persist in this regime. . . .

Yes, we know perfectly well that there will be no effective solution as long as everyone, each man, does not feel . . . the need for art among the pressing demands of his spirit or the inclination to promote the production and purchase of works of art; yet given that this inclination does not exist in the quantity or quality that corresponds to a modern people, we believe it is up to the authorities to come up with a solution to this problem, taking the initial steps and initiating movement on its own account.

This is why our words . . . are directed, first of all, to . . . the authorities who are responsible for the destinies of official Spain at this moment. . . . [The author then addresses the minister of public instruction.]

Spain, Mr. Minister, has been living, in that which concerns the plastic arts, completely on the margins of world culture for about a century. One cannot be any further from history than Spain has been.

The world of the plastic arts has, in the last hundred years, gone through the most splendid, the most essential, and the most profound century that has ever existed in the history of the arts. . . . Yet this movement, which has taken up an entire century and has filled and is filling the whole world *has never come to Madrid*, and has almost never come to Spain at all. . . . Hundreds of respected masters from throughout the world—some of them Spaniards who have exhibited in European and American museums—have not managed to come here, to enter our museums, or to show their work to the Spanish public. . . . The Modern Museum of Spain will never ever put on a show, not even a modest one, representing the century of which we have spoken, because today it would cost millions to acquire a few paintings, which could once have been acquired for very little money.

This crime of neglect alone has caused the Spanish public—including that which considers itself enlightened—to find itself, in regard to this question of living art, in the most total lack of civilization: it does not know anything about and has not seen the works that constitute that of an entire period, nor has it been able to teach itself by viewing them. . . .

It is not a question, as such—as your excellency can see—only of art; it is, indeed, a matter of public instruction; it is a matter of public dignity; it is a matter of whether Spain can keep up . . . with culture, receiving the education it deserves, as other cultures do. . . .

We wish to live in the modern era, and that is all; we thus wish to create a kind of official University of the Arts, in which one tries to inform and to develop people's tastes and ideology through exhibitions, lectures, courses, magazines, monographs, and books. That which we can do on our own we shall do, of course, without asking for any help; for that which we cannot do, we will have to turn to Your Excellency and the government when necessary.

"Declaration of Principles," *Octubre*, May 1933

Our magazine is born under the red sign of the revolutionary epic. *Octubre* is neither temporary nor local, nor national. It is much more. *Octubre* represents a clear break, where one civilization ends and another emerges. *Octubre* is the culminating high point of the revolutionary proletariat. It is its victory. From now on, the proletariat will have a common fatherland and a universal mission: to broaden its limits, going beyond barriers and differences.

The need for a common organ that would bring together the voices and the force of revolutionary literature was in the consciousness of numerous comrades. *Octubre* will fill that need. . . .

It is essential that our magazine, *Octubre*, establish, at the outset, in a precise manner, the basic points upon which its activities will be based. There are five of these points:

1. *Octubre* is not the magazine of any minority group. It is the magazine of all the revolutionary artists and writers who wish to collaborate in it. . . .

2. *Octubre* accepts the general points approved in the General Congress of Revolutionary Literature, held in Kharkov (1930): (a) against imperialist war; (b) for the defense of the Soviet Union; (c) against fascism; (d) with the proletariat.

3. *Octubre*, within the national arena, will never be a magazine of irresponsible and uncontrolled struggle. We will combat all the forms and expressions of bourgeois literature more with persuasion than with immoderation; not with anarchy, but rather using our effective weapon, dialectic materialism. Our task will consist of revealing to the eyes of young writers and artists the fallacies and obsolescence of bourgeois rule, attracting them toward the revolutionary cause.

4. *Octubre* will be a proponent of the development of global revolutionary literature. At the same time, it will dedicate special attention to literature and art in the Soviet Union, since in that country, where socialism has triumphed, the problems and development of art follow a distinct path.

5. *Octubre* rejects the bourgeois claim that art is the product of a "superior caste." *Octubre*, thinking differently, will publish correspondence from workers, impressions from the factories and the fields, articles about struggle, etc. Our mission is to welcome the rudimentary expression of a nascent art form and to stimulate its authors, to guide them with our consciousness and our experience to be able to enrich tomorrow's proletarian literature.

These are, expressed synthetically, our foundations. The current hour has its imperatives of struggle and its urgent duties. To our comrades, artists and writers! Our duty obliges us not to remain indifferent in the contest between two worlds, one that is being born and one that is dying! Out of duty, out of sensibility, out of instinct, let us struggle with our weapons for the global triumph of the proletariat!

"Manifesto of the Association of Friends of *Nuestro Cinema*," *Nuestro Cinema*, October 1933

Comrades: No one can properly deny the critical circumstances that the world is going through, nor can one remain unmoved by the closeness of the events whose consequences still cannot be predicted, events provoked by capitalism, which, having become arrogant through the pompous triumph of Mussolini, Hitler, and the other repressive dictators manipulated by the bourgeoisie, is hastening to unleash an offensive against the international proletariat, with the desire of crushing it once and for all.

In order to secure its victory, the bourgeoisie will not fail to use any weapon at its disposal, nor will it miss the slightest opportunity that could help it attain it; therefore, naturally, well aware of the decisive influence that a properly oriented cinema can have on the people, the high bourgeoisie, already the owners of the most important film production companies, will continue distorting the educational and cultural mission of the cinema and will try to show its imperialistic, warmongering films, and its fascist, religious, capitalist, and arch-bourgeois propaganda on screens throughout the entire world in order to make all the unwary and unaware believe in the beauty of its regime and its already-corrupted civilization.

It therefore seems strange that in the face of these maneuvers that are so clear and so cynically undertaken, no voice has been raised to denounce and unmask them; on the contrary, this whole bourgeois and "independent" press that proclaims itself antifascist has silenced any hint of protest in its pages, under the golden pressure of the donations and the liberally distributed subsidies of the magnates of this dirty little cinematic world. Nor has any of our professional magazines, equally in the service of those magnates, considered it necessary to pay the slightest attention to the problems that this use of the cinema creates for the world proletariat, and also for the Spanish proletariat, which, lacking production of its own, is a colony of Yankee, German, and French cinema, almost all of which is undesirable.

Alone, in frank and hopeful contrast with this base and biased press, one Spanish magazine with a high and universal outlook, *Nuestro Cinema*, has opportunely launched the sound of alarm, denouncing these maneuvers and the invasion of a fascist policy in the cinema, and this in spite of the pressure that the cinema companies have put on its development, of the indifference of the petit-bourgeois public, of the permanent sabotage aimed at it through the organizations that distribute it, and of the attacks that it systematically receives from the capitalist press, hypocritically interested in the advent and expansion throughout Spain of this reactionary cinema.

This is why we, aware of the economic difficulties that *Nuestro Cinema* is going through, wishing to overcome the obstacles to its distribution, fully convinced of its value and of the nobility and clarity of its inflexibly anti-bourgeois criticism and commentary, have created an "Association of Friends of *Nuestro Cinema*," with the goal of helping it, distributing it, and defending it, certain not only of helping sustain a necessary magazine but also to contribute effectively to the struggle against the cinema of fascist, militarist, and bourgeois cinema, and for the possible establishment in our country of a proletarian cinema. Consequently, we have begun to prepare a series of public lectures that will be given throughout Spain, and through which we propose to intensify the movement of struggle against capitalist cinema and for proletarian cinema launched by *Nuestro Cinema.*

"Exposition of Revolutionary Art," *Octubre*, April 1934

From December 1 to 12 1933, in the salon underneath the Atheneum of Madrid, organized by the magazine *Octubre*, revolutionary artists and their sympathizers celebrated their first exposition. A great resonance among the workers. Daily, hundreds of them, upon leaving work, paraded before the works. While the bourgeois expositions die of solitude and boredom and the purchaser of paintings disappears from the broken scene of the crisis [the Depression], a new public, a new class, with clear vision and a clean conscience, is bursting enthusiastically on to the scene of revolution and culture. Now today, the working class is the only one capable of turning the pages of a book with enthusiasm, of overflowing the theaters and the exhibition halls. We have seen this in the Soviet Union. We will see this fully taking place in Spain. The painters and artists who took part in this exposition at the Atheneum are already beginning to know this. Never have their works been seen so attentively by so many eyes. It was art in the service of the revolution, giving a boost to the working masses.

In one of the corners of the salon, the following sign was seen: "The fact of attending this exposition means being against imperialist war, against fascism, for the defense of the Soviet Union, and together with the proletariat." . . .

For the first time, both artists who have come from the bourgeoisie and authentically proletarian artists have appeared together in one exhibition hall. And as one might expect, this new upsurge in the world of painting . . . was received with the silence of the press and the bourgeois critics.

46. *El Debate*, "A Large Catholic Majority" (1933)

The Second Republic, like other European democracies, featured a parliamentary system in which governments rested on the support of a coalition of parties holding a majority of the seats in parliament. From 1931 to 1933, Manuel Azaña had served as prime minister with the support of the Socialist and Radical Parties, among others. Yet significant ideological rifts separated the parties of the left, and when an attempted revolutionary insurrection in January 1933 led to the shooting of a number of peasants at Casas Viejas in Andalusia, some on the left felt they could no longer support the government. With Azaña having lost his majority in the parliament, the Republic's president used his powers to dissolve the parliament and call new elections.

Conservatives had been stunned by the rapidity of events in 1931, but by 1933 they had begun to marshal their forces and find new leaders. The most prominent of these was José María Gil Robles, a young deputy from Salamanca who in 1933 oversaw the formation of a new coalition of parties known as the Confederación Española de Derechas Autónomas (CEDA). Partly because of the right's political recovery, and partly because of popular disillusionment with the government of the left in the midst of the Great Depression (and the abstention of anarchists, who rejected the very idea of electing governments), the right won the November 1933 elections. *El Debate*, a newspaper representing conservatives willing to accept the Republic and work within it, commented on the election results.

SOURCE: *El Debate*, November 21, 1933; the text also appears in Fernando Díaz-Plaja, ed., *Historia de España en sus documentos (nueva serie): El siglo XX*, vol. 2, *Dictadura. . . República (1923–1936)* (Madrid: Instituto de Estudios Políticos, 1965), 593–96.

Exemplary elections, those of the day before yesterday. Because of the number of voters, as the enormous mass mobilized to vote for ideas and not persons, because of the liberty with which people generally voted. The Spanish people can feel legitimately proud.

This Is Spain

As a consequence of the recently completed election . . . a picture of what Spain is has emerged from the ballot boxes. At the moment this is being written we do not yet know the exact figures . . . but they show some 125 deputies for the right, some 50 for the Socialists, an equal number for the Radical Republicans, and small numbers for other leftist groups. And no one can doubt that Spain strongly resembles the collection of these sums: a large Catholic majority, a not inconsiderable force inclined toward socialism, even if it is principally owing to labor unions, a minority of men of the left, leftovers from the old anticlericalism of the nineteenth century, guided by Masonry. Because one should not forget that one must truly count as Catholics many of the votes cast in favor of candidacies that are not strictly of the right. To what we here are calling by the name of right one must add . . . the conservative Republicans and the progressives, and many of those who voted for the Radical Party, and we would even dare to say more than a few of those who, guided solely by class interest, gave their votes to socialism.

If we judge by the proclamations, the speeches, and all the spiritual agitation that preceded the elections, the vote on Sunday was cast, primarily and above all, against the sectarian policies of the government over these last two years. Secondly, it has meant a rejection of the socialistic policies that have damaged . . . legitimate rights of property and of national labor. And finally, one must see in it a protest against the arbitrariness, cruelty, and despotism that misgovernment has created in the aforementioned period. This, and nothing else, is the meaning of the elections.

The Political Situation

We understand that this produces a delicate political situation. The people have just voted against certain articles of the constitution, against some of the constitutional laws, [and] against many practices and acts of the government. . . . But despite what we are saying, . . . we do not believe that any great political problem has now been created, nor that there is any danger threatening public tranquility.

We are not unaware that on the left there are some who are lurking and maneuvering, hoping to take advantage of the interim nature of the government, and who would like to take the battle they have just lost at the ballot box to the streets. But the government must remain completely calm, and it can be if it continues to fulfill its mission of guarding public order, as it has up until now. Peace and order are, in reality, guaranteed. We believe that the government has at its disposal the necessary forces specifically intended to maintain security. But if, which we hope will not happen, the moral support of the entire nation should become necessary to energetically repress any attempt to disturb public peace, we do not hesitate to say that this support will be given. . . .

The Future Solution

Once the new parliament is formed . . . we believe that a government of the center will be constituted, with the collaboration of certain elements of an anti-Marxist character. . . . Obviously that force . . . that from the first moment raised its banner for religion, the fatherland, the family, order, property, and work, will enjoy great influence, and at times decisive influence, in the new parliament. . . . Young elements with a rapid and brilliant future make up this force. Before long, the government will have to be placed in its hands. This force is today, without a doubt, the largest of all the country's political forces; both inside and outside Spain it distinguishes itself as the holder of the secret of the nation's political future. Its ascent has been rapid and triumphal in these two years, and events have shown us what it can soon become. In a matter of months, it can complete its team of members, prepare its slate of governors, specify its program, broaden its following even more, and thus ready itself to receive the reins of the government of the state, which it should begin influencing from today on.

We have grounds for profound satisfaction. Yesterday's events announce a historic moment: the impending arrival of the day when a genuinely Spanish government, faithful to the purest patriotic traditions, formed by young, cultured men very much of their times can hold power, supported by the unconditional allegiance of good Spaniards. Those Spaniards have learned a lesson from the ballot box, one they should not forget: that they are the majority, that they have worthy leaders in whom they can place their confidence and the firm conviction that they will achieve all their demands without going beyond legal procedures, even those of a law dictated by their enemies to serve petty party interests rather than the common good.

And to close these considerations, we raise our hearts and express our gratitude to the exceedingly wise providence of God, who guides and directs peoples and seeks their well-being, even in those moments when it appears that he is punishing and afflicting them.

47. José Antonio Primo de Rivera, Ideas of the Falange (1934)

In interwar Europe, the new movement known as fascism (which first came to power in 1922 under Benito Mussolini in Italy) was attracting support from conservatives and nationalists who were alarmed at the rise of communism and disgusted with parliamentary democracy and liberalism. In Spain, a new organization very much in the fascist mold appeared in late 1933. Headed by José Antonio Primo de Rivera (1903–1936), the son of General Miguel Primo de Rivera, the Falange, or "phalanx," quickly attracted considerable attention. José Antonio, as he was generally known, was widely considered a charismatic young man, and after he was killed by Republicans at the beginning of the Civil War, he became a cult figure on the right. The Falange outlived its leader, and General Franco absorbed the movement and its ideas into his own regime by the late 1930s. This manifesto, sometimes referred to as "The Twenty-Six Points," explains the Falange's ideas.

SOURCE: *Nacional-Sindicalismo* (Zaragoza: n.p., 1936); this text appears in the Blodgett Collection, Harvard University.

Nation, Unity, Empire

1. We believe in the supreme reality of Spain. To strengthen it, elevate it, and promote its greatness is the urgent collective task of all Spaniards. The interests of individuals, groups, and classes must inexorably be subordinated to the realization of that task.

2. Spain is a unity of destiny in the universal. All conspiracy against this unity is abhorrent. All separatism is a crime we shall not pardon. The current constitution, insofar as it promotes disintegration, attacks the unity of Spain's destiny. We therefore demand its immediate repeal.

3. It is our will to maintain the empire. We affirm that Spain's historical fulfillment is the empire. We demand for Spain a preeminent place in Europe. We will tolerate neither international isolation nor foreign interference. With respect to the countries of Hispanoamerica, we seek the unification of culture, economic interests, and political power. Spain declares itself the spiritual axis of the Hispanic world as a title of preeminence in global enterprises.

4. Our armed forces—on land, sea, and air—must be as skilled and large as necessary to assure Spain at all times of complete independence and the leading place in the world it deserves. We shall give back to the forces of land, sea, and air all the public dignity they merit, and in their image we shall see to it that a military sensibility pervades all Spanish life.

5. Spain will once again seek its glory and wealth by the pathways of the

sea. Spain must aspire to be a great maritime power for reasons of security and of commerce. We demand for the fatherland a similarly dominant position for our navy and our air force.

The State, the Individual, Liberty

6. Our state will be a totalitarian one in the service of the fatherland's integrity. All Spaniards will participate in it through their membership of families, municipalities, and trade unions. No one will participate through political parties. The whole system of political parties will be abolished without fail, along with all its consequences: inorganic suffrage, representation by clashing factions, and parliaments of a notorious kind.

7. Human dignity and the integrity and liberty of man are eternal and intangible values. But the only free men are those who are part of a strong and free nation. No one will be allowed to use his liberty against the unity, strength and liberty of the fatherland. Rigorous discipline will prevent any attempt to poison or divide the Spaniards or to inspire them to act against the fatherland's destiny.

8. The national-syndicalist state will allow any private initiative that is compatible with the collective interest and will even protect and stimulate those that are beneficial.

The Economy, Labor, Class Struggle

9. In economic matters, we envision Spain as one giant syndicate of producers. We shall organize Spanish society along corporate lines, using a system of vertical unions for the various branches of production, all in the service of national economic integrity.

10. We reject the capitalist system, which ignores the people's needs, dehumanizes private property, and lumps the workers into shapeless masses prone to poverty and despair. Our spiritual and national sensibilities also lead us to reject Marxism. We shall direct the impetus of the working classes, currently led astray by Marxism, in the direction of demanding their direct participation in the great task of the national state.

11. The national-syndicalist state will not cruelly ignore economic struggles among men, nor will it remain impassive before the domination of the weaker class by the stronger. Our regime will take radical steps to make the class struggle impossible, seeing to it that all those who cooperate in production constitute an organic whole. We denounce and shall prevent at any cost abuses by private interests and anarchy in the system of labor.

12. The primary purpose of wealth, as our state will affirm, is to improve the living conditions of all the people. It is intolerable that enormous masses should live in poverty, while a few others enjoy every luxury.

13. The state will recognize private property as a legitimate means of attaining individual, family, and social ends, and it will protect it against the abuses of great financial capitalists, speculators, and lenders.

14. We defend tendencies toward the nationalization of banking and major public services, through the means of public corporations.

15. All Spaniards have the right to work. Public institutions will necessarily support those who are unwillingly unemployed. While we are moving toward the new total structure, we shall maintain and intensify all the advantages offered to workers under the current social legislation.

16. All Spaniards who are able to have the duty to work. The national-syndicalist state will not have the slightest consideration for those who fulfill no function and aspire to live like guests at the cost of others' efforts.

The Land

17. We must, at all costs, raise standards of living in the countryside, the eternal foundation of Spain. For this purpose, we are committed to carrying out economic and social reforms of agriculture without any hesitation.

18. We shall boost agricultural production (economic reform) by the following means:

Guaranteeing minimum prices for all products of the land.

Demanding that a large part of what the cities now absorb as payment for their intellectual and commercial services be returned to the countryside, to give it sufficient means.

Organizing a true national agricultural credit system, which, in lending money to the worker at low interest with the guarantee of his property and harvests, will rescue him from usury and oppression by bosses.

Disseminating the teaching of agriculture and fishing.

Ordering land usage based on its conditions and the possible placement of its products.

Orienting customs policies in the direction of protecting agriculture and herding.

Speeding up irrigation projects.

Rationalizing agricultural enterprises in order to do away with both wasteful latifundios [excessively large properties] and tiny properties that are uneconomical because of their small output.

19. We shall organize agriculture socially by the following means:

Distributing arable land once again to institute family holdings and energetically stimulate the grouping of workers into syndicates.

Rescuing the human masses from the poverty in which they live, as they wear themselves out farming unproductive lands, and transferring them to better lands.

20. We shall undertake a tireless campaign of reviving herds and replanting forests, punishing with severe measures those who obstruct these things, and also having recourse to forced temporary mobilization of all Spanish young people for this historic task of reconstruction of the national wealth.

21. The state will have the power to expropriate without compensation any land that has been acquired or developed improperly.

22. It will be a high priority of the national-syndicalist state to give villages back their communal properties.

National Education, Religion

23. It is an essential mission of the state, through rigorous educational discipline, to forge a strong and united national spirit and to implant in the souls of future generations contentment and pride in their fatherland.

All men will receive premilitary training that will prepare them for the honor of joining the national and popular armed forces of Spain.

24. Culture will be organized in such a way that no talent will go to waste for lack of economic support. All those who deserve it will have easy access even to higher education.

25. Our movement incorporates the Catholic outlook—traditionally glorious and predominant in Spain—into the task of national reconstruction. The Church and the state will harmonize their respective capacities, without [the state] allowing any interference or any kind of activity that weakens the dignity of the state or national integrity.

The National Revolution

26. The Spanish Falange of the J O N S [Juntas de Ofensiva Nacional Sindicalista, a right-wing political group that merged with José Antonio's Falange Española in 1934] wants a new order, as described in the preceding principles. To implement it, and to defeat the resistance of partisans of the prevailing order, it calls for a national revolution.

In its style, it will favor direct, ardent, and combative means. Life is a militia, and it must be lived with a spirit purified by service and sacrifice.

48. Conservatives on Women and Feminism (1932, 1933, 1935)

The years of the Second Republic saw sweeping changes in Spanish society, and those changes certainly affected the role of women. Although feminism hardly constituted a massive movement, women did acquire the right to vote, and more women also began to assert themselves in various professions and sectors of society. Spain, however, had been one of the West's more traditional societies regarding gender roles, so these changes provoked considerable opposition.

The following three texts give a sense of this opposition. The first is by Santiago Ramón y Cajal, a very distinguished and respected physician and scientist; the second piece is from a daily newspaper based in Cádiz; the last piece is by the founder of Spain's fascist party, the Falange.

SOURCES: Margarita Nelken, ed., *La mujer* (Madrid: Aguilar, 1932), 160–66, 169–70, 174–75; *Revista Portuense* (Cádiz), November 28, 1933; José Antonio Primo de Rivera, *Obras completas*, vol. 1, *Discursos fundamentales y otros discursos de propaganda* (Madrid: FET y de las JONS, 1939), 179–83. These texts also appear in Ana María Aguado et al., eds., *Textos para la historia de las mujeres en España* (Madrid: Cátedra, 1994), 408–9, 427–28, 430.

Santiago Ramón y Cajal, "Concerning Feminism" (1932)

What feminist extremists call the emancipation of women is at heart nothing but the imposition of the formidable yoke of exhausting work without the consoling compensation of love and family. . . . Feminism, or "man-ism," as poor [José] Gómez Ocaña calls it, leads to a vicious circle. The more political rights and freedom to work outside the home women are granted, the more men will distance themselves from marriage. And the fewer marriages there are, the more invasive and demanding women will become, as they are tormented by neglect, exhausting overwork, and the impossibility of satisfying their intimate and sacrosanct yearnings for motherhood legally and with dignity. And although the number of legal marriages is not yet falling, the poorly raised child and the neglected husband are foreshadowing the decline of the race rather than the elevation of its morality and its productive capacity.

If there were not intelligent and tireless old maids and unsheltered widows, I would dare to say that the woman, in demanding the man's political privileges and the exercise of all kinds of mechanical trades, is, without realizing it, demanding the right to ugliness and premature old age. . . .

I am very fearful that in the future the angel of the home will turn into a repulsive virago, and that love, the supreme joy of life, will become a heavy burden imposed by the state to produce workers and soldiers at will. . . . In this era of militant and belligerent feminism, I am amazed that women are not demanding for themselves and their children the right not only to repudiate their husband's names, but even that they use the mother's name. . . .

The tendency toward the homogenization of the sexes, noted by Azorín as a consequence of the European war [World War I], . . . will turn out . . . to be damaging to our race. It is well known that the man and the woman are not equal, but rather complementary, like the bee and the flower. And there is a great danger that working in factories or as laborers, which is fatal to women's beauty and health, will eventually produce a kind of aborted woman. . . . I consider it beyond any doubt that the physical and moral difference between the sexes, an ancient product of nature, constitutes an inestimable advantage for the prosperity of the species.

Revista Portuense, "Return to Your Home, Woman" (1933)

"Woman, go back to the home, close your door, but leave your window half-open to hear the noise of the streets and be ready to come out to defend what is dearest to you, if need be, as is happening now," said the deputy, Mr. Cortés, in a speech filled with high spirituality, given at a banquet.

Yes, return, woman, to the home, where you have a valuable mission to fulfill as a mother, as a wife, as a daughter, and set aside today's struggles, which keep you away from this placid environment where you exercise sovereignty with full rights and without the bitterness of political struggle, creating good citizens for the fatherland through the influence of your benevolent action. . . .

The typical Spanish woman was always withdrawn, modest, powerful, devoted to her house and her family, and the holder of the holy ideals that made our fatherland great. Like a holy relic, she has guarded them in her heart, and like a heroine she has known how to defend them tenaciously throughout these two years in which some have tried to take them away; [she has done so] today, with serene dignity, through the weapon of the vote.

To her traditional virtues, to her delicate sentiments, to her religiousness . . . are owed the triumph won by her exercising the right and the duty the constitution granted her, showing the whole world her readiness to wield a decisive influence on Spain's destiny.

For the woman, the best school for apprenticeship in citizenship is not in institutes, academies, or political or recreational associations, but rather in the home, where virtues of citizenship of great esteem and value are taught and learned. Cultured women, yes, but not learned, or apparently learned, with sentiments or ideas deformed by the reading of books of an annoying modernism, which engender ridiculously audacious acts of imported feminism, manly ways, and misguided and bold sentiments.

The great sense of the Spanish woman, who is worth more than all the erudition of the foreign intellectual woman, or the foreign-imitating Spanish woman, makes up for her lack of culture, in many cases, many times over . . . as we have been able to see in the recent elections. The Spanish woman is a good citizen because she is a good mother, a good wife, a good daughter, and a good sister.

Return to the home, as Mr. Cortés said, assured that when they come calling at your door because the spiritual patriotism of the Spaniards is in danger, or because the proper administration of your towns calls for your intervention, you will once again know, as you did this time, how to earn respect for your exceptional qualities as an exemplary citizen.

José Antonio Primo de Rivera, "Feminine Dignity" (1935)

Perhaps you do not know about the profound affinity that there is between women and the Falange. There is no other party with which you can be closer, precisely because in the Falange we are accustomed to using neither gallantry nor feminism.

Gallantry was nothing other than a hoax for the woman. She was bribed with a bit of flattery, to corner her in a state of deprivation of any serious consideration. She was distracted with some sweet words, she was encouraged to be stupid, to relegate her to a frivolous and decorative role. We know how important the woman's proper mission is, and we will make sure that we never treat her like a silly object of flattery.

Nor are we feminists. We do not believe that the way to respect the woman consists of taking her away from her magnificent destiny and directing her toward masculine functions. It has always saddened me to see women doing men's work, all excited and agitated by a rivalry . . . in which she has every chance of losing. True feminism should not consist of wanting women to carry out functions that are now considered higher, but rather of surrounding feminine functions with more and more human and social dignity.

But because we are neither gallants nor feminists, I believe it is undoubtedly our movement that in certain essential aspects has the best sense of the meaning of feminine existence. . . . The spiritual movements of the individual or the group always respond to one of these two modes: egoism and self-denial. Egoism seeks the direct achievement of sensual satisfaction; self-denial renounces sensual satisfaction in service of a higher order. And so, if one had to assign the sexes a primacy in relation to these two modes, it is obvious that that of egoism would correspond to the man and that of self-denial to the woman. The man—I am sorry, girls, if I am contributing with this confession to lowering the pedestal where you may have placed men—is incorrigibly self-centered; the woman, on the other hand, almost always accepts a life of submission, of service, of a self-sacrificing offering to a task.

49. *El Socialista*, On the Victory of the Popular Front (1936)

After the right's victory in the November 1933 elections, Spain's president, who had the power to invite one of the party leaders to form a government, chose not to pick José María Gil Robles, the head of the main right-wing party, CEDA, because of his refusal to swear loyalty to the Republic; in his place, Alejandro Lerroux, leader of the Radical Party, was chosen. Lerroux governed with the right's support, and his policies generally satisfied the moderate right. A reshuffling of the government in 1934, however, brought Gil Robles's CEDA into the cabinet for the first time. At that point, many workers began striking, and those strikes turned violent in Asturias in October 1934. The government sent troops, who shot many strikers and imprisoned thousands of others. Many on the left feared Spain was heading for fascism.

Amid the unrest, President Alcalá Zamora used a corruption scandal as grounds for calling new elections. The parties of the left then put aside their disputes and formed a coalition known as the Popular Front, which won a majority in the February 14, 1936 elections. (For years, communists in Europe had refused to participate in "bourgeois" governments, but on Moscow's instructions, the Communist Parties in France, Spain, and elsewhere changed course and agreed to ally with socialists and others in order to defeat fascism.) The formation of that coalition proved essential in Spain, for the vote totals in the 1936 elections did not show a massive shift of opinion toward the left; rather, it was the various left-wing parties' willingness to cooperate—and thus to make their votes translate into more seats in parliament—that allowed the left to take control of the new parliament. The victory of Spain's Popular Front, like a similar French version also elected in 1936, can now be seen as a landmark event in the left's struggle for power, but in part because the parties in the coalition had very different aims, it was not immediately clear just what the Popular Front's victory meant. Hoping to clarify, the Socialist Party newspaper offered the following comments in the aftermath of the election.

SOURCE: *El Socialista*, February 18, 1936; the text also appears in Fernando Díaz-Plaja, ed., *Historia de España en sus documentos (nueva serie): El siglo XX*, vol. 2, *Dictadura . . . República (1923–1936)* (Madrid: Instituto de Estudios Políticos, 1965), 839–40.

After the Victory. A Single Demand: The Power to Govern

Victory was obtained on Sunday, and through it the Popular Front has successfully established its claim on the government. No one and nothing can now stand in the way of the conclusive and overpowering mandate of the people. No one—and of this we are sure—will stand in the way. . . .

At this time it is necessary to show great calm. It is not a question now, as it was on April 14, [1931], of swiftly changing the names of the streets and toppling certain statues. Nor is it a matter of the victory producing only some joyous cries and noisy demonstrations. Let us avoid, first of all, letting candor produce delirium in us again. Let us also avoid allowing people who have an interest in stirring up a provocation . . . to succeed. Nothing would be more damaging to all of our purposes than to reawaken something that was dead. . . .

February 16 is not April 14. . . . In April [1931], we leapt over an enemy that was already dead. . . . February 16 is the victory over a well-prepared enemy. . . . Between the two dates there were experiences that we Republicans and socialists had to learn at the cost of many sacrifices. . . . Our victory will make our struggle easier and will give us the certainty of completing it with the absolute defeat of our enemies. And it is to this, concretely and conclusively to this, that we must dedicate all of our efforts. . . .

It is urgent that the powers of government be handed over to the Popular Front. To the whole clamor of the country, to all the anxiousness that now moves Republicans and socialists to demand that those most fundamental aspirations be fulfilled, we only wish to add one: the handing over of the powers of government. It is the Popular Front that should liberate our prisoners. As of yesterday, the jails have started to be opened, allowing our comrades to go free. The people must now ask for a single thing: the powers of the government. They belong to them. They have conquered them and no one can oppose their falling into their hands. Once the powers of the government are in their hands, they will no longer have to ask for anything.

50. Francisco Franco, Manifesto of July 18, 1936

After years of discussions among military officers outraged by the course of events in Republican Spain, a group of generals decided, following the recent murder of the leading conservative politician, José Calvo Sotelo, to mount an armed uprising against the government. The officers had no single commander yet, but one of their leaders was the young general Francisco Franco Bahamonde (1892–1975), who as head of Spain's Army of Africa was based in the Canary Islands. Franco made this speech over the radio. It is unlikely that many Spaniards actually heard it, but nevertheless, the speech illustrates the soldiers' grievances and the kind of arguments they made in defense of their actions.

SOURCE: *Historia de la Cruzada*, vol. 3, part 10 (Madrid: Ediciones Españolas, 1940), 71; the text also appears in Alfonso García-Gallo, *Manual de historia del derecho español*, vol. 2 (Madrid: A.G.E.S.A., 1967), 1231–32.

Spaniards!

To all of you who feel holy love for Spain, to all of you who in the ranks of the army and the navy have sworn to serve the fatherland, to those of you who swore to defend it from its enemies with your lives, the nation calls you to defend it.

The situation in Spain has been growing worse every day: anarchy reigns in most of the countryside and the towns; authorities named by the government preside over revolts, when they do not directly promote them. Pistols and machine guns are used to settle differences between groups of citizens, who murder each other treacherously and treasonously while the public powers do nothing to impose peace and justice.

Revolutionary strikes of all kinds paralyze the life of the nation, ruining and destroying its sources of wealth and creating a situation of hunger that will throw working men into a state of desperation.

Artistic monuments and treasures are the object of the most frenzied attacks by revolutionary hordes obeying the commands they receive from foreign directors, who count on the complicity or negligence of governors and officials.

The most serious crimes are committed in the cities and countryside while the forces of public order remain in their barracks, restrained by the desperation caused by blind obedience to governors who intend to dishonor them. The army, the navy, and other military forces are the target of the lowest and most slanderous attacks by the very ones who should safeguard their prestige.

States of emergency and alarm only serve to muzzle the people and to keep Spain from knowing what is happening outside the gates of their towns and cities, as well as to jail supposed political adversaries.

The constitution, constantly suspended and violated, has been completely eclipsed; there is neither equality before the law nor liberty, enchained by tyranny, nor fraternity, when hatred and crime have replaced mutual respect, nor unity of the fatherland, threatened by the tearing apart of the national territory . . . that the governing powers themselves are promoting, nor solidity and defense of our borders, when in the heart of Spain people listen to foreign broadcasts preaching the destruction and division of our soil.

The judiciary, whose independence the constitution guarantees, also suffers persecutions that exhaust or neutralize it, and it is the target of withering attacks on its independence.

Electoral pacts made at the cost of the integrity of the very fatherland, together with assaults on civil governments and vaults [intended] to falsify their acts, created the mask of legality that rules over us. Nothing restrains the appetite for power. . . .

In addition to the revolutionary and ignorant spirit of the masses deceived and exploited by Soviet agents, who hide the bloody reality of that regime that has sacrificed 25 million people for its existence, there is the maliciousness and negligence of authorities of all kinds, who, protected by an incompetent government, lack the authority and prestige to impose order and the rule of liberty and justice.

Can we consent to the shameful spectacle we are presenting to the world for one more day? Can we abandon Spain to the fatherland's enemies by cowardly and treasonous actions, surrendering it without a struggle and without resistance? No! The traitors may do so, but those of us who have sworn to defend it will not.

We offer you justice and equality before the law. Peace and love among the Spaniards. Liberty and fraternity free from libertinage and tyranny. Work for all. Social justice, carried out without rancor or violence, and an equitable and progressive distribution of wealth without destroying or endangering the Spanish economy.

But first, a war without quarter against the exploiters of politics, against the deceivers of the honorable worker, against the foreigners and would-be foreigners who, directly or indirectly, seek to destroy Spain.

At this moment, it is Spain as a whole that is rising up and demanding peace, fraternity, and justice; in all of the regions, the army, the navy, and the forces of public order are rushing to defend the fatherland. The energy devoted to upholding order will match the magnitude of the resistance offered to it.

Our motives do not derive from the defense of a few illegitimate interests, nor from the desire to go backward along the path of history. . . . Because the purity of our intentions prevents us from stifling those advances that represent an improvement in the political and social realm, and because the spirit of hatred and vengeance has no place in our hearts, we shall be able to salvage those legislative efforts which are compatible with the internal peace of Spain and its much-desired greatness, bringing about, for the first time in our country, the three-part order, ***Fraternity, liberty, and equality***.

Spaniards: Long live Spain!!! Long live the honorable Spanish people!!!

51. Ideological Struggles of the Left (1936, 1937)

The Spanish left in the 1930s was full of schisms and bitter factional infighting. One group was a party founded in February 1936: the Partido Obrero de Unificación Marxista (POUM), or Workers' Party of Marxist Unification, based in Barcelona. That party was made up of two splinter groups that had left Spain's Communist Party, and its status as a Marxist but anti-Stalinist party led the pro-Stalinist Spanish Communists to call its members "Trotskyists" (after Leon Trotsky, a Russian Bolshevik who had fallen out with Stalin). Ironically, when the Civil War began, Moscow and the Spanish Communists argued that because defeating the military rebels required the support of the middle classes, Spain should not launch a social revolution until the war was won. The anarchists and the POUM, however, both disagreed. In December 1936, the POUM published the following pamphlet in Barcelona.

SOURCE: Comité Ejecutivo del POUM, *Qué es y qué quiere decir el Partido Obrero de Unificación Marxista* (Barcelona: Ediciones "La Batalla," 1936), 7–9; the text also appears in Fernando Díaz-Plaja, ed., *Historia de España en sus documentos (nueva serie): El siglo XX*, vol. 3, *La guerra (1936–1939)* (Madrid: Gráficas Faro, 1963), 362–63.

The Problem of Marxist Unification

The great Revolutionary Socialist Party that the revolution needs still does not, unfortunately, exist in Spain. . . .

The Communist Party of Spain is not the Bolshevik Party of our revolution. Being subject, as an official section of the Communist International, to the fluctuations of the Soviet state's foreign policy, it finds itself obliged to act in accordance not with the revolutionary needs of the moment in our country, but rather in conformance with the convenience of Soviet diplomacy, which frequently is in open contradiction with those needs. . . .

The Workers' Party of Marxist Unification . . . believes it is not possible to bring all the Marxists together in an already existing party. The problem is not one of entry or absorption, but rather of revolutionary Marxist unification. It is a new party that needs to be formed through the fusion of the Marxist revolutionaries. . . .

The Workers' Party believes that the fundamental prerequisites for revolutionary Marxist unification to become a reality are the following:

1. The Spanish revolution is a revolution of the democratic-socialist type. The choice is: socialism or fascism. The working class will not be able to take power peacefully, but rather through . . . armed insurrection.

2. Once power has been taken, a provisional dictatorship of the proletariat should be established. The organs of power will be the Workers' Alliances.

The dictatorship of the proletariat presupposes the broadest and most complete workers' democracy. The party of the revolution cannot, must not, smother workers' democracy.

3. The necessity of the Workers' Alliance locally and nationally. The Workers' Alliance must necessarily pass through three phases: first, as the organ of the Unified Front, carrying out legal and extralegal offensive and defensive actions; second, an insurrectional organ; and third, as an organ of government.

4. Recognition of the problem of the [regional] nationalities. Spain will be structured in the form of the Iberian Union of Socialist Republics.

5. A democratic solution, in its initial phase, of the problem of the land. The land for those who work it.

6. Regarding the war, transformation of an imperialist war into a civil war. No hope should be placed in the League of Nations, which is a unified front for imperialism.

7. The Unified Party will remain outside the Second and Third Internationals—both of which are failures. . . .

8. Defense of the U.S.S.R., though not favoring its policy of pacts with the capitalist states, but rather through the international revolutionary action of the working class. The right to criticize the policy of the leaders of the U.S.S.R., which can be counterproductive for the progress of the world revolution.

9. A permanent regime of democratic centralism within the Unified Party.

The Communist newspaper *Frente Rojo* published the following article on February 6, 1937.

SOURCE: *Frente Rojo,* February 6, 1937. This text also appears in Fernando Díaz-Plaja, ed., *Historia de España en sus documentos (nueva serie): El siglo XX,* vol. 3, *La guerra (1936–1939)* (Madrid: Gráficas Faro, 1963), 370–71.

The rabble of the POUM, unmasked in all its infamy before the workers, is now reacting with all the desperation of one who is accused and discovered in the false position created by a deliberately demagogic campaign directed against the solid wall of antifascist unity, with all the perseverance and the intention that its foreign masters dictate to it.

We have therefore come forward to accuse them, demonstrating their conspiratorial plans, pointing them out as a faction organized behind our lines. It is not a matter of ideological dissension, nor even of physical repugnance toward a party of traitors, but rather something more profound and sweeping. It is a question of the distance there can be between those of us who make up the vanguard of our people's interests and the henchmen of the Gestapo. It is a question of the gang of bandits that fascism has still left among us.

Right now, in the Barcelona publication entitled *La Batalla*, they put forward inconsistent and ridiculous arguments such as the following: referring to the trial of the Trotskyists, they call it a "wicked farce," but in the article's final line it says that the ambassadors of France and the United States were present. That is to say that a trial carried out before hundreds of foreign journalists, before the diplomatic corps, with legal guarantees for the accused like those found in no other country, merits the term "farce" in the POUM's view. Naturally, their accomplices in Spain are not going to recognize the justice carried out against a band of assassins. The day when the Trotskyists are judged in Spain—for we . . . ask that a people's tribunal judge the fascist leaders of that organization—their accomplices . . . will say that the justice of our people has been a wicked farce. . . .

In this same issue of *La Batalla* . . . , it is written that they have received a multitude of protests from "comrades and sympathizers,". . . protests that they did not print . . . for lack of space. And it is clear that they are not going to print their congratulations from Franco.

Their cynicism leads them to say elsewhere . . . that "Trotsky's portrait did not appear at a meeting organized by the POUM in Barcelona." These wretches, aware of the indignation that the figure of the chief of these international gangs awakens everywhere, did not dare show his portrait even before their own affiliates. . . . Perhaps the name Trotsky, one so filled with crime, is starting to be uncomfortable for them. We do not know what new schemes they will try in order to go on serving the calculations of the fascist rearguard among us. . . .

If everyone who sabotages the government and insults its defenders must be considered a fascist, then these POUM provocateurs are fascists. And what is needed to finish off this gang of bandits is to give them their due treatment and carry out justice on them, as fitting with their condition as fascists.

52. Decree Closing Religious Institutions (1936)

The Catholic Church in Spain had an old tradition of intense political involvement, and though some Church leaders favored a policy of reconciliation with the new Republican regime, others openly declared their bitter hatred for the Republic from its very outset. At the same time, anticlerical feeling ran high on the left, and the 1931 constitution had established the separation of church and state and authorized measures such as a ban on members of religious orders teaching in Spain. Among the legislation passed in the wake of the new constitution's adoption was the Law of Religious Confessions and Congregations (passed by parliament in May 1933, signed into law on June 2, 1933), which called for the closing of religious secondary schools by October of that year and religious primary schools by 1934.

When the Civil War began in July 1936, this political conflict turned violent, as anarchists and others began shooting thousands of priests and sacking monasteries and convents, while priests and others within the Church either took up arms for the military rebels or urged their followers to do so. In the eyes of the Republic's leaders, then, the members of the Church were part of a "fifth column" aiding the rebellion against Spain's legally elected government. In August, the Republican government issued the following decree.

SOURCE: *Gaceta de Madrid*, August 13, 1936

Decreed in Madrid, August 11, 1936
[President] Manuel Azaña
Minister of Justice, Manuel Blasco Garzón:

By article 23 of the Law of Religious Confessions and Congregations, it has been prohibited for the orders and congregations of said character to exercise any kind of political activity, sanctioning the infraction of said precept, when the activity referred to constitutes a danger for the security of the state, with the preventative closing of the establishments of the religious society to which it may be imputed and, in its case, with the dissolution of the institution. And having observed that some religious associations have cooperated more or less directly in the insurrectional movement declared on July 18, application is made of that which is ordered in article 23 of the law of June 2, 1933.

Based on this, in accordance with the Council of Ministers and on the proposal of the Ministry of Justice, the following is decreed:

Article 1. All establishments of the religious orders and congregations existing in Spain, which in any way may have intervened in the present insurrectional movement, participating in it directly or indirectly, favoring it or helping it, or favoring or helping the rebels or subversives in any way, are closed as a preventative measure.

Article 2. It will be understood that the orders and congregations to which the previous article refers have participated in the insurrectional movement whenever any of their members have committed any of the following acts:

First. Joining the seditious movement by participating in the combatant groups, in the army staff, teams, or organizations of provision or oversight, political or military committees, services of liaison or espionage, or carrying out any kind of task or job, even as a subordinate, under the orders of the rebels or subversives.

Second. Favoring the subversive movement through the provision to the rebels of any quantity [of money], whether in metal or currency, or the cession or delivery, even temporary, of their movable or unmovable property, including the mere momentary use for lodging, installations, or services of any other kind.

Third. Having joined the insurrectional movement in any way, even without active participation in it; having made vows or said prayers for the triumph of the rebellion, or propagated or promoted its objectives in any way or spread false rumors.

Fourth. Having or possessing arms of any kind without proper directives or authorization.

Fifth. Having opened fire on or committed hostilities against the forces loyal to the legitimate government from the buildings occupied by the religious orders and congregations.

Sixth. Having committed any other act that, although not included in the previous cases, can be considered as direct or indirect participation or as indirect or direct assistance to the seditious movement.

Article 3. For the execution of what is ordered in this decree a commission will be formed by three judicial functionaries, with one presiding. . . .

Article 4. The Cortes will be informed of the measures adopted by the Council of Ministers, so that it may decide on the definitive closing of the establishments or the dissolution of the institutions implicated in the subversive movement.

In the case of the dissolution of any religious order or congregation, its property will be nationalized.

53. Germany and the Spanish Civil War (1936–1937)

When the Civil War began in July 1936, Hitler had been in power in Germany for over three years. The ideological affinities between the Nazis and Franco's Nationalists (sometimes referred to in German documents as "White Spain," as opposed to "Red Spain") were clear at once, but the German government, like Mussolini's Fascist government in Italy, was reluctant to risk recognizing Franco's side as the true government of Spain until it was confident it would win the war. It granted that recognition on November 18, 1936.

Throughout the war, Hitler often sought to assist Franco without attracting international attention, and indeed the German government was not alone in seeking involvement. France's Popular Front government, under the Socialist Leon Blum, had begun to offer the Republicans assistance, but Blum, concerned primarily about threats to French security from a militarily resurgent Germany, did not wish to anger its British ally, and when London made clear its opposition to helping the Spanish Republicans, France's government reversed its course. At that point, the French pushed for the creation of an international "nonintervention" agreement, which the Germans and Italians (among others) were willing to sign, but which they soon violated. Attempts to enforce the nonintervention pact soon turned out to be ineffective, but Hitler remained at least somewhat concerned with preserving the image of his country's adherence to the pact. The diplomatic correspondence presented here shows German officials' concerns for their own interests as well as assessments of the situation inside and outside Spain.

SOURCE: *Documents on German Foreign Policy, 1918–1945*, ser. D, vol. 3 (Washington, D.C.: U.S. Government Printing Office, 1950), 103–4, 137–39, 206–7, 256–57, 277–79, 392–94.

The Acting State Secretary to the [German] Legation in Portugal, Berlin, October 3, 1936

General Franco has sent the following telegram to the Führer and chancellor:

"Upon assuming the leadership of the Spanish state and the office of Generalissimo of the Nationalist troops, I have the honor to convey my warmest wishes to Your Excellency as chief of the great German nation for the well-being of Your Excellency and the prosperity of the noble nation with which we are united by so many bonds of sincere friendship and deep gratitude."

Please dispatch Du Moulin to Franco with instructions to express to him orally the thanks of the Führer and of the German nation for his friendly wishes; the Führer's most sincere congratulations on his assumption of power and designation as Generalissimo and his best wishes for the further success of the work of liberation undertaken by Franco; and admiration for the heroic conduct of the Spanish army and of the Spanish population loyal to Franco. In carrying out this commission please explain that the Führer refrained from giving a telegraphic or written reply to the telegram because the world might have considered this to mean recognition of the Nationalist government, but that recognition at the present moment would compromise our work in Spain and therefore serve neither Franco nor Germany's interest.

For your confidential information only: we have asked Rome to proceed in like manner and do not intend to accord de facto recognition until the Nationalist troops have taken Madrid.

The [German] Minister in Portugal to the [German] Foreign Ministry, October 8, 1936

Du Moulin has returned from Salamanca, Franco's new headquarters. He carried out the instructions.

General Franco expressed his heartfelt thanks for the Führer's gesture and complete admiration for him and the new Germany. He expressed the hope soon to be able to hoist his banner beside the banner of civilization that the Führer had raised. He asked that his thanks be conveyed for the valuable moral and material help thus far given. . . .

The [German] Embassy in Spain (at Seville) to the [German] Foreign Ministry, Seville, November 24, 1936

Reception of the [German] Embassy by officials and population was decidedly friendly and cordial, from the point of disembarkation, Sanlúcar, to Seville. . . . Yesterday evening a great demonstration of friendship was held by the population in the square before the city hall, which was festively illuminated, and a banquet followed.

First impressions of the situation in White Spain:

1. [General] Queipo de Llano, who took Seville for the military in July with 150 men, is apparently a determined, energetic personality with political ability. He is very popular with the people, whom he knows how to captivate in a daily radio address. He has a remarkable understanding of propaganda.

2. The external aspect of city, country, and population is very different from that of Red Spain; this has both its positive and its negative sides.

(a) On the positive side: Social order, discipline, security, and tradition are maintained. Military and civil authorities function unimpeded by the interference of the irresponsible forces which have local power everywhere in Red Spain. The country gives the impression of peace and complete tranquility.

(b) On the negative side: The importance and gravity of the war has thus far obviously not been recognized and experienced by the masses and by the majority of the ruling class. Opinion is optimistic and frivolous. Willingness to serve, accordingly, is entirely inadequate and falls far below that on the Red side, where mobilization of the people for war has progressed much further. Whereas the Red government weeks ago decreed militarization of the male population between twenty and forty-five years of age, no similar measures were taken here; they are already being studied. Accordingly, the number of fighters at the front is completely insufficient. . . .

3. While with the Reds divergent political groups have come to terms, here sharp differences have arisen between the Fascist Falange and the monarchist-clerical Requetés [Carlist militias]. Revolutionary tendencies in the working population are suppressed by energetic measures, to be sure, but are not eliminated. There is also rivalry among the leading generals. Whereas the Reds have an extensive Communist social and economic program, there is no corresponding program here for the solution of social questions, which are at the root of the Civil War. The same is true with respect to propagandizing and mobilizing large strata of the population, which is being done effectively on the Red side under Russian leadership, but here only in a very rudimentary way, with really wretched press conditions.

4. The military situation is not very satisfactory. Operations have been conducted to date principally with shock troops of Moroccans and Foreign Legionnaires. These are in danger of wearing themselves out before Madrid even if they succeed in capturing the capital. The difficulty of taking Madrid is obviously underestimated. The Red government's announcement that Madrid would fall into White hands only as a field of ruin and carnage threatens to become a reality. On other fronts there is only weak protection for the troops, so that a surprise attack by the Reds at another point would necessarily lead to a dangerous situation.

5. The principal goal of our endeavors here should therefore be to see to it that mobilization and employment of the population are expedited. This is of primary importance because the necessity of crushing Bolshevism here, come what may, would force us to make up the deficit with German blood, if not enough Spaniards were employed.

6. Even in leading government circles the opinion is already fairly prevalent that the war is not being fought in the interest of Spain but is a

showdown between Fascism and Bolshevism on Spanish soil. This is a rather dangerous obstacle in the way of continued German-Spanish collaboration.

7. The economic problems seem no less difficult than the political and military ones. It is urgently necessary to study the question of how our deliveries are to be paid for and how our economic interests will be safeguarded and indemnification made after the war is over. The war will result in serious financial and economic exhaustion of the countries [*sic*] and in widespread destruction. The export possibilities, especially for the raw materials in which we are principally interested, are relatively small, considering the volume of our deliveries, which will greatly increase in the course of a probably long war . . . and can probably be increased only by investing considerable capital. The danger that countries strong in capital will get ahead of us by granting credits after the war should not be lightly dismissed. . . .

The [German] Chargé d'Affaires in Spain to the Foreign Ministry, Salamanca, January 7, 1937

Since I reported orally in Berlin on December 17, 1936, the military situation has improved. . . . General Queipo de Llano, the commander of the southern army . . . told me that there are rather large stores of olive oil in the captured territory. On the assumption that this information is correct I have taken steps to obtain these stores of olive oil for us.

A further improvement in the military situation may be seen in the arrival of considerable Italian reinforcements. When I was in Seville five days ago, 4,000 Black Shirts had already arrived. . . .

The arrival of the first German instructors, who immediately started their work of training the Falange units, likewise resulted in improving morale. Since we have anticipated the Italians in the field, and Spain's future depends on the ideas held by the Falangists, I consider that cooperation with the Falangists holds certain possibilities for the future.

Altogether approximately fifty German instructors can be expected to arrive in the course of the next six weeks, most of whom were active in Spain until a few months ago as merchants, etc., and who will now have the opportunity of reestablishing themselves here in their former occupations as soon as the situation permits. . . .

The gratitude and joy over German aid is currently finding expression in a variety of ways. Streets are named "Alemania" [the Spanish word for Germany]; German flags can frequently be seen together with those of Italy and Portugal; I am receiving letters of thanks with hundreds of signatures from entire towns and villages. When I am asked by a military governor or commander to inspect a troop detachment or a Falangist unit . . . I am usually greeted with cries of "Viva Alemania" and "Viva el Führer."

Protocol, Salamanca, March 20, 1937
TOP SECRET

The German government and the Spanish Nationalist government, convinced that the progressive development of the friendly relations existing between them serves the welfare of the German and Spanish peoples and will be an important factor for the maintenance of European peace, which is close to both their hearts, are agreed in their desire to lay down even now the guiding principles for their future relations, and for this purpose have come to an understanding on the following points:

1. Both governments will constantly consult with one another on the measures necessary to defend their countries against the threatening dangers of Communism.

2. Both governments will constantly maintain contact with one another in order to inform each other concerning questions of international policy which affect their joint interests.

3. Neither of the two governments will participate in treaties or other agreements with third powers which are aimed either directly or indirectly against the other country.

4. In case one of the two countries should be attacked by a third power, the government of the other country will avoid everything that might serve to the advantage of the attacker or the disadvantage of the attacked.

5. Both governments are agreed in their desire to intensify the economic relations between their countries as much as possible. . . .

6. Both governments will treat this protocol, which becomes effective at once, as secret until further notice. . . .

The Ambassador in Spain to the Foreign Ministry, Salamanca, May 1, 1937

The last few days have led to a temporary, severe tension in the internal situation. . . . The chief of state [Franco] had [Falangist leader Manuel] Hedilla and twenty other leading Falangists arrested. . . .

I again urgently advised the chief of state to calm the excited feelings in certain parts of the Falange by hastening the announcement of certain social measures. . . . I gave him a number of written or printed documents, among others a Spanish translation of our "Law Regulating National Labor," and informed him that we could also put at his disposal this or that specialist for social legislation, etc. if he liked. . . . With a reference to the inadequate propaganda in White Spain, I also recommended to Franco that he not only announce his social decrees in the *Official Gazette* and just once in the press, but make them generally known and therefore more effective through repetition over the radio and in newspaper articles. . . .

In the present situation, . . . [Franco's government needs] the immediate announcement and execution of social reforms which would bring relief to the very poorest of the population and bring the Falangists the certainty that their party program will be executed.

Franco has assured me again and again that he intends to do this. But as questions of social legislation are somewhat out of his personal province, and as he has hitherto had no suitable advisers around him in this field and is, in addition, fully occupied with the military command and with foreign policy and economic questions, the social measures are getting started only very gradually. The best thing Franco could do would be to put into immediate effect some of the proposals for reform which have already been prepared by the Falange, partly with German collaboration. . . .

There is no doubt that [after] a war won because of our intervention a Spain socially ordered and economically reconstructed with our help will in the future be not only a very important source of raw materials for us, but also a faithful friend for a long time to come. . . .

The Ambassador in Great Britain to the Führer and Chancellor, London, July 4, 1937

No serious complications for the general European situation are to be expected from the present tension in nonintervention policy. England desires peace, as does France also; in spite of the sharp line followed at present, neither of them will push things to the limit. We can continue to count on this as an absolutely certain factor and can make our future decisions without being influenced or disturbed. . . .

If it is to be considered at all in Berlin that the ending of nonintervention would be favorable to Franco, we would operate in such a way that the responsibility for the failure will be attributed as far as possible to England and France as a result of the rejection of our plan. . . .

Since the ending of nonintervention would, however, make possible the influx of volunteers, especially from France, Russia, etc. . . . and as a result would also necessitate starting a new influx of volunteers from Italy, Germany, etc., the intensity of the Spanish war would probably increase considerably—a condition which in the long run would involve the possibility of complications of greater magnitude.

Therefore it appears from here that for the time being it is in our interest to work toward maintaining the principle of nonintervention and finding a compromise acceptable to us.

54. British Parliamentary Debates on Spain (1937)

Many of those who viewed Spain's Civil War as a conflict between fascism and democracy expected that Britain, France, and the United States would support the Republican side, which was Spain's legally elected government. At first, the French government, itself based on a Popular Front, sent supplies to the Republicans. But France was also deeply concerned about the rise of German power, so it sought to coordinate its policies with its ally, Britain.

In Britain, opinions were sharply divided over the Spanish conflict. The Labour Party sided with the Republicans, but the Conservatives, under Prime Minister Neville Chamberlain, were currently in power. The Conservatives, some of whose supporters had investments in Spain and were concerned about expropriation by a leftist government, generally favored Franco's side. Moreover, Britain, which hoped to avoid any future wars after the disaster of World War I, feared antagonizing Hitler, who was in the midst of a massive military buildup. Britain thus declined to assist either side, giving its support to the Non-Intervention Committee formed in September 1936 and continuing to support nonintervention even in the face of extensive evidence of cheating. In these excerpts from a debate in Britain's House of Commons on June 25, 1937, Prime Minister Chamberlain explains the government's view, while Clement Attlee presents Labour's view.

SOURCE: United Kingdom, *Parliamentary Debates*, Commons, 5th ser., vol. 325 (1937), cols. 1545–56, 1574–77, 1589–1600.

THE PRIME MINISTER (Mr. Chamberlain): I rise . . . to say a few words about one aspect of foreign policy, and it is one which at present is uppermost in all minds in Europe, the situation arising out of the civil war in Spain. . . . There is a tendency, amid the strong feelings that are aroused in this connection, to forget what it is that the government really are aiming at.

In this Spanish situation there is one peculiar feature which gives it a specially dangerous aspect. That is that to many people looking on from outside, it presents itself as a struggle between two rival systems each of which commands an enthusiastic, even a passionate, body of support among its adherents in their respective countries, with the result that supporters of these two rival systems cannot help regarding the issue of the struggle in Spain as a defeat or a victory . . . for the side to which they are attached. I am not expressing an opinion as to whether that view of the struggle is correct or not, but I say that the fact that it is held constitutes a perpetual danger to the peace of Europe because, if some country or government representing one of these two ideas attempts to intervene beyond a certain point, then some other country taking the opposite view may find it difficult, if not impossible, to refrain from joining in, and a conflict may be started of which no man can see the end.

In these circumstances, the policy of His Majesty's government has been consistently directed to one end, and one end only, namely, to maintain the peace of Europe by confining the war to Spain. It is for that purpose that, in conjunction with France, we have worked to set up and . . . to maintain the Non-Intervention Agreement. No body could have had a harder task than the committee, and we in this country have suffered the usual fate of those who have tried to be impartial. We have been deliberately accused by both sides of partiality towards the other. But although we have had to express as a government our dissatisfaction with the failure of the scheme of non-intervention, we maintain, though it is true that intervention . . . is going on in spite of the Non-Intervention Agreement, that it is also true that up to the present we have succeeded in achieving the object which has been at the back of our policy the whole time. We shall continue to pursue that object and that policy as long as we feel that there is a reasonable hope of avoiding a spread of the conflict. . . .

The situation is serious, but it is not hopeless, and, in particular, although it may be true that various countries or various governments desire to see one side or the other side successful, there is not a country or a government that wants to see a European war. Since that is so, let us try to keep cool heads and neither say nor do anything to precipitate a disaster which everybody really wishes to avoid. I think we are bound to recognise that as long as this civil war is going on in Spain—

MR. GALLACHER: Invasion.

THE PRIME MINISTER: Incidents are bound to occur which involve foreign powers. The very duties which foreign powers have imposed upon themselves in trying to stop the importation of weapons and ammunition into Spain—(An Hon. Member: "What foreign Powers?")—means that there must be an interference with the course of hostilities. Each side is being deprived of supplies of material of which it feels itself in urgent need.

MR. S. O. DAVIES: Rubbish, absolute rubbish.

THE CHAIRMAN: Order. . . .

THE PRIME MINISTER: . . . I was trying to put the case to the committee that the very fact that we are trying to maintain a policy of non-intervention, which is exercised through a patrol by ships belonging to various powers stopping ships taking arms and ammunition into Spain, involves an interference with the hostilities and, therefore, is bound to create strong feelings of resentment among those in Spain who feel that they are thus being handicapped. That leads to accusations of want of impartiality and counter-accusations, and then to such deplorable incidents as the bombing of the "Deutschland" and destruction by bombing—(An Hon. Member: "And the bombing of Almeria.")—And the bombing of Almeria. Once this chain begins it goes on, first on one side and then on the other. . . .

In my view, the best thing we can do now is to turn our minds back again to the two practical steps which have to be taken, the first one being to fill the gap in the patrol which has now been left open and the other to re-start our endeavours to obtain the withdrawal of foreign volunteers in Spain.

That is all I have to say at present, and I want to conclude with a very earnest appeal to those who hold responsible positions both in this country and abroad—to weigh their words very carefully before they utter them on this matter, bearing in mind the consequences that might flow from some rash or thoughtless phrase. I have read that in the high mountains there are sometimes conditions to be found when an incautious move or even a sudden loud exclamation may start an avalanche. That is just the condition in which we are finding ourselves to-day. I believe, although the snow may be perilously poised it has not yet begun to move, and if we can all exercise caution, patience, and self-restraint we may yet be able to save the peace of Europe.

MR. ATTLEE: I agree with the prime minister that the condition of the world is serious, and that everyone who speaks on these subjects must speak with a full sense of responsibility; but that does not mean, in my view, that there should be a lack of plain speaking, but that we ought to see the facts as they really are. I must say that I was profoundly disappointed with the speech of the prime minister, because it seemed to me that he had misconceived the whole issue that lies before us. He suggested that there was being fought in Spain, in the opinion of some people, a struggle between two sides, two rival systems. I do not think that is the issue that is facing us to-day. The world to-day is faced with a contest between two sides, and those two sides are whether the rule of law in international affairs shall prevail, or the rule of lawless force. That is the issue that faces us, and we must look at this Spanish struggle in its true perspective.

This Spanish struggle is not as isolated as one might expect. This

Spanish struggle is the result of the steady decadence of the situation in the world for the last five or six years. It is merely one step in the continual disregard of the rule of law and increasing aggression all over the world by those who claim to be bound by no rules except that which they conceive to be the interests of their own particular state. That is the thing that has destroyed trust between nations, and has rendered treaties and instruments of agreement of little value, and has brought us all face to face with this position: How is this continual decadence of the situation to be brought to an end? That is the point on which I want to challenge the government, because I have not got from the prime minister any suggestion of any action that will really deal with the position. Let me remind the House of what the situation is. I suggest that we have reached a stage in the tragedy of the massacre of the people of Spain by foreign soldiers, foreign sailors, foreign airmen, equipped with all the most frightful of modern weapons, and we have reached also a stage in a farce—the farce of non-intervention.

What was the case for non-intervention? Non-intervention did not rest on any question of right, justice or international law. The Spanish government had the right of a government to seek arms where it could. The Spanish government, like any government, had the right to resist rebellion. The Non-Intervention Agreement rested solely on the basis of expediency, which could be justified only by success. Let me remind the prime minister what were the reasons for the adoption of that Non-Intervention Agreement. The first was that there was great danger that this local struggle might spread into a world struggle, and it was also a great danger that it should be prolonged. The prime minister has quite forgotten to-day that non-intervention was not only to try to put a cordon round this struggle, but that it should end soon, because the outstanding danger in the situation was that there might be incidents, and the longer it continued the more likely would be the incidents.

We accepted at the time with great reluctance this Non-Intervention Agreement only providing that the participants in it were honestly determined to make it work, and that the scales were held evenly. I say that it has not been honestly worked, that the scales have not been held evenly and that it has not been a success. At every stage whenever restrictions have been put on they have always been put on first on the Spanish government, and later on the rebels. Our government have been extremely chary of admitting the facts of the situation. All the way through we have had constant denial of the sending of arms, the sending of munitions, and the sending of men to Spain, and always a little later these facts were established. Overwhelming proof has been shown of the armed and active intervention of foreign powers in Spain, and it is not the least good to suggest that non-intervention has been successful. It is really ridiculous to suggest that this intervention has not been done through the active will of foreign governments. . . .

What we have had all through is really no genuine attempt to carry out the agreement. The boastings and congratulations in foreign countries really condemn those governments out of their own mouth that they have not attempted to work the Non-Intervention Agreement. . . .

What, I think, is abundantly clear is that non-intervention has not removed international tension, has not, as a matter of fact, done anything effective to shorten the contest. The contest has been dragging on now month after month, and, so far from non-intervention having stopped the engagement of other states in this struggle, intervention has gone on and on. The government say that they have been impartial, that they are attacked from either side. I think that all through they have shown decided partiality. I think that they have entirely failed to hold the scales evenly, or to see that the scales are held evenly. We have never demanded that the government should intervene on its own in Spain. What we have demanded is that they should honestly carry out what they have undertaken. Take the question of Bilbao. [The Nationalists besieged and took the Basque town of Bilbao in 1937, with extensive assistance from the Italians and Germans.] Bilbao fell owing to three things—foreign artillery, foreign aircraft, and the blockade. And that blockade was not a blockade by the fleet of General Franco. He could not effect a blockade. It was a blockade by the action of the British government. . . .

I say that we were accessories after the fact to the fall of Bilbao, and the government must take a heavy responsibility. . . . But far more than that, throughout the whole of this contest the government has never taken up a strong line and a clear line. We on this side of the House have made our position perfectly clear. We accepted non-intervention only with the greatest reluctance. We said that it could not be justified except by success. We say that it has failed to prevent incidents and has failed to restore the international situation. Therefore, we demand that it should be ended. . . .

We claim that it is perfectly useless to shut our eyes to the fact that there is deliberate intervention in Spain. There is no need to produce evidence; you have the confession of the governments concerned. Their whole action shows that they are actively supporting intervention in Spain, and we say that the League [of Nations] must act under the Covenant [the League's charter] and take up its responsibilities. We say that the government of Spain should be allowed to take its armaments wherever it may.

55. Spanish Bishops, On the War in Spain (1937)

That the Catholic Church detested the Republic had always been well known, so when the Civil War began there was no doubt which side the Church favored. Yet given the savage violence of the war—as well as fears about the fate of priests and other Catholics in the Republican zone—there was reason to wonder what official position the Church would take. This statement by the country's bishops, issued on July 1, 1937, clarified that point.

SOURCE: *Carta colectiva de los obispos españoles a los de todo el mundo con motivo de la guerra en España* (Pamplona: Gráficas Bescansa, 1937). This text appears in the Blodgett Collection at Harvard University, and in Jesús Iribarren, ed., *Documentos colectivos del episcopado español, 1870–1974* (Madrid: Biblioteca de Autores Cristianos, 1974), 219–42.

Our country is suffering a profound disturbance; it is not only an extremely cruel civil war that fills us with tribulation, but also a tremendous commotion that shakes the very connections of our society and has even endangered our existence as a nation. . . . It is a fact, proved by extensive documentation, that the thinking of a large part of foreign opinion is out of touch with the reality of events in our country. . . . Since God has willed that it should be our country that will serve as a place for testing the ideas and processes that aspire to conquer the world, we want the damage to be reduced to our country alone, saving the rest of the nations from ruin. . . .

The war in Spain is the product of the conflict between irreconcilable ideologies; in its very origins one finds very grave questions of a moral and legal, of a religious and historical order. . . .

When the war broke out, we lamented that painful fact more than anyone, because it is always an extremely serious evil . . . and because our mission is one of reconciliation and peace. . . . The Church did not want and did not seek this war, and we do not consider it necessary to justify it against the charges of belligerence that foreign periodicals have leveled at the Church in Spain. It is true that thousands of her children, obeying the dictates of conscience and patriotism, and on their own personal responsibility, rose up in arms to save the principles of Christian religion and justice that have for centuries informed the life of the nation; but whoever accuses it of having provoked this war or of having conspired to start it, or even of not having done everything in its power to avoid it, ignores or falsifies reality. . . . The Church has been the principal victim of the fury of one of the contending parties, and it has not ceased to work with its prayers, its exhortations, and its influence to lessen the damage and shorten the ordeal. . . .

The Five Years That Preceded the War

Setting aside minor causes, it was the legislators of 1931, and the executive power of the state . . . that suddenly twisted the path of our history in a direction contrary to nature and the demands of the national spirit, and especially contrary to the prevailing religious sentiment in the country. The constitution, along with the laws that developed its spirit, was a violent and relentless attack on the national conscience. Having done away with the rights of God and harassed the Church, our society was weakened, in the legal order, in the area that primarily sustains social life, namely, religion. The Spanish people, for the most part, kept alive the faith of their elders, suffered patiently repeated attacks on their conscience by wicked laws. . . .

The burning of churches in Madrid and the provinces in May 1931, the disturbances of October 1934, especially in Catalonia and Asturias, where anarchy reigned for two weeks, the turbulent period from February to July 1936, during which 411 churches were destroyed or profaned and roughly three thousand serious attacks of a political or social character were committed, all foreshadowed the total collapse of public authority, which was frequently seen to succumb to the force of hidden powers that controlled it.

Our political regime of democratic liberty came unhinged through the arbitrariness of state authority and through the action of a government that violated the popular will, forming a political machine struggling against the majority of the nation, proved by the fact that, in the last parliamentary elections in February 1936, the right-wing parties had more than a half million votes more than the left-wing parties, but obtained 119 deputies fewer than the Popular Front because of the arbitrary rejection of the returns from entire provinces, destroying in this way the parliament's legitimacy.

And as our nation began to disintegrate through the loosening of social bonds, and our economy began to be bled white, and the rhythm of labor was stupidly altered, and the force of the institutions of social defense were maliciously weakened, another powerful country, Russia, working hand in hand with communists here, prepared the popular spirit for the impending outbreak of revolution, using the theater and the cinema, with rites and customs that were foreign to Spain. On February 27, 1936, based on the triumph of the Popular Front, the Russian Comintern decreed the Spanish Revolution and financed it with exorbitant sums. . . .

It is a documented fact that in the detailed plan of Marxist revolution, which would have broken out throughout the country if the civil-military movement had not blocked it in many areas, the extermination of the

Catholic clergy and of designated right-wing politicians, as well as the sovietization of industry and the implantation of communism, were ordered. . . .

It is a basic affirmation of this document that a five-year period of continual clashes with the Spanish subjects in the religious and social order placed the very existence of the public good in very grave danger and produced enormous tension in the spirit of the Spanish people; that it was in the national consciousness that, with all legal means exhausted, there was no other way than that of force to maintain order and peace; that powers outside legitimate authority decided to subvert the constituted order and implant communism through violence; and, finally, that through the fateful logic of events Spain no longer had any alternative but this: either to succumb to the final assault of destructive communism, already planned and decreed (as has already happened in the regions where the national movement did not triumph), or to attempt, in a titanic effort of resistance, to free itself from the terrible enemy and save the basic principles of its social life and its national character.

The Military Uprising and the Communist Revolution

Note first that the military uprising did not occur . . . without the help of the healthy part of the people, which joined en masse a movement that must be called civil-military; and second that this movement and the communist revolution cannot be viewed separately. . . . Going together from the very outset of the conflict, they mark the profound division of the two Spains that are fighting in the battlefields. . . .

Judging the excesses of the Spanish communist revolution as a whole, we affirm that in the history of Western peoples there has never been a phenomenon like this . . . of attacks on the fundamental rights of God, society, and human beings. . . . The anarchist revolution has been "exceptional in history." Let us add that the slaughter was "premeditated." Just before the revolt, seventy-nine professional agitators had arrived from Russia. The National Commission of Marxist Unification at the same time ordered the creation of revolutionary militias in all areas. The destruction of the churches, or at least of their possessions, was systematically planned. . . . A "black list" had been formed for the elimination of notable persons considered enemies of the revolution. . . .

The revolution was extremely cruel. The forms of assassination showed characteristics of horrendous barbarity. Barbarous in their number, for example: the number of those murdered has been calculated as more than 300,000, killed only for their political and especially their religious ideas; in Madrid, more than 22,000 were murdered in the first three months. There is scarcely a village where the most notable rightists were not killed. Barbarous also in their lack of form: without accusations, without proof, usually without any trial. . . . Many have had their limbs amputated or horribly mutilated before being killed; they have had their eyes gouged out, their tongues cut off, their throats slit, been burned or buried alive, killed by hatchet blows. Maximum cruelty has been carried out against the ministers of God. Out of respect and mercy we will not be more specific. . . .

The revolution was barbarous, in destroying works of centuries' worth of civilization. It destroyed thousands of works of art, many of them universally famous. It sacked or burned archives, making historical research impossible. . . . Hundreds of paintings have been slashed, sculptures mutilated, architectural marvels destroyed forever. . . . The famous collections of art in the cathedral at Toledo, in the palace at Liria, in the Prado Museum have been stupidly damaged. Numerous libraries have disappeared. No war, no barbarian invasion, no social disruption in any century has caused ruins like this one in Spain. . . .

The revolution was essentially anti-Spanish. The destructive work was carried out to cries of "Long live Russia!" under the shadow of the international communist flag. Sayings painted on walls, defenses of foreign personages, military commands in the hands of Russian leaders, the despoiling of the nation in favor of foreigners, the international communist anthem, are more than enough proof of the hatred for the national spirit and a sense of the fatherland.

But above all the revolution was anti-Christian. We do not believe that in the history of Christianity a similar explosion has ever occurred in such a short period, affecting all forms of thought, will, and passion, of hatred against Jesus Christ and His holy religion. . . .

The National Movement: Its Characteristics

Let us now give a sketch of the character of the movement known as "national." We believe this term is just. First, in its spirit. Because the immense majority of the Spanish nation was detached from a state that could not represent its profound needs and aspirations; and the movement was greeted with hope by all the nation. . . . It is also national in its objectives. . . . We express a reality and a general yearning of the Spanish citizens. . . .

We have seen an outburst of real charity that has had its fullest expression in the blood of thousands of Spaniards who have cried out, "Long live Spain!" and "Long live Christ the King!" . . .

The movement has guaranteed order in the territory it controls. We contrast the situation in the regions where the national movement has prevailed with those still dominated by the communists. . . . Without priests, without churches, without religion, without justice, without authority, they are prisoners of a terrible anarchy, of hunger, of misery. On the other hand, because of the effort and the terrible pain of war, the other regions live in tranquility of internal order, under the tutelage of a true authority, which is the basis of justice, peace, and progress. . . .

Responses to a Few Points

It is said that this war is a class war and that the Church has placed itself on the side of the rich. Those who know its causes and its nature know this is not true. Even though the Church acknowledges some carelessness in the fulfillment of its duties of justice and charity, which it has been the first to urge, the working classes were already greatly protected by laws, and the nation had already entered on the path of a better distribution of wealth. . . . Nor can we forget our advanced social legislation and our prosperous institutions of public and private assistance of Spanish and Christian origins. The people were fooled by unrealistic promises, incompatible not only with the country's economic life, but also with any kind of organized economy. . . .

Crimes similar to those committed by the Popular Front have been attributed to the leaders of the national movement. . . . Every war has its excesses, and the national movement has undoubtedly had its share as well. Nobody defends themselves with total serenity against the insane attacks of a heartless enemy. Condemning in the name of justice and Christian charity all excesses that may have been committed, by mistake or by low-level personnel, and which the foreign press has methodically exaggerated, we declare that the judgments we are refuting do not correspond to the truth, and we affirm that there is an enormous distance between the principles and practice of justice on the two sides.

56. George Orwell, *Homage to Catalonia* (1938)

Many people around the world viewed the Spanish Civil War as the beginning of an armed showdown between fascism and either democracy or communism (or both). As a result, thousands came to Spain to fight, with most of the volunteers fighting on the Republican side. Among the most famous of the volunteers was the British writer George Orwell, who went to Spain in 1936 to write about the war.

Soon after his arrival in Barcelona, Orwell decided to join a military unit affiliated with the Partido Obrero de Unificación Marxista (POUM), or Workers' Party of Marxist Unification. Despite that choice, Orwell initially sympathized more with the Communist Party's view that military victory should take precedence over launching a social revolution (which might alienate middle-class Republicans and thus harm the war effort), but in time he grew disillusioned with the Communists and moved closer to the POUM's outlook. Orwell was wounded in the war, and while he was recovering in Barcelona a purge of POUM members and sympathizers forced him to flee to France. He later described his experiences in *Homage to Catalonia*, first published in 1938.

SOURCE: George Orwell, *Homage to Catalonia* (New York: Harcourt Brace Jovanovich, 1952), 4–9, 27–28. Excerpts from *Homage to Catalonia* by George Orwell,

This was in late December 1936, less than seven months ago as I write, and yet it is a period that has already receded into enormous distance. . . . I had come to Spain with some notion of writing newspaper articles, but I had joined the militia almost immediately, because at the time and in that atmosphere it seemed the only conceivable thing to do. The Anarchists were still in virtual control of Catalonia and the revolution was still in full swing. To anyone who had been there since the beginning it probably seemed even in December or January that the revolutionary period was ending; but when one came straight from England the aspect of Barcelona was something startling and overwhelming. It was the first time that I had ever been in a town where the working class was in the saddle. Practically every building of any size had been seized by the workers and was draped with red flags or with the red and black flag of the Anarchists; every wall was scrawled with the hammer and sickle and with the initials of the revolutionary parties; almost every church had been gutted and its images burnt. Churches here and there were being systematically demolished by gangs of workmen. Every shop and café had an inscription saying that it had been collectivized; even the bootblacks had been collectivized and their boxes painted red and black. Waiters and shop-walkers looked you in the face and treated you as an equal. Servile and even ceremonial forms of speech had temporarily disappeared. Nobody said "Señor" or "Don" or even "Usted"; everyone called everyone else "Comrade" and "Thou," and said "Salud!" instead of "Buenos días." Tipping had been forbidden by law since the time of Primo de Rivera; almost my first experience was receiving a lecture from an hotel manager for trying to tip a lift-boy. There were no private motor cars; they had all been commandeered, and all the trams and taxis and much of the other transport were painted red and black. The revolutionary posters were everywhere, flaming from the walls in clean reds and blues that made the few remaining advertisements look like daubs of mud. Down the Ramblas, the wide central artery of the town where crowds of people streamed constantly to and fro, the loud-speakers were bellowing revolutionary songs all day and far into the night. . . . In outward appearance it was a town in which the wealthy classes had practically ceased to exist. Except for a small number of women and foreigners there were no "well-dressed" people at all. Practically everyone wore rough working-class clothes or blue overalls or some variant of the militia uniform. All this was queer and moving. There was much in it that I did not understand, in some ways I did not even like it, but I recognized it immediately as a state of affairs worth fighting for. Also I believed that things were as they appeared, that this was really a workers' State and that the entire bourgeoisie had either fled, been killed, or voluntarily come over to the workers' side; I did not realize that great numbers of well-to-do bourgeois were simply lying low and disguising themselves as proletarians for the time being.

Together with all this there was something of the evil atmosphere of war. The town had a gaunt untidy look, roads and buildings were in poor repair, the streets at night were dimly lit for fear of air-raids, the shops were mostly shabby and half-empty. Meat was scarce and milk practically unobtainable, there was a shortage of coal, sugar, and petrol, and a really serious shortage of bread. Even at this period the bread-queues were often hundreds of yards long. Yet so far as one could judge the people were contented and hopeful. There was no unemployment, and the price of living was still extremely low; you saw very few conspicuously destitute people, and no beggars except the gipsies. Above all, there was a belief in the revolution and the future, a feeling of having suddenly emerged into an era of equality and freedom. Human beings were trying to behave as human beings and not as cogs in the capitalist machine. In the barbers' shops were Anarchist notices (the barbers were mostly Anarchists) solemnly explaining that barbers were no longer slaves. In the streets were coloured posters appealing to prostitutes to stop being prostitutes. To anyone from the hard-boiled, sneering civilization of the English-speaking races there was something rather pathetic in the literalness with which these idealistic Spaniards took the hackneyed phrases of the revolution. At that time revolutionary ballads of the naivest kind, all about proletarian brotherhood and the wickedness of Mussolini, were being sold on the streets for a few centimes each. I have often seen an illiterate militiaman buy one of these ballads, laboriously spell out the words, and then, when he had got the hang of it, begin singing it to an appropriate tune.

All this time I was at the Lenin Barracks, ostensibly in training for the front. When I joined the militia I had been told that I should be sent to the front the next day, but in fact I had to wait while a fresh centuria was got ready. The workers' militias, hurriedly raised by the trade unions at the beginning of the war, had not yet been organized on an ordinary army basis. . . . The Lenin Barracks was a block of splendid stone buildings with a riding-school and enormous cobbled courtyards; it had been a cavalry barracks and had been captured during the July fighting. My centuria slept in one of the stables. . . . All the horses had been seized and sent to the front, but the whole place still smelled of horse-piss and rotten oats. I was at the barracks about a week. Chiefly I remember the horsy smells, the quavering bugle-calls (all our buglers were amateurs—I first learned the Spanish bugle-calls by listening to them outside the Fascist lines), the tramp-tramp of hobnailed boots in the barrack yard, the long morning parades in the wintry sunshine, the wild games of football, fifty a side, in the gravelled riding-school. There were perhaps a thousand men at the barracks, and a score or so of women, apart from the militiamen's wives who did the cooking. There were still women serving in the militias, though not very many. In the early battles they had fought side by side with the men as a matter of course. It is a thing that seems natural in time of revolution. Ideas were changing already, however. The militiamen had to be kept out of the riding-school while the women were drilling there, because they laughed at the women and put them off. A few months earlier no one would have seen anything comic in a woman handling a gun.

The whole barracks was in the state of filth and chaos to which the militia reduced every building they occupied and which seems to be one of the by-products of revolution. In every corner you came upon piles of smashed furniture, broken saddles, brass cavalry-helmets, empty sabre-scabbards, and decaying food. There was frightful wastage of food, especially bread. From my barrack-room alone a basketful of bread was thrown away at every meal—a disgraceful thing when the civilian population was short of it. We ate at long trestle-tables out of permanently greasy tin pannikins, and drank out of a dreadful thing called a porrón. A porrón is a sort of glass bottle with a pointed spout from which a thin jet of wine spurts out whenever you tip it up; you can thus drink from a distance, without touching it with your lips, and it can be passed from hand to hand. I went on strike and demanded a drinking-cup as soon as I saw a porrón in use. To my eyes the things were altogether too like bed-bottles, especially when they were filled with white wine.

By degrees they were issuing the recruits with uniforms, and because this was Spain everything was issued piecemeal, so that it was never quite certain who had received what, and various of the things we most needed, such as belts and cartridge-boxes, were not issued till the last moment, when the train was actually waiting to take us to the front. I have spoken of the militia "uniform," which probably gives a wrong impression. It was not exactly a uniform. Perhaps a "multiform" would be the proper name for it. Everyone's clothes followed the same general plan, but they were never quite the same in any two cases. Practically everyone in the army wore corduroy knee-breeches, but there the uniformity ended. Some wore puttees, others corduroy gaiters, others leather leggings or high boots. Everyone wore a zipper jacket, but some of the jackets were of leather, others of wool and of every conceivable colour. The kinds of cap were almost as numerous as their wearers. It was usual to adorn the front of your cap with a party badge, and in addition nearly every man wore a red or red and black handkerchief round his throat. A militia column at that time was an extraordinary-looking rabble. But the clothes had to be issued as this or that factory rushed them out, and they were not bad clothes considering the circumstances. The shirts and socks were wretched cotton things, however, quite useless against cold. I hate to think of what the militiamen must have gone through in the earlier months before anything was organized. I remember coming upon a newspaper of only about two months earlier in which one of the P.O.U.M. leaders, after a visit to the front, said that he would try to see to it that "every militaman had a blanket." A phrase to make you shudder if you have ever slept in a trench.

On my second day at the barracks there began what was comically called "instruction." At the beginning there were frightful scenes of chaos. The recruits were mostly boys of sixteen or seventeen from the back streets of Barcelona, full of revolutionary ardour but completely ignorant of the meaning of war. It was impossible even to get them to stand in line. Discipline did not exist; if a man disliked an order he would step out of ranks and argue fiercely with the officer. The lieutenant who instructed us was a stout, fresh-faced, pleasant young man who had previously been a Regular Army officer, and still looked like one, with his smart carriage and spick-and-span uniform. Curiously enough he was a sincere and ardent Socialist. Even more than the men themselves he insisted upon complete social equality between all ranks. I remember his pained surprise when an ignorant recruit addressed him as "Señor." "What! Señor! Who is calling me Señor? Are we not all comrades?" I doubt whether it made his job any easier. . . .

The essential point of the system was social equality between officers and men. Everyone from general to private drew the same pay, ate the same food, wore the same clothes. . . . If you wanted to slap the general commanding the division on the back and ask him for a cigarette, you could do so, and no one thought it curious. In theory at any rate each militia was a democracy and not a hierarchy. It was understood that orders had to be obeyed, but it was also understood that when you gave an order you gave it as comrade to comrade and not as superior to inferior. There were officers and N.C.O.s, but there was no military rank in the ordinary sense; no titles, no badges, no heel-clicking and saluting. They had attempted to produce within the militias a sort of temporary working model of the classless society. Of course there was not perfect equality, but there was a nearer approach to it than I had ever seen or than I would have thought conceivable in time of war.

But I admit that at first sight the state of affairs at the front horrified me. How on earth could the war be won by an army of this type? It was what everyone was saying at the time, and though it was true it was also unreasonable. For in the circumstances the militias could not have been much better than they were. A modern mechanized army does not spring up out of the ground, and if the Government had waited until it had trained troops at its disposal, Franco would never have been resisted. Later it became the fashion to decry the militias, and therefore to pretend that the faults which were due to lack of training and weapons were the result of the equalitarian system. Actually, a newly raised draft of militia was an undisciplined mob not because the officers called the privates "Comrade" but because raw troops are *always* an undisciplined mob. In practice the democratic "revolutionary" type of discipline is more reliable than might be expected. In a workers' army discipline is theoretically voluntary. It is based on class-loyalty, whereas the discipline of a bourgeois conscript army is based ultimately on fear. (The Popular Army that replaced the militias was midway between the two types.) In the militias the bullying and abuse that go on in an ordinary army would never have been tolerated for a moment. The normal military punishments existed, but they were only invoked for very serious offences. When a man refused to obey an order you did not immediately get him punished; you first appealed to him in the name of comradeship. Cynical people with no experience of handling men will say instantly that this would never "work," but as a matter of fact it does "work" in the long run. The discipline of even the worst drafts of militia visibly improved as time went on. In January the job of keeping a dozen raw recruits up to the mark almost turned my hair grey. In May for a short while I was acting-lieutenant in command of about thirty men, English and Spanish. We had all been under fire for months, and I never had the slightest difficulty in getting an order obeyed or in getting men to volunteer for a dangerous job. "Revolutionary" discipline depends on political consciousness—on an understanding of *why* orders must be obeyed; it takes time to diffuse this, but it also takes time to drill a man into an automaton on the barrack-square.

57. Francisco Franco, Letter to Hitler (1940)

In helping Franco militarily during Spain's Civil War, Hitler had certainly expected a victorious Franco to become a reliable German ally. When World War II began on September 1, 1939, Hitler asked Franco to join the war on the German side, but on September 4 Spain declared itself neutral.

From that point on, negotiations continued between Spanish and German diplomats. For Hitler, Spanish help was not crucial militarily, and the Germans knew what poor shape Spain's forces were in at the time. More important than Spanish troops in Hitler's eyes were Spanish minerals and other raw materials, though Hitler did hope that Spain might help him seize Gibraltar from the British.

For Franco, there were ideological reasons to back Hitler, and some of his domestic supporters also favored Germany. Yet others (including some members of his cabinet) were less sympathetic to the Nazis, and Franco's top priority was maintaining his political control within Spain. Franco was also worried about the international consequences of backing the losing side in a European war, which led him to pursue his usual policy of refusing to commit himself until things played out. When Hitler invaded France in May 1940, negotiations intensified, and on June 3, 1940, Franco sent Hitler the following message.

SOURCE: *Documents on German Foreign Policy, 1918–1945*, ser. D, vol. 9 (Washington, D.C.: U.S. Government Printing Office, 1956), 509–10.

Führer: At the moment when the German armies, under your leadership, are bringing the greatest battle in history to a victorious close, I would like to express to you my admiration and enthusiasm and that of my people, who are watching with deep emotion the glorious course of a struggle which they regard as their own, and which is realizing the hopes that already burned in Spain when your soldiers shared with us in the war against the same, though concealed, enemies.

The great upheavals which Spain underwent in the three years of war, where to our own losses and wear and tear were added the innumerable losses inflicted in Red territory, have put us in a difficult position; it has been made even more difficult by the present war which forces us to develop in a world which is hostile toward us and hinders our recovery wherever possible to the great detriment of our military preparedness, so that we must perforce lag behind in industry as well as in the procurement of raw materials and motor fuels.

In this general situation we must also consider the special conditions of our islands and of the territories separated from the motherland by the sea, which have forced us to make our official attitude a neutral one, while we remain continually on the alert in order to ward off most energetically any attack which might, in connection with the expansion of the war, be launched against us by the eternal enemies of our fatherland.

I do not need to assure you how great is my desire not to remain aloof from your cares and how great is my satisfaction in rendering to you at all times those services which you regard as most valuable.

I have thought it right, in view of present circumstances, to choose General Vigón, chief of the high general staff and outstanding participant in the battles of our campaign, to bring you this letter, since he can best inform you on the situation and on everything which touches and concerns our country.

With my best wishes for the future and the greatness of Germany, and with the expression of my unchanging friendship and regard.

58. Francisco Franco, Laureate Cross Acceptance Speech (1940)

At the outset of the Civil War, Franco was only one of a group of generals leading the rebellion, but he soon emerged as the most capable leader, and the others accepted his leadership of the Nationalist side. The deaths of Generals José Sanjurjo and Emilio Mola (in separate plane crashes) and that of José Antonio Primo de Rivera (at the hands of a Republican firing squad) certainly helped Franco establish his authority, as did his control of the Army of Africa (the best fighting force in the Spanish army) and his ties with the German and Italian governments; soon his followers were referring to him as El Caudillo, a term referring to a political boss or military leader. Although Franco was by training and inclination a soldier rather than a political leader, and although by most accounts he lacked the kind of charisma Hitler and Mussolini had, he did his best to grow into his position as Spain's head of state.

Franco gave the following speech in July 1940 while accepting an award, the Laureate Cross of San Fernando, Spain's highest military honor. As a young officer fighting in Morocco, Franco had been nominated to receive this honor, but he was denied it in 1918. Now, in 1940, Franco, being the head of the government, was essentially awarding himself the Laureate Cross. In this acceptance speech given before an assembly of military officers, Franco expressed many of his new regime's central principles.

SOURCE: Fernando Díaz-Plaja, ed., *La España franquista en sus documentos (La posguerra española en sus documentos)* (Madrid: Plaza and Janés, 1976), 53–56.

My dear generals, chiefs, and officials of the armies of land, sea, and air:

You have been so generous as to grant this precious reward, wishing to be the ones who offered as a demonstration of affection and loyalty this precious Cross of San Fernando—who brought together all the ideals of any military man—as a sign of service to the fatherland.

We cannot, on this day and at this moment, fail to note its significance, and as this Cross of San Fernando has been intertwined, day after day, with the hopes, dreams, and laurels of the successive victories, as it has also signified the respects paid with the blood of our fallen, on the swords and bayonets of our soldiers. That is to say that on my chest is a sign of a mandate from our dead, and over my heart is a symbol of esteem, of chivalry that brings us closer to the fallen. . . .

May this evocation of bloody swords embellished with laurel leaves be a reminder that brings us closer to those who fell, without being ostentatious. May it take us further from the petty miseries in order to bring us closer to the grandeur of our fatherland. And in times of discord, when weakness tries to invade our spirits, let us recall those other moments as soldiers, of grandiose eloquence of truth and enormous fortitude when in the presence of a dark shirt, in the presence of the rigid body of the fallen soldier, the differences and the pride died out, leaving room only for the silent testimony of admiration before grandeur and heroism; may this be the model for our honorable ambitions.

I say this to you because we Spaniards are a forgetful people, because we are used to living for the moment, because we do not look back, because we do not know how to see the chain of heroes, because we do not contemplate the sum of sacrifices.

We have made a pause in the battle, but only a pause; we have not finished our work. We have not carried out the revolution. The blood of our dead was not spilled so that we could return to the decadent times of the past. We do not want to return to the feeble times that brought us the sad days of Cuba and the Philippines. We do not want to return to the nineteenth century. We have spilled the blood of our dead to make a nation and to forge an empire. And in saying that we have to make a nation and create an empire, these cannot be vain words in our mouths, and they will not be.

We have to forge the unity of Spain, a better Spain, full of grandeur and political content; we must engage in politics, gentlemen, a great deal of politics. And I say politics while filling my heart with the word. Not the bad politics of the nineteenth century. Not the liberal politics that pitted one brother against another. Not the politics of division of our classes, which awakened our disdain and justly summoned you from the barracks, but rather the politics of the unity of Spain. For you must know that that golden age of our history, those centuries we look upon as the base and foundation of the Spanish nation, those centuries in which Isabella and Ferdinand displayed their banners throughout Spain, are related to what we now can see. A divided Spain, a subjected Spain, a Spain full of misery, a Spain full of miserliness and selfishness, was what they found. And what did the Catholic monarchs do? What was the first act of Isabella's marriage? The first political act was that of preparing the unity of Spain by uniting the two great pieces in which it was divided, while also sacrificing the conveniences and the heart for the grandeur of the fatherland. It was an act that was political, eminently political, by an exemplary queen, and one that signified the downfall of the power of the local lords and the relief of the misery of the classes of the people with the suppression of the secular despotism of the lands of Spain; these were eminently political acts of the Catholic monarchs.

And when the King assumed all powers and linked the masters of the military orders—the shock troops of that era—to the Crown, what was he doing other than carrying out an enormous political act of blending the power of the armies with that of the sovereign? And what did Cisneros and Mendoza do, at the side of the king, working closely with him, other than create the unity of the cross and the sword and watch over a people? And what meaning did the epics of the Reconquest have other than the constant and systematic execution of the political directives of the nation? And what was the expulsion of the Jews other than a racist act like those of today, because of the obstacle created for the achievement of unity by a foreign race that had come to own a people and one that was a slave to material desires? Are these acts not eminently political? And when the conquest of the Indies was undertaken, along with our wise laws and our provincial governors went the universalistic policy of Spain, with its flags and its cross, and an evangelizing Catholic spirit pervaded the policies of that era. And even up to her final moments, when that holy queen placed her signature on her final will and testament, she created a political testament for her people: the mandate of Gibraltar, the African vision, political unity, political expression, political mandates that over the past four centuries have remained an eternal lesson.

This is my concern: that you appreciate all of this life of Spain. That you open your hearts to unity. That we learn from the lesson we are receiving. We are living through the most interesting moments of our century. We do not want an easy and comfortable life. We want a hard life, a difficult life, the life of manly people. We display ourselves before Europe with just and legitimate titles. five hundred thousand dead for the salvation and unity of Spain we offered in the first European battle for the new order. We are not absent from the problems of the world. Our rights and ambitions have not been subjected to limits; the Spain that created and gave its life to a continent now has a pulse and virility. It has two million warriors ready to do battle in defense of its rights. But these warriors would be nothing, our weaponry and supplies would be nothing, nor would our strength, if the enemy could open a breach within the divisions of a people.

I am sure that now and forever you will close ranks around me. I am convinced that you, who live among the people, will be able to understand them. . . . If the life of Spain must be that of a militia, it will need the military virtues and the spirit of discipline. The army is a mirror in which the nation may see itself, and so today, when Spain's great concerns are incarnated in the National Revolution that must elevate so many classes and must bring satisfaction, . . . you must be the strongest marker we must put along the path, with all the understanding, with all the grandeur of spirit, with all your loyalty, and with all your discipline.

Discipline, which is the essence of the military virtues. Discipline and unity, which are the secret of these fantastic victories on the battlefields of Europe. There can be no reservations, conditions, or half-hearted measures. Discipline, which finds a shining example in . . . this fallen man in a dark shirt who asked neither where he was going nor how he was being commanded. That is discipline. One who commands, responsible . . . before the supreme judgment of history, and others who follow and obey blindly, as they followed Ferdinand and Isabella, as they followed our caudillos in the distant lands of America, and as you will follow me.

In homage to our dead, in memory of them, affirm with me: "Arriba España!"

(All present cry out: "Arriba!")

"Viva España!"

(They answer unanimously: "Viva!")

59. The Nationalist Movement, Law of Syndical Organization (1940)

As a career military man, Franco tended to pay little attention to social issues, but his advisers—including German and Italian diplomats—repeatedly urged him to pay more attention to matters such as the organization of labor. Franco authorized the drafting of the following law on the organization of labor—a law that reflected the corporatist outlook then prevailing in Germany and Italy, as well as among the Spanish Falangists.

The "movement" referred to here was the political organization Franco had formed in consolidating all of the conservative political groups into one unit in 1937. The complexity of the full name of that state party, the Falange Española Tradicionalista y de las Juntas de Ofensiva Nacional Sindicalista (FET y de las JONS), reflected the range of groups he had fused in creating his party.

SOURCE: Fernando Díaz-Plaja, ed., *La España franquista en sus documentos (La posguerra española en sus documentos)* (Madrid: Plaza and Janés, 1976), 69–75.

The current increase in the syndical efforts of the movement, in which the majority of the components of the Spanish economy are already organized, calls for the dictating of a law of the foundations of the syndical organization of the regime. . . . This law will only establish the basic outlines of the syndical order, the hierarchy of its organisms, an index of its functions, and its connections with the state and the movement.

The political foundations of the syndical system . . . thus acquire a new concrete and orienting expression . . . drawing on our guild tradition . . . [and on] measures that the state dictated at the moment necessary to clear the way for the efforts of the leaders of the party [FET y de las JONS] and the syndicates to begin disciplining the forces of production.

The law begins by considering all Spanish producers members of a great national and syndical community. The system of the regime's syndicates, however, is not set up as a network of private associations to which the state grants more or less authority; syndication, instead, is the political form of the entire economy of Spain—in accord with that principle in the [Falangist] Twenty-Six Points [see reading 47] that conceives Spain, economically, as a gigantic syndicate of producers. Those who contribute to the power of the fatherland through some form of production are thus organized as a militia, following the guidelines of our movement. . . .

The national-syndicalist centers and the national syndicates . . . convey to the government the desires and specific needs of each branch of production, and they have the responsibility of ensuring the fulfillment of the orders and directives that the state, as supreme ruler of the economy, dictates.

[They] . . . will gather together the various social categories of labor in Christian and Falangist brotherhood, to ensure the obedience of each producer, manager, technician, and worker to the discipline of the syndicate; [they will] see to it that the relation of work is born and lives in the spirit of justice and service that its charter assigns to it, and that through the establishment of powerful works of education, social assistance and provision, etc., the standard of living that Spain demands for its workers is achieved. . . .

The representation and discipline of all the producers is the responsibility of the syndical organisms. . . . With all democratic illusions now having been destroyed, the syndical organisms are now constituted by those who voluntarily mobilize themselves to serve in constituting and commanding them. . . . The law guarantees the subordination of the syndical organization to the party, since only the latter can give it the discipline, the unity, and the spirit needed for the national economy to serve national policy.

The subordination and discipline with respect to the state are, as is logical, fully guaranteed. Only by decree approved in the Council of Ministers is the personality of each syndicate officially recognized.

We therefore decree:

Article 1. The Spaniards, insofar as they participate in production, constitute the national-syndicalist community as a militant unit under the discipline of the movement. . . .

Article 9. In accordance with . . . the Labor Charter, the national syndicate is a corporation under public law, constituted for the integration within a unitary organism of all the elements that devote their activities to the fulfillment of the economic process, and within a specific service or sector of production, organized hierarchically under the supreme direction of the state. . . .

Article 12. The chief of each national syndicate will be named by a national order from the movement. . . .

Article 16. The national-syndicalist centers and local syndical brotherhoods will . . . have the following functions under their control:

1. To establish the social discipline of the producers on the principles of unity and cooperation, dictating the necessary rules for this.

2. To represent their affiliates in legal matters.

3. To settle individual labor conflicts, as an obligatory preliminary to intervention by the Magistracy of Labor.

4. To seek professional improvement and a proper distribution of the labor force. . . .

6. To cooperate in the gathering of statistics on the conditions of labor and production, the situation of the market, and any management issues of

a socioeconomic character that can help inform the decisions of the syndical organization of the government.

Article 18. These are functions of the national syndicate:

1. To propose to the government the ordinances necessary for the discipline and promotion of the production, preservation, and distribution of products, as well as the regulation of their prices in the various phases of the production process; also to dictate the regulations and take the measures conducive to these goals.

2. To assist the national delegation of syndicates in the development of proposals and reports for the regulation of labor.

3. To exercise disciplinary power over the lower syndicates in the form established by the syndical statute.

Article 19. All the positions of command in the syndicates will necessarily be held by militants of the FET y de las JONS.

Article 20. The action of the syndicates on the national, provincial, and local levels will be carried out under the discipline of the movement and under the hierarchies of the corresponding authorities of the FET y de las JONS, which will act under the political authority of the party and subordinated to the statutes of the party.

60. José Rodríguez Vega, *Impressions of Franco's Spain* (1943)
Translated Anonymously from Spanish

The author of this description of life under the Franco regime in its early years was a member of the Printers' Union and a secretary of the Unión General de Trabajadores, or General Workers' Union. He was arrested in Alicante at the end of the war and spent time in prison awaiting execution, but he managed to escape and flee the country. Like many other Spanish exiles, he made his way to Mexico, where he gave speeches such as this one from March 1943. Although it offers but one perspective on the Franco regime and living conditions during World War II, this speech, which was translated into English and published as a pamphlet in Britain in 1943, represented part of a broad effort by exiles to build support outside Spain for measures to topple Franco's regime.

SOURCE: José Rodríguez Vega, *Impressions of Franco's Spain,* no translator listed (London: United Editorial Limited, 1943); the text appears in the Blodgett Collection, Harvard University.

I shall try to give you this evening—although in a somewhat unpolished way as, unfortunately, I am not accustomed to oratory—some of my impressions of the period from the end of the Spanish war until my departure from Spain a few days after the Anglo-American landing in North Africa [in 1943]. . . . In the last months, particularly in the last two months of our war, an idea had got about, as a result of Francoist propaganda, that there was a possibility, seeing that the war was lost militarily, of coming to an understanding with the enemy in the belief that the latter would be generous and would only take steps against those persons who might have committed crimes of a common character. This belief, propagated during the month of March 1939 throughout the part of Spain which had remained loyal to the government of the Republic, became almost unanimous in the Spanish people. Worn out by an extremely hard war, lacking food, without the help of the representatives of parties and organizations . . . it was possible for this idea to take hold in such a way that the immense majority thought, in the last days of March 1939, that Franco would keep his oft-repeated promises. In numerous newspaper articles, the Caudillo had promised to take steps only against so-called criminals. . . .

[At the war's end in Alicante] we were transferred to a concentration camp which will go down in history as one of the most notorious together with the very notorious one of Dachau in Germany: the concentration camp of Albatera. . . . I shall not refer here to the vicissitudes and bitter troubles endured by the seventeen or eighteen thousand men who found themselves here. It will suffice if I tell you that in Albatera, a camp established by the Republic for 800 persons, that multitude lived—if it can be called living—for many months, in the open, with hardly any food, many days without water. For some time, at certain periods, two or three times a week, there were executions of compatriots making attempts at escape or accused of such intentions. . . .

As regards myself, after a little while . . . I was taken to Madrid. . . . I was taken to a notorious, a terribly notorious, police station situated in the Calle de Almagro, No. 36. The entry into Madrid—an entry I shall never forget—gave us an idea of the panorama of horror, pain, and tragedy which we were to witness or live for a period of years: beatings of companions, among them many very dear to us and who are still in prison; blows given without respect for sex or age, blows rained on an old man as well as on a woman; refined tortures, which led to three suicides while I was in that police station. . . . Elsewhere I have already referred to the sport indulged in by the Franco police at the expense of a companion, Regatero, who was, I believe, a doctor with the Army of the Levant. After beating him with irons and subjecting him to innumerable tortures, really frightful tortures, they used to put his head in a bath of water. When they reckoned that he was on the point of drowning, they would pull him out, beat him again, and then again put him in the bath. Our companion at last freed himself from this martyrdom by committing suicide. Out of fifteen of us there, I think only three or four are alive today. There I had to hear the horrible cries of those being martyrized, and afterwards see the wounds produced on the bodies of our comrades. Women do not escape these torments either, some of them wives of lovable comrades and friends, nor does there exist even for children the respect which an animal has for its little one. . . .

There were in Madrid at that time seventeen prisons, four of them for women, without counting numerous buildings where prisoners were crowded, some of the buildings housing a thousand persons. . . . The number in the Madrid prisons at that time, without of course counting those in the concentration camps, was possibly fifty thousand. . . .

In the list of established crimes, it was enough to have been a member of a left-wing organization to be considered hostile to the regime and be condemned, as minimum penalty, to a sentence of twelve years and a day. . . . As regards the trial, there were no guarantees of any kind for the prisoner. It might happen—and generally did happen—that he would be tried for and be asked at the War Council totally different things to those which had been the object of the interrogation in the police station or by the judge. In reality, it was a question of "taking people for a ride" and disguising same. . . .

The death penalties imposed by the military tribunals were very frequent. If they were not more than the others, at least they reached a number equivalent to those of temporary or perpetual imprisonment. Executions took place three, four, five times a week, all the Madrid prisons contributing contingents for the wall. Even though the sight of friends and dear companions leaving us in order to appear before the execution squads engendered a certain insensibility, nevertheless on occasions we were overcome by a profound emotion, an emotion which it is necessary to have experienced in order to be able to give an idea of it. . . .

But what happens outside the prisons? Outside, the most outstanding feature . . . is the state of terrible hunger through which nearly the whole of the Spanish people is passing. . . . Food has diminished considerably in our country. [The speaker then gives the prices of certain items on the black market.] In view of these prices . . . everyone's position is unbearable and is the cause of the irritation and discontent now existing in Spain. . . . There has arisen, I say, a tremendous movement of irritation and disgust against the Francoist regime. If we take into account the fact that many people desired the end of the war, not because they wanted the triumph of fascism, but because they wanted an end to their material sufferings, you will understand the terrible disillusionment of these nuclei of excessively ingenuous population who hoped for little less than that Franco would bring abundance and plenty. . . .

The spirit of the people, which was never favorable to the dictatorship, not even in its moments of natural depression after a struggle on the scale and extent such as ours, is becoming firmer and its sentiment of hostility to the situation is now greater. This spirit of rebellion has led to an increase in Spain in the numbers of organizations which are functioning, more or less well, at great risk, as well as to an increase in the campaign against the present regime. . . . Opposition in Spain to the fascist regime is to be found among the popular masses, among the classes which had desired the coming of Franco and his triumph in our war, as well as throughout all the regions where, as regards these feelings, there is no difference whatever between them. . . . In Catalonia there is a notable revival of the regionalist feeling due, as has always occurred when there has been a desire to wound the Catalan people's soul, to the brutality and stupidity of the Francoist elements. . . . As regards the Basque country, I can tell you that it is one of the regions where the greatest coolness against fascism exists. On a journey which Franco made some time ago to Bilbao, he met with an icy reception because, together with the popular classes, who detest him, were the nationalist and monarchist bourgeoisies, who are maintaining attitudes of open hostility or, at least, of suspicion against the present regime. . . .

As was to be expected, the world war has had a great influence in Spain. . . . For a long time in Spain it was thought by the elements which supported the Franco regime, that the end of the war would be favorable to the totalitarian regimes. Not so, the popular elements. . . . Everybody, the workers, democrats, and liberals of our country expect their liberation on the termination of the war. Nobody can believe it to be true that, according to what the American ambassador said recently, the triumph of the United Nations [the Allies] would not affect the Spanish regime in any way. There is not a single Spaniard, unless he be in a lunatic asylum, who believes that this can happen. Neither they—the Francoists—nor we. They are convinced that the triumph of the democratic countries is going to be, though they do not wish it, the triumph of liberty in Europe and the triumph of liberty in Spain.

61. The United States and Franco's Spain, 1945–1954

As the fortunes of war gradually shifted in Europe, and as the prospects of long-term Nazi control of Europe gave way to expectations that the Allies would be able to defeat Germany, Franco's position in Spain looked increasingly precarious. By the time of the Allied invasions of Europe in 1943 and 1944, his strong ties with the Nazis and Italian Fascists and his image as the head of a fascist regime raised serious questions about whether his government would survive, and some even called for the Allied armies to invade Spain and overthrow Franco as part of their war effort. Even when it became clear that the Allies would not send troops to Spain, their hostility toward Franco and the desperate economic situation Spain faced in the aftermath of the Civil War of 1936–1939 raised the possibility that the regime could be toppled simply by international isolation.

Yet over a remarkably brief period from the close of World War II to the early 1950s, Franco managed to defy expectations and thwart his domestic and international opponents, escaping from almost-total isolation (and surviving in large part because of grain purchased from Juan Domingo Perón's Argentina) to secure important measures of international acceptance and support by 1953. Leading the campaign to allow Spain back into the community of Western nations were the Vatican, which signed a crucial concordat with Spain in August 1953, and the United States government, which signed agreements in September of that year creating American military bases in Spain, in exchange for American economic and military assistance to Franco's government.

The American accords with Spain essentially crowned a long effort by Franco to ensure his long-term survival, and they therefore also helped fuel the anti-Americanism that lingers in Spain even today, at least on the left. The following series of American diplomatic reports and letters on Spain show the path by which the two countries moved so dramatically in such a short time. The American documents in large part provide their own explanation for Washington's changing attitude, but understanding that shift also requires recalling the atmosphere and expectations of the early cold-war years, when hostility between the West and Stalin's Soviet Union became acute, and when fears of an invasion of western Europe by the imposing military forces the Soviets maintained in central Europe did not seem at all imaginary. In addition to revealing how Franco's relationship with the outside world changed, these American texts also offer a valuable glimpse of internal conditions and patterns of popular opinion in Spain under Franco.

SOURCE: U.S. Department of State, *Foreign Relations of the United States* (Washington, D.C.: U.S. Government Printing Office, 1948–), *1945* (1967), 5: 667–68, 679–80; *1948* (1974), 3: 1017–19, 1031–32; *1949* (1975), 4: 750–53; *1951* (1985), 4:773–74, 814–16; *1952–1954* (1986), 6: 1980–82.

President [Franklin D.] Roosevelt to the Ambassador in Spain ([Norman]Armour), Washington, March 10, 1945

My Dear Mr. Armour: In connection with your new assignment as ambassador to Madrid I want you to have a frank statement of my views with regard to our relations with Spain.

Having been helped to power by Fascist Italy and Nazi Germany, and having patterned itself along totalitarian lines, the present regime in Spain is naturally the subject of distrust by a great many American citizens who find it difficult to see the justification for this country to continue to maintain relations with such a regime. Most certainly we do not forget Spain's official position with and assistance to our Axis enemies at a time when the fortunes of war were less favorable to us, nor can we disregard the activities, aims, organizations, and public utterances of the Falange, both past and present. These memories cannot be wiped out by actions more favorable to us now that we are about to achieve our goal of complete victory over those enemies of ours with whom the present Spanish regime identified itself in the past spiritually and by its public expressions and acts.

The fact that our government maintains formal diplomatic relations with the present Spanish regime should not be interpreted by anyone to imply approval of that regime and its sole party, the Falange, which has been openly hostile to the United States and which has tried to spread its fascist party ideas in the Western Hemisphere. Our victory over Germany will carry with it the extermination of Nazi and similar ideologies.

As you know, it is not our practice in normal circumstances to interfere in the internal affairs of other countries unless there exists a threat to international peace. The form of government in Spain and the policies pursued by that government are quite properly the concern of the Spanish people. I should be lacking in candor, however, if I did not tell you that I can see no place in the community of nations for governments founded on fascist principles.

We all have the most friendly feelings for the Spanish people and we are anxious to see a development of cordial relations with them. There are many things which we could and normally would be glad to do in economic and other fields to demonstrate that friendship. The initiation of such measures is out of the question at this time, however, when American sentiment is so profoundly opposed to the present regime in power in Spain.

Therefore, we earnestly hope that the time may soon come when Spain may assume the role and the responsibility which we feel it should assume in the field of international cooperation and understanding.

Very sincerely yours,
Franklin D. Roosevelt

The Ambassador in Spain (Armour) to the Secretary of State [Edward R. Stettinius, Jr.], Madrid, June 2, 1945

General Franco gave a dinner for us at the Pardo last night. It was the first opportunity I had had to see him since presenting my credentials on March 24, and I took advantage in a short conversation to stress again our government's viewpoint.

I expressed my disappointment at what I felt to be the lack of any real progress in the evolution of the regime in the two months since our last talk. Franco pointed to certain steps taken, freedom from censorship of foreign press correspondents, the bill of rights now before the Cortes, proposed municipal elections, etc. as evidence of a gradual change. I said that while the two latter matters cited might have some significance internally . . . so long as the Falange continued to occupy its present position in the structure of the government and the totalitarian aspect of the regime remained unchanged, he could not expect any improvement in our relations. I said that I felt the important thing was that they should get started as soon as possible along the right road even though attainment of the ultimate goal might not be immediately realized. . . .

Franco fell back on his usual arguments stressing the Communist menace to Europe including Spain. He admitted that the danger of a clash between the Western Allies and Russia might have been exaggerated, particularly in their own press (plans for relaxation in the press control are now, he said, under way). . . . He emphasized that Spain was the particular target for Communist propaganda and that France was playing Russia's game. The combined Soviet-French attacks, he said, made it necessary for them in accomplishing their evolution not unduly to weaken the central authority.

Franco said that he sincerely desired the closest relations with the United States and Great Brit[ain] and he could not believe that with the many grave problems that confronted us in Europe we would not be disposed to show a sympathetic understanding of Spain's difficulties, having in mind the nearness of their own civil war and therefore give them time to work out their problems in their own way. . . .

I said [that] we considered this to be an internal problem for Spain [and] that, as he knew, it was not our policy to interfere in the internal affairs of other countries, but he must realize that until they at least made a real start in bringing this regime more into line with the new world currents he could not expect relations on the basis that we would like to have them.

The Chief of the Division of Western European Affairs ([Theodore C.] Achilles) to the Chargé in Spain ([Paul] Culbertson), Washington, January 5, 1948

TOP SECRET

Dear Paul: I will try in this letter . . . to give you our general thinking on the subject of our policy toward Spain:

1. We want to bring about gradual normalization of relations between Spain and the United States and, incidentally, between Spain and other Western countries.

2. While popular opinion in this country and western Europe with respect to Spain has cooled off to a very considerable extent, complete normalization would be difficult, if not impossible, without some democratization in Spain.

3. We emphatically would not want to see the Spanish state weakened to a point at which civil disorders might ensue.

4. Changes in the form or composition of the Spanish government are the business of Spaniards alone. . . .

5. International pressure to "kick-Franco-out-now" has failed and has served only: (1) to strengthen his resistance to any liberalization under foreign pressure; (2) to increase support for him in Spain among those who would like a more democratic government but object to foreign pressure or fear renewed disorders; and (3) to give the communists everywhere one more chance to cause trouble and embarrassment. . . .

7. We had reasonable success in trying to hold down the United Nations pressure at the 1947 assembly. This should be, and apparently is, evidence to Spaniards of a change in our basic attitude. However, the provisions of the 1946 resolution on isolation from agencies connected with the United Nations and the recall of chiefs of mission still hold and we are not at this time considering any action contrary to that. . . .

8. We do not want to see the economic situation in Spain deteriorate further. . . .

9. We are not at this time prepared to extend governmental credit

(Export-Import Bank), but would be glad to consider it as and when the regime gives concrete signs that it has the intention of moving toward greater democratic and economic efficiency. Inclusion of Spain in the European Recovery Program [Marshall Plan] would be a question for the sixteen countries concerned. They would be most unlikely, judging from their attitude at the UN Assembly, to agree on inclusion of Spain in the absence of substantial political and economic changes within Spain. . . .

10. From the foregoing, it should be obvious that we are thinking in terms of persuading Franco to inaugurate gradual and orderly liberalization rather than trying to force him out.

11. Persuading him to adopt such a course will naturally be difficult. . . .

13. Assuming that you get anything short of a complete rebuff from Franco . . . I think you should take substantially the same line with all other elements in Spain—army, Church, monarchists, and the moderate left. The extreme left is seeking disorder and communism rather than democracy in Spain and we do not care what they think. Other leftist elements may well react unfavorably, possibly bitterly, but we believe with complete sincerity that there is no chance whatever of achieving a really democratic regime in Spain through the former policy of attempting international coercion and that there is a reasonable possibility of bringing it about through the new one.

The Chargé in Spain (Culbertson) to the Secretary of State [George C. Marshall], Madrid, March 29, 1948

SECRET

It is my understanding that in general American military authorities consider continental Spanish territory to be of major importance to strategic military operations in the Mediterranean and to the keeping of operational lines open to the Middle and Near East. Certainly our military authorities have not at all times seen eye to eye with the State Department with regard to American policy toward Franco Spain, and this has been true presumably because of the value of Spain in the event of hostilities with forces in the east of Europe. Problems of political ideology and American public resentment against Franco were and are of less importance to military thinking than to diplomatic thinking, but military considerations in time of crisis may well override ideological objections and change purely political policy. . . . If we are interested in Spain for purely military reasons and we can foresee the need to use Spain and Spanish territory, it should be borne in mind that Spanish transport and her military establishments are presently so antiquated that considerable time would be required to build them up to a point of real value and usefulness.

Our present policy is designed to encourage the Spanish regime to liberalize its structure and practices to a point where we and other nations can in the light of public opinion justify acceptance of Spain into the community of nations. . . . At the very best Spain, under our present interpretation of the 1946 [UN] General Assembly resolution, cannot hope for inclusion in United Nations organizations prior to sometime in 1949. The immediate incentive to Spain to adjust her policies is, therefore, not very great.

Of course, one would think that people with normal reactions would welcome a friendly hand by demonstrating through action a desire to be accepted into the community of nations—the Western nations, that is. Spanish reactions are not however exactly what I would call normal. Likewise, Spanish psychology is different—a psychology influenced by individualism and an inferiority complex which evidences itself in an effort to relive the greatness that was once Spain's. Add to this their conviction that Spanish territory is strategically indispensable and that the Western powers, principally the United States, will require Spain in their self-defense interest and you get a stubborn, self-righteous, injured attitude that it is up to the world to change, not Spain. Furthermore, with the iron curtain daily moving further upstage, the regime becomes increasingly convinced of the correctness of its policies.

For ten years Spain has been kicked around internationally and kicked with vigor, although less vigorously in recent months. She has been ostracized and excluded from international cooperative effort. Small wonder, therefore, that she has a head-in-the-sand reaction to participation in the Western European Union or even to responsibilities concurrent with participation, if she were invited, in ERP [the European Recovery Program, also known as the Marshall Plan].

The Chargé in Spain (Culbertson) to the Secretary of State [Dean Acheson], Madrid, June 22, 1949

CONFIDENTIAL

In the possibility that a restatement of policy is under consideration, I submit the following comments. . . .

I recognize that realism and consistency in the formulation and conduct of foreign policy are not easy of complete realization. Political reasons, domestic or foreign, emotional considerations and many other factors contribute to the state of affairs. Another factor I recognize is that anyone discussing policy toward Spain in any other light than that of damning Franco is subject to attack by some elements at home as condoning or supporting all the practices and forms of the present Spanish regime, many of which stink to high heaven and are repugnant to our own democratic concepts. However, I am not a supporter of the idea that we should base policy on the concept of molding the rest of the world in our own democratic image. It would be fine if the nations of the world could thus be molded, but peoples the world over are not the same and won't mold the same. Certainly not the Spanish.

Stable democracy in Spain is a possibility only in the indefinite future. Past efforts at democracy have produced instability and chaos. These people, high or low, do not know the difference between liberty and license. In probably no other country is individualism more pronounced than in Spain. Anarchism has had its greatest success in Spain because of this. It is, and has been, the characteristic of all Spaniards to object to or criticize whatever government is in control at any given time. They have always had pretty sound reasons, but historically the present Spanish regime is no worse than its predecessors, and with them I include the last Republic with its chaos, disorder and repression.

Internal Spanish objections to the Franco regime are however quite different, in most respects, than our objections. For instance, our objection to the regime because it was helped to power by our recent enemies—Germany and Italy—plays no part in Spanish objection. On the other hand, Soviet assistance to the Republic is an element supporting Franco. We do not like Franco himself but here in Spain Franco as an individual has less opposition than the regime. As an example: Spain's economic difficulties are laid at the doorstep of the Minister of Industry and Commerce [Juan Antonio Suances Fernández] and not on Franco's. Monarchists object to Franco not so much because he is a dictator but because they feel Franco did not keep faith with them, they having fought with and supported Franco during the Civil War because they thought they were fighting for the restoration of the monarchy. Another factor, and an important one, with regard to Franco is that while there is opposition and objection to him, there is no majority desire to see him thrown out on his neck because there is no visible alternative that could assure internal security.

We find religious intolerance in Spain repugnant to our democratic concepts. It is repugnant but when attacks are directed against that intolerance, they should be directed against the Spanish people and not against the Franco regime. . . . Franco is not to blame for all the things that are wrong here in Spain and, while he himself is a devout Catholic, there is no indication that he or his regime members support that old inquisition spirit found in the Spanish Catholic Church and among the people. From the standpoint of religion the Spanish church and people are bigoted and backward. Franco may be a dictator but he would never get by with any crusade on behalf of Protestants. . . .

Political repression and persecution in any form or degree go against the grain of American ideas and we therefore object to that side of the Spanish régime. We are more conscious of and impressed by this repression and persecution because of the Fascist origins and trappings of the regime. Spain is a police state and, as one prominent Spaniard remarked the other day, it "is a country occupied by its own army." However, the vast majority of the Spanish people are little, if at all, affected by repression and persecution as practiced today. The peasant, the laborer, the clerk and on up the line are more concerned today with the actual problem of living than they are with the establishment of political liberties such as we know them. It is the economic situation in Spain and its economic inequalities that are of the greatest importance today to the individual Spaniard and, I suppose, our basic interest lies more in the welfare and well-being of the people of Spain than in the individual who happens to be at the head of the state at any given time. The refusal of material aid to Spain punishes the Spanish people, not Franco and his cohorts or the rich. There are lots of very hungry folk in Spain today, and there are going to be more before the end of the year.

I assume that our broad policy toward Spain continues to rest on our desire to see Spain integrated economically, politically and militarily into the Western community of nations. . . . As the Department knows, I have talked liberalization to these people but without success. The tragedy of Spain is that Franco takes no measures of an evolutionary character, and without evolution revolution is possible, and, in the event of Franco's death, I think probable. One would think that Franco, if he is honest and I think he is, would see that. However, he is stubborn and provincial, and so long as the nations of the world continue openly to condemn him he may do a Samson and pull the temple down on himself.

Draft Report by the Secretary of State [Acheson] to the National Security Council, January 15, 1951

TOP SECRET

United States Policy Toward Spain

1. Changing conditions resulting from Soviet-inspired aggression and the consequent increasing danger of global war require a reconsideration of

U.S. policy toward Spain which will serve immediate requirements of our national security.

2. The potential military value of Spain's geographic position grows steadily in direct proportion to the deterioration of the international situation. It is necessary to incorporate Spain into the strategic planning for the Western European, Mediterranean and North Atlantic areas which are essential to our national security. This necessity is becoming urgent. . . .

3. Our ultimate objective should be to obtain Spanish participation in the MDAP [Mutual Defense Assistance Program] and the NAT [North Atlantic Treaty]. Although this is still not practicable . . . we should begin now to provide for the contribution Spain can make to the common defense. . . .

4. In the event of a Soviet attack on Western Europe, the Spanish government, spurned for several years by the Western nations, is entirely capable of attempting neutrality. The longer we delay before seeking Spanish cooperation, the more we encourage this neutrality sentiment, or at least encourage the Spaniards to place an exorbitantly high price on their cooperation. On the other hand, the sooner we decide that Spain shall play a role in the common defense of the Western European, Mediterranean and North Atlantic areas, the more time we will have to obtain the detailed information needed to determine what is required to make effective use of Spanish bases and manpower. At present, Spanish forces have no offensive capabilities and only the most limited defensive capabilities; in order to contribute militarily they would consequently require extensive reequipping and training. The use of bases would also require action to overcome such serious handicaps as the inadequacy of Spanish airfields and their limited storage and repair facilities, the absence of radio and navigational equipment, inadequate and debilitated port facilities, railroads and highways and inadequate telecommunication facilities.

5. Thus, if we do not soon determine to exploit Spain's strategic geographic position and to develop its military potentialities, manpower and resources, we may well lose the opportunity. . . .

The Ambassador in Spain ([Stanton] Griffis) to the Secretary of State [Acheson], Madrid, April 24, 1951

SECRET

My Dear Mr. Secretary: May I impose on your busy life to give you a brief summary of the situation in Spain. . . .

1. Generalissimo Franco, despite the Barcelona strike, appears to be firmly in control of the country.

2. The only development, outside of his death or serious illness, which could possibly change this control would be economic, that is, the actual lack of foodstuffs or the further spiraling of prices, which would raise the cost of basic elements of life, such as wheat and rice, beyond the true purchasing power of the masses, and thus throw the army into the scale against him.

3. The only existing power which would have any possibility of upsetting Franco would be the army, whose leaders are afraid or unwilling to upset the military dictatorship of which they are a part. There is always the possibility of a move by Franco to restore the monarchy to save himself.

4. Franco is hardworking, has a thorough knowledge of the Spanish political and economic situations, and is more astute politically than any of his opposition.

5. There is substantially no freedom in Spain either political or economic as affecting labor; nor is there freedom of press or assembly. There is evidence of recent improvement in the freedom of the almost microscopic number of Spanish Protestants, Jews and Moslems as to the practice of their religions.

6. The Spanish army, air force and navy are and would be substantially impotent in modern warfare under their present conditions of equipment. Any talk of their defending the Pyrenees with their present equipment is absurd.

7. The great economic danger period for Spain is between this date and next autumn when the flour and rice from the present crop will become available. The crop shows signs of being the best in recent years, but it is not definitely certain that a period of actual national starvation will not develop before it is harvested and processed.

8. Spain is willing to fight, willing to send troops beyond the Pyrenees, anxious to make a bilateral agreement with the United States if properly armed, and/or would even reluctantly consent to join NATO, despite her old suspicions of England and France, but she must have arms.

9. As the longtime enemy of everything communistic, neither the Spanish government nor its people are able to understand the discrimination against them so far as American aid, either economic or military, is concerned. . . .

11. Spain is nobody's child.

Surely we must act and act promptly to aid Spain even in a small way. . . . Furthermore, we desperately need a military mission here at once. . . . We should have at least fifty more officers here studying the possibilities of transportation rehabilitation, airfields, and lines of defense. . . . If the United

States government wants starvation and a trend toward communism in Spain, they are going to get it very quickly with their present indecision. If they want a militarily impotent Spain, they have it now.

My incorrigible sense of humor in the midst of this tragedy makes me ask your indulgence in closing this letter by quoting a jest that is sweeping the country:

A Frenchman asked a Spaniard: "How much time do you think it would take the Russians to arrive at the Rhine?"

"Six days."

"And at the Pyrenees?"

"Six days."

"And at Gibraltar?"

"Six weeks."

"And why the difference?"

"Because of the roads."

This is a cry for help for an orphan but able child who, on a very small diet, could be made lusty and strong in the defense of the world.

Statement of Policy by the National Security Council, June 10, 1954

TOP SECRET

1. Spain's strategic geographic location is extremely important to the immediate defense of Western Europe and the Middle East and to the security of the NATO area and of the United States. . . .

2. Three agreements signed by the United States and Spain on September 26, 1953, provide for the development and use by the U.S. of military facilities in Spain, and the strengthening of Spain's military posture through economic and military aid. Implementation of these agreements is expected to contribute materially to the defense of Western Europe and to the security of the NATO area.

3. To support this program of military cooperation with Spain, the U.S. informed the Spanish government at the time the agreements were signed that, with respect to the aid envisaged by the agreements, the United States intended to provide a total program in the amount of $465 million over a period of four years, subject to congressional appropriations. The Spanish government was also informally given to understand that approximately $350 million would be allocated to military aid, leaving $115 million for economic and technical assistance. . . .

4. Spain (nominally a monarchy but without king or regent) is an authoritarian state with the strength and stability of the regime due in large part to General Franco's dominant position. The government derives its support principally from the army, the Church, the landed and business interests and the Falange Party. Of these elements, the most important is the army, which is firmly under Franco's control. Its prestige will be further strengthened by the U.S. aid and base programs.

5. Although the threat of popular unrest over living conditions which developed in the spring of 1951 has lessened, the major domestic problem of the government continues to be one of satisfying the requirements of the Spanish people with regard to their standard of living, which is lower than that of any other Western European country except Portugal. The government's position has been strengthened by international developments, particularly the signing of the concordat with the Vatican (August 27, 1953) and the signing of military and economic agreements with the U.S. In the eyes of many Spaniards these agreements brought increased international prestige and the hope of individual economic gain. Furthermore the organized clandestine noncommunist opposition, already weakened by police action, was further discouraged by what was regarded as an alliance with the United States, to which the opposition had looked for ultimate fulfillment of its political aspirations. Consequently, the position of the government of General Franco is probably stronger than at any time since 1940.

62. Spanish Bishops, On Criticism, Propaganda, and Publicity (1950)

Within Franco's authoritarian system, the Catholic Church played a major role in many areas, including the regulation of culture and the media. The government used a formal system of censorship to shield Spaniards from certain ideas and images found in other Western countries, and members of the Church figured prominently in that censorship work. Here the Church expresses its outlook on that task in a document it published in the magazine *Ecclesia* in July 1950.

SOURCE: *Ecclesia* (1950–II), 286–88; the text also appears in Jesús Iribarren, ed., *Documentos colectivos del episcopado español, 1870–1974* (Madrid: Biblioteca de Autores Cristianos, 1974), 249–57.

It is an undeniable fact today that in the world of ideas and customs, the modern means of communication—the press, the cinema, the theater, and radio—have a powerful and dominating influence. They constitute something like a hinge on which society now turns, for they form ideas, and thus they guide humanity, leading it or misleading it.

The periodical press in particular disseminates ideas, manufactures reputations (good or bad), propagates either scandals and infamies or noble ideas, destroys or defends authority, religion, moral sense, even public order and the stability of international affairs. Moreover, the filmmaker, despite obviously being a powerful force for good and evil (and as a professor from Prague who studies the cinema put it, "the most powerful dominator of minds, hearts, and consciences"), nevertheless remains dependent on the press. . . . Without publicity today, no work of art can survive, no form of business can develop; and publicity is largely in the hands of the press, especially daily newspapers.

On the other hand it is an undeniable fact, and one worthy of tears of blood, that all these modern forms of progress, in themselves either good or indifferent, are frequently, indeed mostly, used for evil, as an instrument of corruption and disorder.

Everyone can see the immense damage that bad writers cause. . . . There is no sword, no rifle, no machine gun, that kills as many bodies as the pen of a bad writer kills souls. And there are, unfortunately, so many!

Studies and surveys on the havoc that the cinema wreaks in its wicked work of corrupting minds and misleading spirits are truly stunning; so much that, in 1916, an official of the Spanish Supreme Court, in assessing the previous year's crime rate, made no mistake in calling the cinema "a school for criminals." And the Twelfth Congress of the Russian Communist Party proclaimed: "The cinema must be a powerful means of communist agitation and education."

Regarding plays, the great [Jacques-Bénigne] Bossuet [French prelate and political theorist, 1627–1704], with all his authority and skill, affirmed that the theater had been, with rare exceptions, a school for immorality and a cause of decadence in all times and countries.

Finally, as for radio broadcasting—an admirable portent of our times—one cannot deny that it is often an excellent means of culture and true progress, even serving religion; but along with all that, such frivolity and sensuality! So much influence, deception, and revolutionary propaganda! . . .

Now it often happens that certain literary or artistic works of obviously impious or immoral character are written or produced with such art and style that they seduce many incautious Christians who, through the lure and the bait of literary or artistic beauty, swallow the fatal and corrupting poison. . . .

More than once, these problems have led the Church to intervene and sound the alarm, especially through the Sacred Congregation of the Holy Office, whose job it is to watch out for and prohibit publications that threaten faith or customs. . . .

The Holy Office has properly pointed out, in its message of May 3, 1927, that immoral and obscene things, however artistically they may be presented, are still immoral and obscene. Moreover, the artistic form in which they are presented is a new and powerful incentive to uncontrollable passions. That document denounces the terrible dangers and the damage that this wave of obscene, pornographic, and provocative literature is causing. . . .

Catholic critics and writers should refrain from praising even the purely literary or artistic parts of immoral or heterodox books, plays, or films, for this constitutes a temptation to their readers. Especially in periodicals of general interest, speaking of reproachable aspects [and] praising artistic values necessarily leads many to read the work or see the production.

63. Law of the Fundamental Principles of the Nationalist Movement (1958)

As the Franco regime continued evolving in the 1950s, subtly recasting itself to suit changing times, it issued this statement of the regime's fundamental principles. Careful observers could see some movement away from the regime's Falangist outlook of the 1930s and 1940s toward a more traditional form of conservatism.

SOURCE: Fernando Díaz-Plaja, ed., *La posguerra española en sus documentos* (Madrid: Plaza and Janés, 1970), 330–33.

I, Francisco Franco Bahamonde, Caudillo of Spain, aware of my responsibility before God and history, in presence of the Cortes of the kingdom, promulgate the following principles of the national movement, understood as the community of all Spaniards in the ideals that gave life to the crusade:

1. Spain is a unity of destiny in the universal. The service of unity, grandeur, and liberty of the fatherland is a sacred duty and a collective task of all Spaniards.

2. The Spanish nation considers respect for the law of God a sign of honor, following the doctrine of the Catholic, apostolic, and Roman Holy Church, the only true church and the faith that is inseparable from the national consciousness. . . .

4. Unity among the men and lands of Spain is beyond question. The integrity of the fatherland and its independence are supreme demands of the national community. . . .

6. The natural entities of social life are the family, the municipality, and the syndicate, basic structures of the national community. Institutions and corporations of any other character that satisfy social demands of a general interest must be protected so that they may participate effectively in the attainment of the national community's goals.

7. The Spanish people, united in a state of law, informed by the ideas of authority, liberty, and service, constitute the national state. Spain's political form is . . . a traditional, Catholic, social, and representative monarchy.

8. The people's participation in the task of legislation and other functions of a general interest will take place through the family, the municipality, the syndicate, and other entities of organic representation that the laws will recognize for this purpose. Any political organization of any kind that falls outside this representative system will be considered illegal.

9. All Spaniards have the right to an independent judicial system that is free of charge for the needy; to a general and professional education which can never be forgone for lack of material means; to the benefits of social

security and assistance; to an equitable share of the national income and tax burden. The Christian ideal of social justice . . . will inspire policy and laws.

10. Labor is recognized as the origin of the hierarchy, duty, and honor of the Spaniards, and all forms of private property are recognized as a right contingent on their social use. Private initiative, the basis of economic activity, must be stimulated, guided, and if need be, supplemented by the action of the state.

64. Pilar Primo de Rivera, On the Rights of Working Women (1961)

The Franco regime is known for its traditionalistic views on women, but it also allowed the Women's Section of the Falange, headed by José Antonio's sister Pilar, to play an important role, organizing activities and programs for women. For some observers, the Women's Section served to advance women's interests in Spain, while in others' view it helped control and indoctrinate women and preempt any sort of real feminist movement. On July 22, 1961, Pilar, who was in the Cortes representing the Women's Section, gave this speech there in support of new legislation offering women greater legal equality in the workplace.

SOURCE: *La mujer en la nueva sociedad* (Madrid: Ediciones del Movimiento, 1963), 89–91.

I wish to explain very briefly the reasons why the Women's Section of the Falange has presented this law to the Cortes. It is by no means a feminist law: we would be unfaithful to José Antonio if we did such a thing. It is only a law of justice for women who work, born from the experience of a diligent, cordial, and human relationship with all the problems that concern women. In no way do we wish to make men and women equal beings: neither by nature nor by the objectives of life will they ever be equal, but we do ask that when fulfilling the same functions they have equal rights. Women working is a real and universal fact of life we cannot ignore, and it is precisely because of that fact that we ask . . . that a woman forced to work out of necessity should be able to do so in the best possible conditions; so the law, instead of being feminist, is . . . a support that men offer to women, as a weaker vessel, to make their life easier.

What more could we want than that the man's wages should be lucrative enough that the woman, above all the married woman, should not have to work out of necessity? I assure you that if family life were sufficiently endowed, 90 percent of women would not work. For us it is much more comfortable and desirable to have all problems resolved for us. But there is an unlimited number of families, not only in Spain but also throughout the world, that cannot do without the woman's earnings, precisely so that the attention and education of the children, the primary purpose of marriage, should be sufficient. For this reason, it seems to me, this law is appropriate, as it regulates an existing fact.

On the other hand . . . we have taken all the necessary precautions so that this law will not disturb the life of the marriage. For us the law of God is sacred; perhaps it is the Church that has supported our intentions most warmly. . . . Besides, we are convinced that in protecting the work, and above all the studies, of the woman, we are not committing any offense; an educated, cultured, and sensible woman . . . is a much better educator of her children and a better companion for her husband. We have in the Women's Section thousands of examples of our comrades in universities, and their families are models of understanding and comprehension. The woman, as José Antonio said, cannot be limited to being "a silly object of flattery." Her fundamental virtue, self-sacrifice, can be developed much more consciously and efficiently if she has an educational foundation. But it is a fact that there are many women, single or widowed, whose lives cannot be at the mercy of the generosity or stinginess of their relatives; they can and must live on their own, and if, for example, we have applied the same exams and standards for women in universities as for men, then we must give them the same opportunities. In fair competition, let the one with the most merit win; in any case, Spain will benefit from a raising of cultural levels as those competing have to try all that much harder. . . .

Thank you very much, and please be assured that what you are approving is just. . . . This is also what the Caudillo wants us to do. *Arriba España!*

65. Luis Buñuel, On *Viridiana* (1962)

Like many of Spain's twentieth-century artists, filmmaker Luis Buñuel spent much of his career abroad. Born in 1900, he began working in Paris in the late 1920s—establishing himself as a leading surrealist filmmaker—but for much of his career the Franco regime's strict censorship forced him to remain abroad. In 1961, as Franco's government was seeking to prove that artistic freedom existed in Spain, officials invited Buñuel to return to Spain to make a film. Buñuel accepted (despite protests from some of his colleagues), and amid minimal interference from the authorities, he made *Viridiana* in 1961. Those authorities had not seen the film before it was rushed off to compete as an official Spanish entry in the Cannes Film Festival, where it won the Palme d'Or.

When Spanish officials saw the film, however, they were appalled at its treatment of religion and its images of suicide and sexual obsession. The film was banned in Spain, and those responsible for inviting Buñuel to return were fired. Buñuel's decision to work in Spain then began to look like a shrewd act of resistance to Franco. Here Buñuel explains the ideas behind the film.

SOURCE: Luis Buñuel, "Out of a Cinema Credo," *New York Times*, March 18, 1962, II, 7:7, copyright © 1962 New York Times Co. Reprinted by permission of the *New York Times*.

Viridiana follows most closely my personal traditions in filmmaking since I made *L'Age d'or* thirty years ago. In all my work, these are the two films which I directed with the greatest feeling of freedom. I have been more or less successful with my films, some of which, to be sure, have been banal. For myself I must say that I made them just to make a living. Equally, however, I must say, also, that I have always refused to make concessions and I have fought for the principles which were dear to me.

I went back to Spain from Mexico because that is my country and I could work there with total freedom. I did work there on *Viridiana* with that freedom. What followed was one of the pieces of nonsense that time will take care of.

We do not live in the best of all possible worlds. I would like to continue to make films which, apart from entertaining the audience, convey to people the absolute certainty of this idea. In making such films I believe that my intentions would be highly constructive. Today movies, including the so-called neo-realistic, do not make it clear that we do not live in the best of all possible worlds.

How is it possible to hope for an improvement in the audiences—and consequently in the producers—when consistently we are told in these films, including even the most insipid comedies, that our social institutions, our concepts of country, religion, love, etc., are, while perhaps imperfect, unique and necessary? The true "opium of the audience" is conformity.

In none of the traditional arts exists such a wide gap between the possibilities of what can be done and the facts of what is being done, as in the cinema. Motion pictures act directly upon the spectator. To the spectator, persons and things on the screen become concrete.

In the darkness they isolate him from his usual psychic atmosphere. Because of this the cinema is capable of stirring the spectator as perhaps no other art. But as no other art can, it is also capable of stupefying him. The great majority of today's films seem to have exactly that purpose. They thrive in an intellectual and moral vacuum. They imitate the novel. Films repeat over and over the same stories.

However, for myself, looking across the years I must insist that I have not tried to prove anything and that I do not use the cinema as a pulpit from which I should like to preach. I realize that perhaps I will be disappointing a great many with this statement. But I know that people will draw from *Viridiana* and from my other films many symbols and many meanings.

I want to make some comments about my film *Viridiana*. I feel that it is very Spanish, and it must be understood that Viridiana was a little-known saint who lived in the period of St. Francis of Assisi. The story is born of this situation: a young woman, drugged by an old man, is at his mercy, whereas in other circumstances he could never be able to hold her in his arms. I thought that this woman had to be pure and so I made her a novice preparing to take the final vows.

I know I have been criticized for having shown a knife in the shape of a crucifix. One finds them everywhere in Spain and I saw many of them in Albacete. I didn't invent them. It is the photography which stresses the malice and the surrealistic character of an object fabricated innocently and put into mass production. I am also reproached for my cruelty. Where is it in the film? The novice proves her humanity. The old man, a complicated human being, is capable of kindness toward human beings and toward a lowly bee whose life he does not hesitate to rescue.

In reality, *Viridiana* is a picture of black humor, without doubt corrosive, but unplanned and spontaneous, in which I express certain erotic and religious obsessions of my childhood. I belong to a very Catholic family and from the age of eight to fifteen I was brought up by Jesuits. However for me, religious education and surrealism have left their marks all through my life.

Concerning *Viridiana* once again: I think that it has in it most of the themes which are closest to me and which are my most cherished interests.

66. Dionisio Ridruejo, On Resistance to Franco (1962)

The relationship between Franco and the Falange had always been complex. The two shared a hatred for the republic in the 1930s, and Falangists were eager participants on the Nationalist side in the Civil War. Yet the Falange was devoted to a complex blend of right-wing ideology and vaguely leftist demands for modernization and social change, whereas Franco was a more traditional Catholic conservative opposed to nearly every hint of modernity or social change. During the war, Franco effectively absorbed the Falange into his National Movement—a process greatly aided by the left's execution of José Antonio Primo de Rivera, the Falange's charismatic founder and leader—and from that point on the Falange was an essentially subdued and controlled shadow of what José Antonio and his core followers had wanted it to be.

Resentment over Franco's traditionalistic policies and his treatment of the Falange, however, eventually led to tensions between devoted Falangists and Franco, and as early as the 1940s some Falangists broke with the regime. Their opposition is exemplified and described here by a passage from a 1962 book by one former Falangist, the poet and activist Dionisio Ridruejo. Ridruejo had supported the regime as late as 1950, when he was serving as a correspondent for the Francoist newspaper *Arriba* in Italy, but perhaps because of his experiences living in that country (which had made the transition from fascist dictatorship to parliamentary democracy), Ridruejo became disillusioned with Franco's government and began working for change in Spain. The opposition of former comrades such as Ridruejo often proved more troubling than that of easily dismissible groups such as the Communists, and the regime did not always move against them as decisively as it did against other opponents.

SOURCE: Dionisio Ridruejo, *Escrito en España* (Buenos Aires: Editorial Losada, 1962), 28–29.

In the year 1954, I began making contacts with groups of young people, mostly university students, who offered me new perspectives on plans for the future, less simple but also less clear than those I had presented. I helped one of these groups work within the university, organizing decisive acts and trying to promote some kind of association that would be both intellectual and political. In 1956, in February, a plan was prepared for a student campaign demanding the professionalization and democratization of the Syndicate of Spanish Students [an official student union under the government's control], as well as for the calling of a national congress of young writers.

I presided over the meeting at which agreement was reached on a text to be submitted for signature by the students of Madrid, at a time when, as I noticed, the government was scowling threateningly, continually issuing severe warnings. . . . I warned my young friends that in all probability we would end up in jail, which, in terms of its effects as a form of agitation, could be more useful than gathering signatures or circulating manifestos.

And so it turned out. The young loyal Falangists [supporters of the Franco regime] reacted violently against the gathering of signatures. There were blows and attacks on sacred symbols. This brought a new reaction, assaults on the university—this time by armed Falangist adults. More blows and the intervention of the army. Finally the matter spilled into the streets, and during a clash between student demonstrators [opposed to the official student union] and a troop of young Falangists a shot rang out—from where it is still not known—and one of the Falangists fell injured. [The Falangist appears to have been shot accidentally by a fellow Falangist during the melee.] That night other Falangists kept an armed watch and wrote up lists for possible handgun executions. The following day the government, through the press, officially displayed me to the country and the world as a member of the opposition. After a month and a half of jail, contacts, which had been difficult a month earlier, became child's play. . . .

A few months after my leaving jail, a group of young people from the most diverse backgrounds . . . asked me to look into the possibility of forming with them a group that would take a leading role in renewal, a group of progressive orientation, culturally liberal, politically democratic, economically neosocialist. This was exactly the orientation that corresponded to my ideas, and so without any great pretensions, and aware that the path would be long and the operation bound to involve great sacrifice, we formed the Social Party of Democratic Action, which soon became known simply as Democratic Action. It was neither a political party nor an intellectual organization. It was, with something of both of those things, a center for promotion and action that did not restrict the future decisions of its participants—some of whom were more liberal and others more socialist—but perhaps it would serve to fix the guidelines of a social sector that was neither narrowly class-based nor too amorphous.

The group, lacking economic resources and navigating like a clandestine boat through the passivity of the environment, has certainly not become a danger to the system. But it has been and will continue to be a small focal point that will perhaps not survive the task of opening up a new perspective in Spain, but which will remain—as I will too—fully justified if it should make some contribution to that task. . . .

Carried out in three phases, brutal repression reached a scale whose extent escapes my calculations, but which we must qualify as crushing, both quantitatively and qualitatively.

Regarding informal or spontaneous repression, all the militias, security forces, and opportunistic groups entered into a tragic competition, under the tutelage of authorities who either acquiesced to or inspired that repression, and also with instigation and denunciation by reactionary priesthoods and rural caciques. After the first months [of the dictatorship] the army took exclusive control of the repression, formalizing it through the War Councils, except when it was exercised directly by occupying forces.

Even later, and for many years, it would be directed by . . . the so-called Special Judges of repression. But even as it went through three phases it maintained a single central intention: the physical destruction of the framework of the parties of the Popular Front, the labor unions, and the Masonic organizations, without forgetting about the most moderate democratic parties and the independent personalities who, in the intellectual or professional world, had a reputation of being leftists or decidedly liberal. If, to the abundant number of those executed or condemned to crushing prison terms, we add the number of those who, opting for emigration, managed to save themselves from the flames at the price of losing all contact with their country, then we can speak of a perfect operation of eradication of the political forces that had overseen and sustained the republic, and who represented advanced social currents or simply democratic and liberal currents of opinion.

67. The Nationalist Movement, *The Woman in the New Society* (1963)

Despite the Franco regime's deeply traditionalist view of women's proper place in Spanish society, the Falangist Women's Section, headed by Pilar Primo de Rivera, remained an important voice on women's affairs under Franco. Her ideas, like those of her brother, José Antonio, reflect a mixture of conservative and progressive approaches, as one can see in a 1963 book on women. The book lists no author, but it is published by the "movement" (Franco's national party), and the ideas are those of Pilar or a close associate.

SOURCE: *La mujer en la nueva sociedad* (Madrid: Ediciones del Movimiento, 1963), 5–9, 19–21, 37–39, 59–61, 63–65, 75–77.

The question of what function women should fulfill in future society calls for two kinds of responses. On the one hand, those concerning the woman's role in the socioeconomic order, and on the other hand, those concerning the woman's role as a subject of rights, that is to say, as a fully capable human being, in whose name one calls for legal actions that have long been conceded to men as a privilege.

As for the first kind of responses, it is interesting to note the close parallel that exists, historically, between the evolution of industry starting in 1848 and the series of legal dispositions that have concerned women since that date. The industrial revolution, initially produced by the appearance of the machine, and later by the use of electric energy in industry, and even later, in our own times, by the entry into the industrial world of atomic energy and automation, brought with it, at first, a loss of the qualitative respect for human labor. This was later corrected, and it is still being corrected, but what is important for our purposes is that management, considering human labor an endeavor for which it is not necessary to have much professional training, concluded that a woman was just as well suited to do this work as a man was. . . .

At the dawn of the twentieth century, women were engaged in a battle, for having already obtained the right to work, they wished to obtain other rights and exercise them fully. This they also achieved. The world wars, especially the second one, forced all the participating countries to put all their productive capacity to work. Almost simultaneously, the first women in military uniform appeared in London and Berlin, driving trucks, serving in military offices, or replacing men in the factories. As payment for this contribution, society finally accepted that in principle women had the same abilities as men to carry out important social functions, with the exception of those requiring special physical condition. Today we can already see women who are ministers, governors, and mayors throughout the world. . . . One must admit that women's efforts have been notable and beautiful. . . .

In Spain, women's progress toward their complete acquisition of dignity has been more tentative than in other countries, owing primarily to our economic backwardness, but also to other less acceptable reasons, such as the dead weight of social prejudices. . . . The Second Republic, which failed in this, as in other questions, to the disgrace of all Spaniards, nonetheless managed a certain measure of progress. The female intellectual, although at times taken to an excessive degree, was a republican creation. There had never been a sufficient number of young ladies in our universities until the republic. On the other hand, working women, stirred up by communist movements, also broke free of many bonds, even if the brutal excesses of subversion ended up . . . leading women away from a properly feminine condition.

But it was beginning in 1936, with the National Revolution, when the Spanish woman managed to make decisive gains. The name of an institution, the Women's Section of the Spanish Falange, proved to be the axis around which the entire present and future reality of the women of Spain turns. The Women's Section, which had its baptism of fire in the hard work of the war, and which so often proved its capacity for sacrifice and struggle, is today one of the most authentic realities of Spain. Without excessive measures or unseemly methods, the Women's Section has created a new kind of woman in our fatherland. . . . This kind of athletic, healthy, happy, cultured, and serious woman whom the Women's Section has created is the model for the Spanish woman of the future. . . .

There is a kind of Spanish girl we all know: simultaneously pretty and hardworking, . . . cordial and serious, concerned over these little feminine things . . . [such as] clothing and children, girlfriends and lipstick, but also concerned about the problems of her country, her society, her compatriots, and the whole world. This kind of girl, whose kind has been growing more and more common . . . has been the creation of the Women's Section. In contrast to that great number of careless and ordinary women of which there are so many in our country, and in contrast to all those other women who, because of their defective education, demonstrate their ignorance of the world, these girls of the Women's Section are precisely the role models for the Spanish woman of the future. . . .

The Women's Section has produced journalists, athletes, professors, artists, and at the same time, has produced cooks, dressmakers, farmers, and artisans. Seventy percent of the women in universities—the best 70 percent—are its creation, as are 70 percent of the peasant women. . . . This difficult combination of tradition and modernity . . . has been carried out by the Women's Section. . . .

The Woman and the Family

Of all the functions a woman can fulfill in life, there is none more important than her role as a mother. This is the basis of her character as the foundation of the family, which is itself the essential unit of society. This affirmation does not contradict the outlines of a modern policy that elevates feminine dignity in the world of work and culture. We believe that, quite to the contrary, the greater the woman's knowledge and vital capacities are, the more able she will be to carry out her role in the heart of the family. . . .

The woman whose family situation does not create special obligations—whether because she is a widow, or simply because she has completed the period of the upbringing of her children, who have become independent—must face life with all the abilities and rights that belong to her as a human being. That is to say that the woman must enjoy all the social and professional rights, so we therefore applaud any policy in our fatherland that elevates the woman and makes her equal. But when a woman's domestic duties concern her family, the fulfillment of these duties must take precedence over any other duties. For this reason, the supreme social priority of a woman's work in the home must be recognized, and society must always make it possible, even in the case in which economic circumstances may force her to alternate her family duties with the demands of work outside the home. . . .

It seems natural . . . to say that the man is the one who should support his family by working. . . . So we believe that society should offer its greatest possible assistance to the family, by supporting the work of the head of the family, protecting him from the consequences of a shortage of income and the extraordinary expenses of child-raising and education. . . . But it would be absurd to deny that this is not always possible, and that the work of the married woman is an increasingly common fact of life in today's world. Given this, it is proper to watch over the form in which this work takes place, so that it does not prevent the woman from fulfilling her role in life and her family duties. The most valuable contribution to the common good a woman can make is the personal effort she must make within the family, and so society must be concerned with this, first of all by supplying facilities and helping her through all possible means, namely, through measures to support the head of the family, or to support her directly when the nature of a particular necessary feminine professional activity calls for a compatibility of the two. What would not be fair or reasonable would be for society to be indifferent to circumstances that make the woman's domestic duties even more difficult, preventing her from fulfilling the highest duties entrusted to her.

The Woman and Feminism

The term "feminism" is now more than fifty years old, and it is linked in people's memory with those old photos in the illustrated magazines, which showed suffragettes marching through the streets of European capitals. . . . Yet feminism did not die when women's suffrage was recognized as a right. . . . In all civilized countries, women learned to organize themselves, to participate in public life, and to demand that they be useful in it. As with all human affairs, women's liberation movements were a historical step forward, and no one any longer denies, except in a few places in Asia, an indisputable fact: that the woman is a human being and a citizen capable of exercising and enjoying all of a person's rights.

The libertarian revolutions—communism above all—brought a new conception of the woman. Taking to the furthest limits the cry of the old suffragettes, women began dressing as soldiers, getting drunk in bars, hoisting machine guns, and turning themselves into that sad, beastly, and lamentable picture, the "militia woman," which later, even in Russia itself, gradually began to be erased once the horrifying implications of the image began reaching the most responsible minds.

One must be careful in speaking of these feminist excesses, because those who would like to keep women reduced to the condition of servants usually defend their position by saying they are "saving women's dignity." Behind such high-sounding declarations, what is really going on is often to continue locking all the doors of society to women, preventing them from taking an active role in the adventure of humanity.

José Antonio spoke quite beautifully of flattery as a kind of bribe. It is the custom of all those who defend themselves against the liberation of the woman by all available means to believe that slavery, or perhaps servitude and ostracism, can be compensated for with gallant flattery. We favor neither the "militia woman" nor the woman locked inside the home. The Christian world, which elevated respect for the woman to the highest possible level, has in mind another type of woman, one free and worthy, lively and serious at the same time, which men such as Fray Luis de León described once and for all. The wife is the Western ideal of the woman. But the active and free wife, justly treated as a person, professionally capable, socially active, takes up a role in society, not as a piece of furniture, but as a human being. . . .

Women and Culture

According to custom, which is not always just, despite being grounded in an obvious historical reality, women have not been given enough consideration in cultural matters in our community. It seems that in our collective psychology two strains clash regarding women. On the one hand, perhaps because of our Oriental heritage we like women to be ignorant and silent, staying in the home, but not in a free and dignified way, but rather in the submissive way that the masculine will demands. Those casinos restricted to men in the southern part of Spain and those cities whose nightlife seems reserved to young carousers and shady old men represent . . . a selfish sensibility. The woman for the man, but not with the man, as the Arabic proverb says, is still the prevailing way in many places. Yet time has gradually planted doubts in men's minds. The active presence of women in other countries' societies has created a positive kind of envy. . . . It is obvious that the newer idea has triumphed, fortunately, creating a dilemma, and we now wish that our women be decidedly and totally integrated into the life of the country. . . .

Women's access to universities has been difficult throughout the Western world, and in Spain . . . it has been doubly slow and difficult. It is true that even today the Spanish woman is not sufficiently represented in elite circles of high culture. In comparison with other Western countries, the number of Spanish women studying in universities is small, and even smaller is the number of women dedicated to high cultural work, to scientific investigation and teaching, although it is in the latter field that the most progress has been made. This produces a doubly negative phenomenon: on the one hand, women feel delayed, obstructed, hamstrung, and . . . on the other hand, the country is prevented from having a larger share of its population be more highly cultured. . . .

It seems as if there were some tacit social convention that prohibits women from doing certain things. In the name of what principles such distinctions are made is something that is not clearly understood, but the hard fact of the matter is that a woman biologist, professor of economics, or engineer strikes people as strange in our country, producing reactions of a lack of confidence, of alarm, sometimes even of humor.

This is not really how it should be in these times. We believe that except in those physical activities that truly demand that men exercise them exclusively, women have sufficient ability and the undeniable right to take part [in all activities]. Out of justice, primarily, and because it is necessary for the common good, secondly and essentially.

Women in Rural Society

There is a well-known image of the peasant woman, not only in our country, but also in other places throughout the world, one in which dark and sad colors have been carefully brought out. This woman, old before her time and wasting away, with sunken eyes and hands worn out by work, with her head covered by a dark scarf is, nevertheless . . . something that, all literary exaggeration aside, still exists in our country and others. . . . We would not be truthful if we denied it, and if we did not recognize that in Spain, though many things have changed, this painful type of woman that we would like to see soon converted into a memory of the novelists continues to exist.

This reality has many causes. . . . There are those social prejudices of which we have often spoken . . . [and] the lack of health care in poverty-stricken areas has turned maternity into a tragedy for peasant women. . . . To this we can add disastrous educational conditions, almost completely absent in some regions and very poor in others. A countryside bypassed by modernization, the scarcity of doctors and other health-care workers, the difficulties of transportation and the lack of communication with the outside world have for many years affected the peasant woman much more than the man, who, because of his labor and his privileges possessed some means of developing his personality and feeling truly free.

Currently, things have been improving a great deal. Not only because of initiatives directly seeking to improve the condition of peasant women—especially those of the Women's Section—but also through general changes in the country, through the growth of systems of communication and transportation, through technical improvements in rural labor and the constant creation of schools and health clinics. But all is not done. . . . Many of the tasks of transformation of Spain's agrarian structures . . . must truly seek the redemption of the peasant woman, attending to her cultural and social education and facilitating her access to active levels of common life. Above all, keeping in mind that if women's presence is necessary in all orders of national life, it is especially necessary in rural settings, where the home, the special territory of the woman, retains all its vigor . . . and which women must sustain for most of the year because of the physical absence of the man, who remains in the fields all day. . . .

Tradition and Modernity

Life demands a continual rejuvenation . . . but everything is not susceptible to change. In the world there are certain constants, certain principles that . . . give a foundation and cohesion, a pattern, a meaning, and an end to life. These principles cannot vary with time because they are immutable and eternal. . . .

The difficulty of balance consists in this: in knowing how to distinguish the fundamental from the contingent, . . . what is immutable from what is variable. The desire to be modern and to be up to date cannot permit us to disdain all that is given to us. . . . Change cannot mean a loss of essence. . . . The problem of all periods is that of knowing how to reconcile these constants with modernity.

It is in the family life that this problem presents itself most acutely, because in it one always sees these fundamental principles of religiousness and respect, which are the norms of human life. The work of the woman and the mother in this sense is much more important than one might suspect. The woman has a very keen sense of what concerns modernity. The woman is always up to date, and this is indeed one of her continual concerns. Yet on the other hand, she is the faithful guardian of the traditional, of the intimate that cannot vary, of the fundamental dictates of a Catholic and permanent conception of life. This is why the woman's role in the home is so important.

68. The Abbot of Montserrat, "The Regime Calls Itself Christian" (1963)

By the early 1960s, opposition to Franco's rule was beginning to surface in many areas of Spanish society. Given Franco's close relationship with the Catholic Church over the years, it was surprising when a few Spanish priests began voicing their misgivings about the regime in the 1960s. That development reflected new attitudes within the Catholic Church, as the Vatican itself began articulating social concerns in unprecedented ways, but it also reflected resentment toward Franco's policies in regions such as Catalonia, where the government forbade the use of the Catalan language. One notable example of such opposition to Franco was this interview that a Catalan monk, Aurelio M. Escarré, gave to the French newspaper *Le Monde* in 1963. Spain's bishops and archbishops, however, remained staunch supporters of Franco's regime, and after they relieved the abbot of his duties as punishment for this interview, he fled Spain.

SOURCE: José Antonio Novais, "Le régime se dit chrétien mais n'obéit pas aux principes de base du christianisme," *Le Monde*, November 14, 1963. Reprinted by permission of *Le Monde*.

In the heart of Catalonia, a mountain rises almost vertically out of the plains, one whose strange shape has earned it the name Montserrat (split mountain). According to tradition, the Virgin appeared on one of its peaks, and the holy mountain then became a sacred site visited by a million pilgrims each year, as well as the spiritual home of almost all Catalans. . . .

Watched over by the image and floating among the clouds, on a side of the mountain, is a Benedictine monastery, a focal point for people of the most diverse walks of life, a center of culture that goes beyond the limits of Catalonia and even those of Spain. The soul of this Benedictine community today is the very reverend father Abbot Dom Aurelio M. Escarré. Twenty years in the service of the monks, the reconstruction of a community mutilated by the Civil War (twenty-six monks were murdered in the Republican zone), an intense spiritual life, and a serious illness have not managed to extinguish the fire in the eyes of this fifty-four-year-old abbot, whose passionate voice cannot hide a certain sweetness.

Dom Escarré has been the first authority in the Spanish hierarchy, perhaps the only one, to stand up and denounce the existing contradiction, in his view, between the evangelical truth and the Spanish regime.

"Where there is no real liberty there is no justice, and this is what is happening in Spain," he said in one of his recent homilies. . . .

He welcomed us paternally, with all the love that the sons of Saint Benedict show a guest, who in their eyes symbolizes Christ the pilgrim.

LE MONDE: What does Your Holiness think about the current moment in Spain?

FATHER ESCARRÉ: Spain, and this is the great problem, continues to be divided in two parts. We do not have twenty-five years of peace behind us, but rather twenty-five years of victory. The victors, including the Church, which was forced to fight alongside the victors, have done nothing to end this division between victors and vanquished. This represents one of the most regrettable failures of a regime that calls itself Christian, but one in which the state does not obey the basic principles of Christianity.

The majority of its leaders are honorable and are well-meaning Catholics, but they do not see clearly what it is to be Christian in regard to political principles. They have not reflected upon the [papal] encyclical *Pacem in Terris* [Peace on Earth, a 1963 encyclical of Pope John XXIII calling for peace among individuals and nations], which is the evangelical and traditional expression of our time; in the light of that document, the primary subversion that exists in Spain is its government.

LE MONDE: Why, in Your Holiness's view, is the Spanish state not Christian?

FATHER ESCARRÉ: The people must be able to choose their government and be able to change it if they wish; this is liberty. Freedom of the press, a sincere freedom of information, is needed. . . . The government does not have the right to abuse its power; it must be an administrator acting in the name of God and a servant of the people. The lack of information is contrary to the doctrine of the Church, and that should present problems of conscience to the Catholic leaders of a state, which, if it does not change its political principles, cannot call itself Catholic. . . . I have taken a great interest, and I continue to take an interest, in the political prisoners, whose existence constitutes one of the most embarrassing aspects of the regime. Their presence in the prisons stands in direct relation with this peace that the state has not managed to establish. For the moment what is most worrying is those nonbelieving prisoners in the penitentiary at Burgos, who are in solitary confinement for having followed their consciences, refusing to attend mass. . . .

LE MONDE: Montserrat is the most important center of Catalan culture and the most popular site as well. How does the abbot see the monastery?

FATHER ESCARRÉ: History has made us into the spiritual center and the national sanctuary of Catalonia. Following in the footsteps of my predecessor, Abbot Marcet, I have tried to see to it that the monks have a solid knowledge of all that the evangelical law puts into practice. Montserrat, which is on the margins of the world, takes an interest in the world and in the present time; above all, we maintain contact with the people, and perhaps it is for this reason that we think about many matters. . . .

Catalonia is one of the typical examples that can illustrate the encyclical [*Pacem in Terris*] in regard to its references to ethnic minorities. The state must favor these minorities and their cultural life. The regime is hampering the development of Catalan culture. Using the legally recognized right of petition, I myself, with one hundred other persons, wrote a letter a few months ago to the vice president of the government, Captain General Muñoz Grandes, asking him for full liberty for Catalan culture. We still have not received any reply.

[To speak the Catalan language] has until now been our right as Catalans. . . . To defend one's language is not only a duty but a necessity; when the language is lost, religion has a tendency to be lost as well. This has happened in other places. . . .

LE MONDE: It is said that the Catalans are separatists.

FATHER ESCARRÉ: The great majority of the Catalans are not separatists. Catalonia is one nation among the nationalities of Spain. We have a right, like any other minority, to our culture, to our history, to our customs, which have their own personality within Spain. We are Spaniards, not Castilians.

LE MONDE: Does Your Holiness believe that the [Second Vatican] Council has influence in Spain? [The Second Vatican Council, opened by Pope John XXIII in October 1962, produced many significant reforms in the Catholic Church.]

FATHER ESCARRÉ: The council is in a process of creating a new climate. One cannot live in the past; one must live in the present. I believe very much in tradition, but not in routine. The council confronts us with reality. We Spaniards have many good things and many bad things. We have to change the latter. The Spanish people have transformed themselves. Why haven't we? The Spanish people are much more European than is often realized, especially in the northern regions. . . . Yet the regime does nothing to favor this Europeanism. . . .

At first, the opposition feared another civil war, but now, after so many years and so many injustices, the people are irritated. . . . In principle no one wants a civil war, but I am not afraid. Everything depends on the circumstances. Neither the right nor the state has done anything to avoid another war. The government's legislation is, in general, proper, but the government does not execute the law. The standard of living has improved, but not the level of culture and education, nor the sense of mutual respect. The lack of social justice is frightening. I have recently been in Andalusia, and I have been able to see this for myself. . . .

The future depends on the way in which we resolve today's problems, which are social problems, problems of democracy, of liberty, and consequently, of justice. Basically, it is a problem of Christianity; to be or not to be true Christians, in the individual sense as well as in the collective sense, which is to say, the political sense. Collectively, our political leaders are not Christians.

I am only a monk; my mission consists of preaching the truth and in praying to God that it be made real.

69. ETA Communiqués (1970, 1973)

From its beginnings as a tiny opposition group in the 1950s, Euskadi Ta Askatasuna (Basqueland and Liberty) grew to worldwide fame (or infamy) because of a long series of spectacular bombings and assassinations. ETA rejected Sabino de Arana's conservatism for Marxist ideology, and it also exchanged Arana's racialist definition of the Basque people for a more inclusive view emphasizing knowledge of the Basque language. ETA's main goal has been to create an independent Basque country.

During Franco's rule, ETA battled the security forces of a regime that sought to restrict Basque culture and language. Many of Franco's opponents inside and outside Spain sympathized with ETA in those years, and when the government put sixteen alleged ETA members on trial in Burgos in December 1970 in retaliation for an assassination, sentencing nine of them to death, international protests led Franco to commute their sentences to life imprisonment. In 1973, ETA pulled off its most ambitious feat, assassinating Admiral Luis Carrero Blanco, whom Franco had chosen to perpetuate his system after he died.

SOURCE: The communiqués appeared in various newspapers; see, for example, "L'ETA: nous ne sommes pas une bande irresponsable," *Le Monde*, December 27, 1970, p. 3; "Cette opération est une juste riposte de la classe ouvrière à la mort de nos camarades," *Le Monde*, December 22, 1973, p. 2; they also appear in Fernando Díaz-Plaja, ed., *La España franquista en sus documentos (La posguerra española en sus documentos)* (Madrid: Plaza and Janés, 1976), 502, 522–23.

Communiqué of December 27, 1970

Our primary objective has been to save the life of our compatriots on trial in Burgos. It has been our intention to see to it that the whole world knows of the existence of our people and of our unbreakable will to struggle for their complete liberation, national independence, the reunification of the north and south of Euskadi [the Basque territories of both France and Spain], and the installation of a modern, democratic, and socialist Basque state. We believe that these two objectives have been reached, at least for the moment.

In deciding to return Mr. [Eugen] Beihl [West German consul in San Sebastián, kidnapped in December 1970 but released as part of a clandestine deal with the Spanish government] safe and sound to his family, we wished to show to our people and to the whole world that ETA is not an irresponsible, fanatical, and bloodthirsty band whose greatest pleasure would consist of killing anyone who fell into our hands, whether they were or were not a direct enemy of our cause. This is the image of us that the fascist imperialism of the Spanish state has vainly sought to project. They are the assassins, in the literal sense of the word, including when they seek to give their actions an institutional and legal appearance.

We have a morality, the revolutionary morality of the Basque people. To pursue it, we have executed Melitón Manzanas, chief of the politico-social brigade of the Guipúzcoa Police, struck down on 2 August 1968. Other "manzanas" will suffer the same fate. Let no one be fooled, and above all let our enemies not make the mistake of underestimating our revolutionary aims and our determination to see this to the end. If a single one of our brothers should fall, the reprisals we will take will be instantaneous, and their targets will be those persons who belong to the imperialist occupation force in southern Euskadi.

Communiqué of December 22, 1973

The Basque revolutionary socialist organization of national liberation, Euskadi Ta Askatasuna (ETA) assumes responsibility for the attack that today, Thursday, December 22, 1973, produced the death of Mr. Luis Carrero Blanco, president of the current Spanish government.

Throughout the struggle, in southern Euskadi and in the rest of the Spanish state, repression has clearly demonstrated its fascist character, detaining, jailing, torturing, and murdering those who fight for the liberty of their people.

In very little time the fascist criminal forces in the service of the high Spanish bourgeoisie have assassinated nine of our comrades . . . and other militants and Basque patriots for the simple reason of their having defended their most basic rights.

The operation that ETA has carried out against the Spanish oligarchy's machinery of power, in the person of Luis Carrero Blanco, must be viewed as a just revolutionary response of the working class and of all our Basque people to the deaths of our nine ETA comrades and to those of all who have contributed and are contributing to the securing of a humanity definitively liberated from all exploitation and oppression.

Luis Carrero Blanco—a "hard-liner," and one who was violent in his repressive acts—constituted the keystone that guaranteed the continuity and stability of the Francoist system; it is certain that without him the tensions, in the midst of the governing power, between the different tendencies loyal to the fascist regime of General Franco—Opus Dei,[1] Falange, etc.—will become dangerously sharper.

1. Opus Dei is a secretive Catholic organization founded in Spain in 1928; its members were active in university, business, and government circles during the Franco regime.

We therefore believe that our action carried out against the president of the Spanish government will doubtlessly signify a fundamental step forward in the struggle against national oppression and for socialism in Euskadi, and for the freedom of all those exploited and oppressed under the Spanish state.

Today the workers and all the people of Euskadi, of Spain, of Catalonia, and of Galicia, all the democrats, revolutionaries, and antifascists of the whole world—we all find ourselves liberated from an important enemy. The struggle continues. Ahead with national liberation and with socialism!

Gora Euskadi Askatuta!! [Long Live Free Basqueland!!]

Gora Euskadi Sozialista!! [Long Live Socialist Basqueland!!]

70. Women's Liberation Front, Founding Manifesto (1976)

When Franco died on November 20, 1975, those Spaniards who had opposed his regime looked toward their future with a mixture of hope and fear, the latter because of the possibility that his associates would manage to keep his system in place without him. Among the various groups seeking to create a wholly different kind of society in those crucial months was a group of Spanish feminists, who issued the following manifesto. The document reflects many of the same concerns and demands found in other Western countries in a decade when feminism was making unprecedented progress, but the movement naturally had much further to go in Spain, given that Franco's legislation—against divorce and contraception, for example—remained in force after his death.

SOURCE: María Angeles Duran, ed., *Mujeres y hombres: La formación del pensamiento igualitario* (Madrid: Editorial Castalia, 1993), 227–30.

In Madrid, on January 25, 1976, a group of feminist women formed the Frente de Liberación de la Mujer (Women's Liberation Front).

The FLM is an autonomous group, formed only by women, and independent of the political parties of the Spanish state and the sectoral organizations. We are autonomous because we women, as a specifically oppressed group, must take control of our own struggle, for history offers no example of any oppressed group having been emancipated without having waged its own struggle. That autonomy does not imply the division of the forces of the left. Division arises, instead, from constant negligence in the acts of defense of our real objectives, and from exclusions in the acceptance of all the feminine programs of demands, which tend to do no more than bring a partial improvement in our situation while still keeping us as a marginal group. Therefore, we do not want to take women away from their combat posts; we want, on the contrary, to recognize ourselves and be recognized as citizens with full rights and to align our own struggle with all the struggles of the exploited.

Although there has indeed been oppression of women in all societies, capitalism generates some specific forms of exploitation because it needs the existence of social sectors that are marginal to production, which it cannot absorb, while at the same time it needs a sector of society—women—that assures it the maintenance and reproduction of the labor force. For all those reasons, capitalism relegates women to the status of second-class citizens and uses the institution of the family to perpetuate private property and maintain and assure the social division of labor. Therefore, we affirm that the feminist struggle is directed against capitalism and the division of society into classes, and it seeks to secure a socialist society. We also believe that this society will only be truly socialist if within it the following objectives are met:

- Disappearance of all the structures of domination: economic, legal, and ideological.
- Suppression of the traditional family and of the economic and ideological relations it implies.
  - Elimination of the sexist division of labor.
  - Disappearance of the institution of marriage; in its place we propose free choice in the relationship between the sexes on a basis of equality.
  - Securing of freedom and awareness regarding maternity.
- Incorporation of all women into productive, political, and creative social tasks.
- Socialization of domestic work, of the education of children, and control over its execution by the whole of society.

We characterize the current political moment as a continuation of the Francoist dictatorship. In this situation, the feminist struggle is linked to the combined action of all the oppressed sectors for the securing of democratic liberties:

- Freedom of assembly, expression, association, strikes, and demonstrations.
- A general amnesty and the return of the exiles.
- Repeal of all existing legislation that discriminates against women and penalizes them.
- Repeal of the antiterrorist decree-law, special jurisdictions, the death penalty, and in general, all repressive legislation.
- Self-determination of the nationalities of the Spanish state.

Our struggle, whose ultimate objective is the destruction of capitalist and patriarchal society, takes shape at the present moment around the following list of demands:

- Equal pay for equal work.
- No female unemployment.
- Access to all employment positions with equal decision-making power.
- Equality of education and professional training within a system of co-education at all levels of teaching.

- The woman's right to control her own body, specifically meaning:
  - Free and legal contraceptives with ample information about them.
  - Sex education.
  - Free and legal abortion paid for by Social Security.
- Free day-care centers that function twenty-four hours a day, with specialized and responsible personnel.
- Public cafeterias in workplaces and neighborhoods.
- Equality of responsibility between men and women in domestic work.
- Elimination of moral double standards.
- Disappearance from the media of sexist roles and of the image of the woman as consumer and demander of consumption.
- Suppression of the discriminatory treatment women receive as a function of their civil status.

The FLM invites all women who are conscious of these issues to join it.

The FLM also wishes all groups of feminist women who are struggling for their liberation to unite for concrete action.

Women, unite for your liberation!!

71. The 1978 Constitution

The key moment in Spain's transition to democracy after Francisco Franco's death was the drafting of a new constitution. In June 1977, voters elected a Constituent Cortes, which entrusted the work of drafting a new text to a committee of seven deputies—including three from the governing Unión de Centro Democrático (Center Democratic Union), and one each from the Socialists, the Communists, a Catalan party, the Convergència i Unió (Convergence and Union) and the conservative Alianza Popular (People's Alliance). Unlike previous constitutions, then, this one would not simply be imposed by one victorious faction or party. The draft underwent several modifications, including the addition of references to the Catholic Church (following a campaign by Spain's bishops). The revised text was then put to a referendum in December 1978. Abstention was about one-third, with particularly high rates in the Basque region—where Basque nationalists dissatisfied with the text urged voters to abstain—but those who voted overwhelmingly supported the new constitution.

The text addressed many sensitive topics that had long divided the country, which is partly why it is such a long and complex document. At the time it seemed clear that a majority of Spaniards favored democracy, but the armed forces' willingness to allow democracy and fundamental social change in Spain still remained very much in doubt. Moreover, numerous topics—including the powers of regions such as Catalonia and the Basque country, the political role of the armed forces, the relationship between church and state, the rights of women, and the government's role in the economy—remained highly controversial, and so countless passages contained ambiguities that simply deferred the resolution of crucial matters. Such ambiguities are understandable given fundamental disagreements between those who felt that sweeping changes were long overdue and those wary of a return to what they viewed as Spain's tendency toward political extremism. The 1978 constitution, however, has had much to do with the success and durability of Spain's transition to democracy.

SOURCE: *El País* (Madrid), November 12, 1978.

Preamble

The Spanish nation, wishing to establish justice, liberty, and security, and to promote the well-being of all who are part of it, making use of its sovereignty, proclaims its will to:

Guarantee democratic coexistence within the constitution and the laws in accordance with a just economic and social order.

Consolidate a state of law [and] assure the law's effectiveness as an expression of the popular will.

Protect all the Spaniards and the peoples of Spain in the exercise of their human rights, cultures and traditions, languages, and institutions.

Promote the progress of culture and the economy to assure everyone a suitable quality of life.

Establish an advanced democratic society, and

Collaborate in the strengthening of peaceful relations and effective cooperation among all the peoples of the earth.

Consequently, the Cortes approves and the Spanish people ratify the following constitution.

Preliminary Title

Article 1

1. Spain is constituted as a social and democratic state of law, which proclaims liberty, justice, equality, and political pluralism as the highest values of its legal order.

2. National sovereignty resides in the Spanish people, from whom all the powers of the state emanate.

3. The political form of the Spanish state is a parliamentary monarchy.

Article 2

The constitution is based on the indissoluble unity of the Spanish nation, the common and indivisible fatherland of all Spaniards, and it recognizes and guarantees both the right of autonomy of the nationalities and regions that make it up and solidarity among all of them.

Article 3

1. Castilian [Spanish] is the official Spanish language of the state. All Spaniards have the duty to know it and the right to use it.

2. The other Spanish languages shall also be official in the respective autonomous communities in accordance with their statutes.

3. The richness of Spain's different linguistic modalities is a cultural patrimony that shall be the object of special respect and protection.

Article 4

1. The flag of Spain is formed by three horizontal bands, red, yellow, and red, with the yellow band being twice as wide as each of the red bands.

2. Statutes may recognize flags and ensigns belonging to the autonomous communities. These shall be used alongside the flag of Spain in their public buildings and in their official acts.

Article 5

The capital of the state is the city of Madrid.

Article 6

Political parties express political pluralism, work together on the formation and expression of the popular will, and are a basic instrument for political participation. Their creation and their activities are free within the framework of observance of the constitution and the laws. Their internal structure and functioning must be democratic.

Article 7

Workers' unions and employers' associations contribute to the defense and promotion of the economic and social interests that correspond to them. Their creation and their activities are free within the framework of observance of the constitution and the laws. Their internal structure and functioning must be democratic.

Article 8

1. The armed forces, comprising the Army of the Land, the Navy, and the Air Force, have as their mission to guarantee Spain's sovereignty and independence [and] to defend its territorial integrity and the constitutional order. . . .

Title 1: On Fundamental Rights and Duties

Article 10

1. The dignity of the person, the inviolable rights that are inherent to each person, the free development of the personality, and respect for the law and the rights of others are the basis of the political order and social peace.

2. The norms concerning the fundamental rights and liberties that the constitution recognizes shall be interpreted in accordance with the Universal Declaration of Human Rights and the international treaties and accords on such matters that Spain has ratified.

First Chapter: On Spaniards and Foreigners

Article 11

1. Spanish nationality is acquired, kept, and lost in accord with what the law establishes.

2. Native Spaniards cannot be deprived of their nationality.

3. The state is authorized to agree on treaties of double nationality with the countries of Iberoamerica or with those countries that have had or have some particular link with Spain. In those same countries, even when they do not recognize a reciprocal right for their citizens, Spaniards shall be able to be naturalized without losing their original nationality. . . .

Article 13

1. Foreigners in Spain shall enjoy the political liberties this title guarantees, under the terms established by treaties and the law. . . .

3. Extradition shall only be granted in fulfillment of a treaty or a law, following the principle of reciprocity. Excluded from extradition are political crimes, with acts of terrorism not being considered as such. . . .

Second Chapter: Rights and Liberties

Article 14

Spaniards are equal before the law, and there can be no discrimination of any kind for reasons of birth, race, sex, religion, opinion, or any other personal or social condition or circumstance.

First Section: On Fundamental Rights and Public Liberties

Article 15

Everyone has the right to life and to physical and moral integrity, without in any case being subjected to torture or to cruel and degrading punishment or treatment. The death penalty is abolished, except for what military penal laws may establish in wartime.

Article 16

1. The manifestations of liberty of ideology, religion, and worship are guaranteed to individuals and communities without any limits except for those necessary for maintaining the public order protected by law.

2. No one can be forced to declare his or her ideology, religion, or beliefs.

3. No religion shall have official status. The public powers shall take into account the religious beliefs of Spanish society and shall maintain consequent relations of cooperation with the Catholic Church and the other faiths.

Article 17

1. Everyone has the right to liberty and security. No one can be deprived of liberty except following the provisions of this article and in the cases and forms envisioned by the law.

2. Preventative detention shall not last longer than the time strictly necessary to carry out investigations tending to clarify the facts, and, in any case, within the time limit of seventy-two hours the detainee must either be freed or brought before judicial authorities.

3. All detainees must be informed immediately and in a comprehensible manner of their rights and the reasons for their detention, and cannot be forced to make any declaration. . . .

Article 18

1. The right to honor and to the privacy of one's person, family, and image are guaranteed. . . .

Article 20

1. The constitution recognizes and protects the right:

a) to express and disseminate thoughts, ideas, and opinions freely through words, writings, or any other means of reproduction.

b) to literary, artistic, scientific, and technical production. . . .

2. The exercise of these rights cannot be restricted by any kind of prior censorship. . . .

Article 21

1. The right to peaceful and unarmed meetings is recognized. The exercise of this right shall not need prior authorization.

2. In cases of meetings in places of public transit and of demonstrations, advance notice shall be given to authorities, who can only prohibit them when there are reasons based in the disruption of public order, endangering persons or property.

Article 22

1. The right of association is recognized. . . .

5. Secret associations and those of paramilitary character are prohibited.

Article 23

1. Citizens have the right to participate in public affairs directly or through representatives, freely elected in periodic elections by universal suffrage.

2. Similarly, they have the equal right to hold public functions and positions, following requirements established by the laws. . . .

Article 27

1. Everyone has the right to education. Freedom of instruction is recognized. . . .

3. The public power shall guarantee parents' right to have their children receive the religious and moral training that corresponds to their own convictions.

4. Primary education is obligatory and free of charge. . . .

Article 28

1. Everyone has the right to unionize freely. . . . No one can be forced to join a union.

2. Workers' right to strike in defense of their interests is recognized. . . .

Second Section: On the Citizens' Rights and Duties

Article 30

1. Spaniards have the right and duty to defend Spain.

2. The law will specify the military obligations of the Spanish people and shall regulate, with the necessary guarantees, the status of conscientious objection, along with the other grounds for exemption from military service, retaining the authority, in such cases, to impose alternative social service. . . .

Article 31

1. All shall contribute to supporting public expenses in accordance with their economic capacities through a just system of taxation inspired by the principles of equality and progressiveness, which, in no case, shall reach the level of confiscation.

2. Public expenses shall seek an equitable allocation of public resources, and their design and execution shall follow criteria of efficiency and economy. . . .

Article 32

1. The man and the woman have the right to engage in contract of matrimony with full legal equality. . . .

Article 33

1. The rights of private property and inheritance are recognized. . . .

3. No one shall be deprived of property or rights unless for causes justified by public utility or social interest, in exchange for appropriate compensation. . . .

Article 35

1. All Spaniards have the duty to work and the right to work, to free choice of profession or trade, . . . and to remuneration sufficient to satisfy their needs and those of their family, and in no case may there be discrimination based on sex. . . .

Article 38

Freedom of entrepreneurship within the framework of a market economy is recognized. The public powers shall guarantee and protect its exercise and the defense of productivity, in accordance with the demands of the overall economy, and, as the case may be, economic planning.

Third Chapter: On the Guiding Principles of Social and Economic Policy

Article 39

1. The public powers shall assure the family's social, economic, and legal protection. . . .

Article 40

1. The public powers shall promote conditions favorable for social and economic progress and for a more equitable regional and personal distribution of income, within the framework of a policy of economic stability. Those powers will especially pursue a policy of seeking full employment.

2. Similarly, the public powers shall pursue a policy that guarantees professional training and retraining; shall watch out for safety and health in the workplace; shall guarantee necessary rest by limiting the working day; [and shall guarantee] periodic paid vacations. . . .

Article 41

The public powers shall maintain a public regime of social security for all citizens, one that guarantees sufficient assistance and social spending to meet situations of need, especially in cases of unemployment. . . .

Article 42

The State shall especially watch out for the protection of the economic and social rights of Spanish workers abroad, and shall orient its policy toward seeking their return.

Article 43

1. The right to the protection of one's health is recognized.

2. It is up to the public powers to organize and oversee public health through preventative measures and the necessary programs and services. . . .

Article 45

1. All have the right to enjoy an environment that is suitable for personal development, [and all have] the duty to preserve it. . . .

Article 47

All Spaniards have the right to enjoy worthy and suitable housing. . . .

Title 2: On the Crown

Article 56

1. The king is the head of state, symbol of its unity and permanence; [he] arbitrates and moderates the regular functioning of the institutions, assumes the highest representation of the Spanish state in its international relations, especially with the nations of its historical community, and exercises the functions that the constitution and laws expressly attribute to him. . . .

Article 61

1. The king, upon being proclaimed before the General Cortes, shall swear an oath to carry out his functions faithfully, to preserve the constitution and the laws and to see that they are preserved, and to respect the rights of the citizens of the autonomous communities. . . .

Article 62

It is the king's responsibility:

a) To sanction and promulgate the laws.

b) To summon and dissolve the General Cortes and to call elections following the terms established in the constitution.

c) To call referenda in those cases established by the constitution.

d) To propose the candidate to be president of the government and, in his case, to name him, and also to put an end to his functions following the framework established by the constitution.

e) To name and dismiss the members of the cabinet, as proposed by its president.

f) To expedite the decrees made in the Council of Ministers, to confer civil and military positions, and to grant honors and distinctions in accordance with the laws.

g) To be informed about matters of state and to preside, to this effect, over the sessions of the Council of Ministers whenever he considers it appropriate, upon the request of the president of the government.

h) To be supreme commander of the armed forces.

i) To exercise the right of pardon in accordance with the law. . . .

Article 63

1. The king shall accredit ambassadors and other diplomatic representatives. Foreign representatives are accredited before him. . . .

3. It is up to the king, with prior authorization by the General Cortes, to declare war and make peace.

Article 64

1. The king's acts shall be countersigned by the president of the government, and when appropriate, by the competent ministers. . . .

Title 8: On the Territorial Organization of the State

First Chapter: General Principles

Article 137

The state is organized territorially in municipalities, in provinces, and in autonomous communities that may be formed. All of these entities enjoy autonomy for the management of their respective interests. . . .

Article 139

1. All Spaniards have the same rights and obligations in any part of the territory of the state.

2. No authority shall adopt measures that directly or indirectly impede either people's freedom to circulate and establish themselves where they wish or the free circulation of goods throughout the entire territory. . . .

Third Chapter: On the Autonomous Communities

Article 143

1. In exercising the right to autonomy recognized in article 2 of the constitution, the frontier provinces with common historical, cultural, and economic characteristics, island territories, and provinces with a historical regional character shall be able to govern themselves and to constitute themselves as autonomous communities. . . .

2. The initiative for the process of [establishing] autonomy belongs to the interested *Diputaciones* [governing bodies in the regions] or to the corresponding inter-island body and to two-thirds of the municipalities whose population represents, at the least, the majority from the electoral census of each province or island. . . .

Article 145

1. In no case shall the federation of autonomous communities be permitted.

Article 148

1. The autonomous communities shall be able to exercise authority in the following areas:

(1) The organization of their institutions of self-government. . . .

(3) The ordering of the territory, urban planning, and housing.

(4) Public works of interest to the autonomous community in its own territory.

(5) Railroads and highways whose extent lies entirely within the autonomous community's territory. . . .

(9) The management of matters involving protection of the environment. . . .

(17) The promotion of culture, research, and, as the case may be, the teaching of the language of the autonomous community.

Article 149

1. The state has exclusive authority over the following matters:

(1) Regulation of the basic conditions that guarantee the equality of all Spaniards in the exercise of rights and in the fulfillment of constitutional duties.

(2) Nationality, immigration, emigration, alien status, and right of asylum.

(3) International relations.

(4) Defense and the armed forces.

(5) The administration of justice.

(6) Commercial, penal, and penitentiary legislation. . . .

(7) Labor legislation, without infringing upon its execution by the constituted authorities of the autonomous communities. . . .

(9) Legislation on intellectual and industrial property.

(10) The customs and tariff regime; foreign commerce.

(11) The monetary system: foreign exchange, exchange rates, and convertibility; the foundations for the ordering of credit, banking, and insurance. . . .

(14) General finance and the debts of the state. . . .

(21) Railroads and ground transportation systems that cross the territory of more than one autonomous community. . . .

(23) Basic legislation on the protection of the environment, without infringing upon the power of the autonomous communities to establish additional measures of protection. . . .

3. Matters not expressly attributed to the state by this constitution shall be up to the autonomous communities, as regulated by their respective statutes. Authority over matters not regulated by the statutes of autonomy shall belong to the state, whose rules shall prevail, in case of conflict, over those of the autonomous communities in every area not attributed to their exclusive competence. The law of the state shall in all cases supplement the law of the autonomous communities.

72. Spanish Reflections on Franco (1979)

In 1979, José María Gironella and Rafael Borràs Betriu published a book containing one hundred written interviews they did with Spaniards across the political spectrum concerning Franco and his regime. Here, the full versions of the questions appear only in the first interview.

SOURCE: José María Gironella and Rafael Borràs Betriu, eds., *Cien españoles y Franco* (Barcelona: Editorial Planeta, 1979), 12, 23–24, 98–100, 173–76, 179–80, 195–98, 223–24.

Víctor Alba

Víctor Alba (the pen name of Pere Pagès) was born in Barcelona in 1916. He worked for various workers' periodicals as a young man, and he fought on the Republican side in the Civil War. After the war, he lived in exile in France, Mexico, and the United States, writing books and articles on Spanish politics and history and teaching political science at the university level.

QUESTION I: General Franco is one of the most controversial political and military figures of our times. His supporters have called him "the sword of the West"; his detractors, "the most nefarious man in the history of Spain." How would you define the general's personality? Was he a great patriot? Was he a cynical egotist, ambitious for power? Intelligent? Merely shrewd? Did he have a prophetic vision or was he pulled along by events? (Et cetera.) Could you give us your personal evaluative judgment?

ALBA: Any evaluation of Franco is necessarily subjective, because he did not let others get to know him and he did not have contact with the people. Yet something of his personality shines through. . . . He had all of the lesser virtues and none of the really important ones. So he was a skillful politician—though here it should be noted that it is easy to govern with bayonets—but he never managed to become a statesman. Perhaps he began as an idealist with ambitions for his country, but he ended up like one of those South American dictators whom the Swiss bankers love so much. . . .

He was one of those people with more schooling than education—without taste, without refinement, without a broad vision, without creative imagination, always ready to apply measures from daily life to politics. In this sense he represented a very common type in Spain. Yet by his temperament he was not a representative Spaniard. . . . He knew how to take advantage of events, like any good politician, but not to cause them. The civil war itself was a surprise to him—as for everyone. I suspect he ended up truly believing he was communicating with Providence. . . .

QUESTION 2: Equally controversial is the work that General Franco carried out throughout his thirty-nine years of authoritarian rule. In your opinion, what are the positive aspects—if there are any—of the general's work? What are—if there are any—the negative aspects? It seems certain that in this period "Spain has changed on the outside" (dams, industrialization, development of tourism, highways, etc.). *Has it also changed in its soul?* (Have some of the basic problems that have traditionally affected the country been resolved: ignorance, lack of civic spirit, the burden of envy and aggressiveness, agrarian reform, the health-care question, the lack of scholarly research, oligarchic pressure, corruption, etc.?)

QUESTION 3: The fact that General Franco stayed in power—which had a personal and absolutist character—for almost four decades is intriguing and calls for reflection. To what would you attribute this long stay in power? To the fact that the general was a born caudillo and a charismatic leader? To the flagrant inability of the opposition to operate? To the official support of the Church? To the fact that a majority of the Spanish people were satisfied with the regime established at the end of the Civil War? Or were there other determining factors?

ALBA: If Franco is hard to know, Francoism can be evaluated objectively, by applying the biblical idea that a tree can be known by its fruits. Franco, when the Civil War ended, could have forgotten the past and transformed Spain, because . . . the people were so sick of the killing that anything would have seemed better to them than going on with it. But by temperament, I suppose, and out of conviction, as well as because of the interests he was defending, he opposed change. The rhetoric, the uniforms, the speeches, the raised-arm salute all helped him hide his desire to keep things as they were. He did not succeed. To keep himself in power he had to give in to the ways of the time: first, fascism, then developmentalism. . . . It was this ability to adapt without really changing that allowed him to remain in power, along with the fact that . . . the leadership of the opposition from the Civil War had been decimated and decapitated. . . .

Franco relied on . . . a system of denunciation and corruption. He who uses such methods so widely shows how much he detests the Spaniards. When the war ended, and until just a few years ago, repression was exercised on the basis of people denouncing others. He turned half of Spain into police informers. And he rewarded it with a tolerated, promoted, and sanctified corruption. . . .

I believe there has not been enough attention paid to a depressing and surprising fact: in forty years, a dictatorship can change a people's way of life. . . . The Spaniard had many faults—envy, above all—but he was honorable. Francoism dishonored him. He did not even have the excuse of having taken advantage of this to resolve the country's basic problems. Those that led to the Civil War remained in place when Franco died. . . . It was only later that the existence of those problems was recognized and solutions were sought. . . . It would not be an exaggeration to say that Franco left everything to be resolved. . . . Of course there was industrialization, and highways and factories were built, but this occurred throughout the whole world, and at a lower human and even material cost than Spaniards had to pay.

QUESTION 4: Do you believe Franco respected "human rights," or that he violated them in a systematic, relentless, and bloody way?

ALBA: Nothing would allow us to think that Franco believed that the Spaniards had rights. He could not respect them. Franco's repression cannot be explained without keeping in mind that he must have sincerely believed he was sent from heaven, and that he felt a total disdain for the Spaniards. The very fact of establishing a dictatorship . . . already indicates the existence of this disdain for his own people. The fact that people have forgotten Franco so quickly is an indication of the volume of the repression. All dictators think they will remain in people's memory, but all are erased from memory once they lose power. And the bloodier a dictatorship has been, the more quickly the dictator's memory is erased. People wish to forget that which hurts them, that which humiliates them; in this way one can measure the brutality and the cruelty of a dictatorship by the speed with which a dictator disappears from memory.

Accepting the most modest figures of the cost in lives of the Civil War and the repression that followed it—a half million dead—and doing some simple division, we can see that . . . each year of Francoism was paid for by twelve thousand five hundred dead, and each day of Francoism by thirty-four dead; every two hours of Francisco Franco Bahamonde's time in power cost three dead. We should say not only Franco, but also Francoism. Because Franco would not have been what he was without the Francoists. And there were plenty of these. . . . The corruption and the denunciation that were used as methods of government make it hard to estimate what portion of the country was Francoist at what point of the regime's history. But to judge by the proliferation of banks, the construction firms, the destruction of the countryside, the plots concerning social security, the fever for automobiles, and the glorified egoism, it could not have been an insignificant portion. . . .

QUESTION 5: General Franco spoke with obsessive insistence about the "unity of the men and lands of Spain." Do you believe that we Spaniards are now more united than in 1936, or do you see signs of equally profound divisions?

ALBA: In the name of an imaginary "unity" Francoism divided. There had never been such great differences between rich and poor, so little confidence toward the centralizing state, the oppressor of all, as under Franco. A few more years of Franco, and the autonomist tendencies, which are healthy and a sign of vitality, would have turned into centrifugal tendencies. The very fact that Castile, Andalusia, and León wanted autonomy indicates how far Franco divided.

Teresa Berganza

Born in Madrid in 1935, Teresa Berganza attended the Madrid Conservatory and went on to a career as an opera singer, performing in the leading opera houses of the world.

BERGANZA: I believe that General Franco loved Spain, that he loved it passionately. In his youth he could even offer to spill his blood for it. . . . But I also believe he did not know or could not accept the submissiveness implied in the very exercise and service of arms. And the Spanish people found themselves forced to be victims of this lack of vision on the general's part. Oh, if only we could forget everything more quickly! I wish we could hasten the process of forgetting the way we hasten to pardon! . . .

QUESTION 2: In your opinion, what are the positive aspects of the general's work? What are the negative aspects?

BERGANZA: A single word: mediocre. Sadly mediocre, because the men who represented him and his governments were mediocre at all levels. . . .

Dams, highways, tourism? These are all things that any government—of any political sign—would have been able to carry out.

Ignorance: The reasons for the literacy campaigns are still valid. The schools still lack materials and properly qualified personnel. . . .

Lack of civic spirit: Those of us who, unfortunately, must keep crossing national borders over and over again have noticed, each time we return, how low this level of virtue is. . . .

Envy and aggression: This existed more than ever. I believe it is already diminishing.

Agrarian reform: A more difficult undertaking than that of settling a confrontation between brothers. It presupposes a sense of justice in those called upon to carry it out.

Health: Have you ever heard anyone mention a ministry of health?

Lack of research: Do you know of the problems and tragedies of our students abroad? Do you know how few scholarships are offered for this purpose? . . .

Corruption: The most profound; but because it resulted from mediocrity it was not able—thank God—to become permanently entrenched.

QUESTION 3: To what would you attribute his staying in power for so long?

BERGANZA: You are asking me to tread on the ground of real politics. I don't know. I do not understand politics. . . . But I do not believe, nor can I believe, in caudillos or kings "by the grace of God.". . .

The Church? The Church is a prostitute, a cheating spouse that is constantly washed, reembellished, and rejuvenated by the love and fidelity of its spouse. . . . Yes I believe it can be said, briefly, that our national Church prostituted itself by aiding and protecting General Franco's work. It prostituted itself and was unfaithful to the demands of the message of salvation it is obliged to announce to all, to the poor, to the needy, to the persecuted. But in the depths of the mystery of the Church there are always forces of redemption. And it is already being redeemed from its sin. It also needs our understanding. It must also find its place in our capacity to forget. I do not condemn it; I love it, and I weep at having to speak and to write this way about it. . . .

QUESTION 4: Do you believe Franco respected "human rights," or that he violated them in a systematic, relentless, and bloody way?

BERGANZA: There was once a good, just, passionate man, a seeker of good, of truth, of beauty. There was once my father, who was jailed without any previous formal accusation of any kind, who spent many months in prison without being given any notice of why he was there, who suffered in his flesh the punctures of all the physical and moral pains, and who one day found himself—free?—and in the street without any explanation, without any verdict.

And there was once my mother, who while still a youth, saw that youth cut off and broken in its splendor. Why? Because of all this. And it was not possible to speak, to write, to demonstrate, to protest, to call for justice. Nothing.

QUESTION 5: Do you believe that we Spaniards are now more united than in 1936, or do you see signs of equally profound divisions?

BERGANZA: Who would invent that concept of "race" that was applied indiscriminately to all the peoples of Spain? Spain has been great and unique when it has managed to maintain the diversity of the peoples who have been influential in its history. But the temptation and the downfall have had traces of an endemic malady for many centuries: the expulsion of the Jews, the expulsion of the Moriscos, the expulsion of the Jesuits. The departure of the Jews undermined the economy, that of the Moriscos undermined agriculture, and that of the Jesuits left the empire without teachers. . . . But I am optimistic. It seems to me that in reality, in truth, it is now that Spain is "beginning to awaken."

Manuel Díez Alegría

Born in Asturias in 1906, Manuel Díez Alegría entered Spain's Army Corps of Engineers in the 1920s and fought on the Nationalist side in the Civil War. After the war, Díez Alegría reached the rank of general, was elected to the Royal Academy of Moral and Political Sciences, and occupied a series of official positions during the Franco regime.

QUESTION 1: How would you define the general's personality?

DÍEZ ALEGRÍA: General Franco was, above all, a human being, and therefore a combination of qualities, some favorable, others adverse. So extremists who use terms such as those in the question err. . . . From our distance of place and time, the latter still being short, it can be argued that the general's patriotism was sincere, even if his way of understanding it did not perhaps accord with everyone else's. He came to power through a series of circumstances, most of which were fortuitous, but for him staying in power became something fundamental. Although he lacked a solid educational base, he had common sense and the ability to master what interested him. More than shrewd, the word that fits him is cautious; he was prudent, secretive, and mistrustful, and he left complex problems to be taken care of by time. He did not have a determined and concrete ideology, but rather a few rigid ideas that his acts always reflected. And so he did not follow a definite policy, acting out of a mere pragmatism that was rather opportunistic. . . . Distance, and a coldness that was strangely compatible with an extreme emotionality. . . . The more outstanding of his qualities were a limitless courage, great force of character, and impassiveness. On the whole, a very complex personality that would merit an objective and detailed study.

QUESTION 2: In your opinion, what are the positive aspects of the general's work? What are the negative aspects?

DÍEZ ALEGRÍA: Setting aside any doctrinaire perspectives . . . the following points could be emphasized. That of rebelling victoriously; that of staying out of the terrible world war; the securing of a very long period of tranquility—totally unusual in our country; the undeniable development of the nation, which has indeed changed not just the outside but indeed the substance of Spain; the fact that during these years a certain notion of the state took form and was spread like never before; the fact of not having used the power of the army in political and social conflicts; the launching of an embryonic social concern; and that of assuring, at least, the succession at the summit, ultimately leaving no other heirs than the people and the king; these are, in spite of the many flaws that are pointed out, positive aspects of his work.

The perpetuation during peacetime of factional divisions, seeking submission rather than consensus; the maintenance, against all opposition, of a strange political regime—sterile, being a hybrid, and fossilized, being autocratic; the resulting absence of an international policy, leaving us as a satellite of America; . . . sluggishness in dealing plainly with internal regional problems; the systematic error—the product more than anything of mistrust—in dealing with the world of culture and the press; and finally, . . . keeping in mind what Lord Acton said [that absolute power corrupts absolutely], the corruption that extended outward from around him; these are negative aspects that are no less important. Which are greater? To posterity goes the hard task of judging. . . .

It is hard to change fundamentally what is intrinsic to a people. Even so, the general level of enlightenment and good sense were incomparably higher at the end of this period than they were at the beginning. . . .

QUESTION 3: To what would you attribute his staying in power for so long?

DÍEZ ALEGRÍA: Strictly speaking, he was not a born caudillo, but rather a distinguished military leader well above those who could have been his peers. Considering his limited qualifications for social communication, his charisma was more the fruit of the victory he attained, the effective creation of order he imposed, and, more than anything, with the passage of time, the very fact of his having stayed in power. The supposed support of the Church . . . was less decisive than people say. . . . General Franco's adversaries, who must have been numerous if we can trust what is said today, were not capable of organizing a coherent internal opposition, hoping for everything from abroad, and their activities seemed polarized around a factionalism that was repulsive to many. On the whole, they strengthened him more than they weakened him. . . . If not absolutely satisfied, a large part of the Spanish people preferred the tranquility and the advantages of development that reached them to launching themselves into adventures that could end up in another conflict. . . .

QUESTION 4: Do you believe that Franco respected "human rights," or that he violated them in a systematic, relentless, and bloody way?

DÍEZ ALEGRÍA: The notion of "human rights," as we understand it today, did not figure in General Franco's agenda. In the time when he was brought up, the most that could be known about this would simply be the Declaration of the Rights of Man and of the Citizen, which was then tainted with being a product of the French Revolution. His later activity in the militia, his fighting in the colonial war, and especially the hard discipline of the Legion did not help him fill this gap. It is undeniable that the liquidation of the civil war was notoriously inhumane. With the passage of the years his actions in this area evolved noticeably. . . . Certainly his attitude in this area was not exemplary, but nor could one . . . assert fairly that he violated human rights "in a systematic, implacable, and bloody fashion.". . .

Pilar Franco Bahamonde

Younger sister of General Franco, Pilar Franco Bahamonde was the mother of ten children, and described her occupation as housewife.

QUESTION 1: How would you define the general's personality?

FRANCO BAHAMONDE: There have been so many lies, so much slander, said about my brother that I cannot understand how a democratic government can allow it. Of course it is not with slander and lies that one creates an authentic democracy. . . . Here the governors have instituted a democracy without order or consensus. . . .

My brother was a unique person in the world, who sacrificed his life, sacrificed his health, and sacrificed everything for the salvation of his fatherland. He was extremely clever and was not pulled along by events, but rather, he went about avoiding those that could do us harm.

The Reds left us a burned and broken Spain, in which one could not get by with what we could gather from impoverished fields, and from that burned and broken land he made a Spain that was so great and so good that he managed to place it, without anyone's help, in seventh place in the world. I said without anyone's help, but I must note one exception: Argentina, with Juan Domingo Perón. . . . [After World War II, the victorious Allies imposed a partial blockade on trade with Spain, but Perón's government in Argentina extended credits to Spain and shipped large quantities of wheat, helping alleviate dire food shortages there.] My brother didn't need anything from anyone. He alone, alone with the help of poor Perón . . . fixed Spain and placed it, I repeat, in the seventh place in the world. And I ask: what place are we in now? . . .

QUESTION 2: In your opinion, what are the positive aspects of the general's work? What are the negative aspects?

FRANCO BAHAMONDE: In my brother's time people came . . . to Spain because things were cheap, they stayed in Spain because there was sunshine, because there was love, they stayed in Spain because we Spaniards all made life pleasant for the foreigner, who came to leave us that currency that we needed so badly. . . . And they were the best of times for Spain. . . . We lived in order, without strikes, without crime, without murders. Spain was a place of paradise . . . and every foreigner who came here and then left later wrote the best things about Spain. . . . And now what do they say about Spain? . . . With the disaster of the strikes, which have caused the closing of hundreds of thousands of factories; the alarming unemployment that there is; the people who can't make ends meet because of the inflation that has been allowed. In my brother's time prices were controlled. To raise the price of an item ten pesetas you needed authorization, and if it was found that the item's price should not go up, then it did not go up. . . . My brother . . . knew how to do things so that we did not have a communist state. And I ask: now that we're so friendly with the Russians, why don't they give us back the gold they took? . . .

QUESTION 3: To what would you attribute his staying in power for so long?

FRANCO BAHAMONDE: He was a great caudillo and he lasted forty years, and people wonder: why couldn't he have lasted sixty? Because in his time we ate well, we lived well, and we were happy, and now we don't eat, nor are people calm, nor happy. So people miss my brother, and you would not believe how many people of the most humble condition stop me in the street when they see me and ask me: "Why can't we bring him back?" One day it is communists who offer to give half their lives to bring my brother back, and another day it is poorer people. "What will become of our little children? Where are we heading? What will happen to our families?" And today they miss my brother's regime so much, so much that I am tired of my eyes filling with tears when people embrace me. . . .

And about this absolutism business. Well, how is it that [Santiago] Carrillo [secretary general of the Spanish Communist Party] lived in Spain if there was such a strong dictatorship? . . . How can you let people say such things? And besides, how can you not remember the long lines of people crying [at Franco's funeral], the lines people waited in, standing for fourteen hours without being able to do their necessities, without being able to drink something warm when it was below freezing? And the ordinary people . . . stood in line for fourteen or twenty hours to be able to say, "Adiós, padre!" And people from the middle class threw their calling cards in his coffin, where he lay dead, and the poor people filled it with little pieces of paper saying: "Generalissimo, you who are in heaven, I have a little girl with cancer; ask all-powerful God to cure her.". . . The people cried for their father, and that is the truth, against all the slander and all the lies being told. The whole people cried for their father—for their father!—who had given them bread, who had sacrificed for them, who had passed labor laws so that they would have their well-being, so that they would have their Social Security, so that they would have their cars, so that they would have everything. . . . This is the death of a dictator? This is the death of a man, of a caudillo who sacrificed himself so for Spain that in the end it cost him his life.

The help of the Church? The Church was helped, of course, by my brother, who was a great Catholic, apostolic, and Roman; but of course, as for influence, I don't think so. . . . They supported each other, it is true, because between the Church and the government there was a concordat. And besides my brother wanted a Christian society, as all of us Spaniards want. A society that, certainly, they do not give us now, in the sense that whereas he banned all kinds of garbage, now they allow all kinds of indecencies, the most disgusting pornography, to the point that people come from France and say: "How can you allow these embarrassments that aren't even allowed in France?"

QUESTION 4: Do you believe that Franco respected "human rights," or that he violated them in a systematic, relentless, and bloody way?

FRANCO BAHAMONDE: A lie, it's a lie and a slander, like everything else this government allows to be said about him, because he was a man who saved Spain and respected human rights, and when he had to sign a death sentence he had to sign it, because it was his duty, and it cost him ten days of thinking about the man whose life he had to take away. I won't hear of this violation of human rights. . . .

QUESTION 5: Do you believe that we Spaniards are now more united than in 1936, or do you see signs of equally profound divisions?

FRANCO BAHAMONDE: He asked for the union of men because it was the union of Spain, . . . [but now] we have never been less united. We have never been more upset with each other, and people have never been more afraid, more frightened, seeing where Spain is heading. It is not democracy's fault, no. If democracy is a good thing for people, then fine, but not a democracy with crime, murders, strikes, and the inability to stop terrorism.

These things they're saying . . . on television, "the Constitution of Concord," most Spaniards do not agree with. Is it up to the constitution to destroy the family, to approve what is wrong, to approve of abortion, to approve crimes? And why are they doing this? Well, they're doing it . . . because they know that united families make a united fatherland. . . . When the war ended we were all united, we were all friends. Not now, no, now hate has spread here and there, and people were never more hated than they are now. So the Constitution of Concord is enough to make you die laughing.

Xabier Echarri

The son of a journalist, Xabier Echarri was born near Madrid in 1936 but grew up in the Basque country. Echarri has worked for and published numerous periodicals.

QUESTION 1: How would you define the general's personality?

ECHARRI: It's hard to find a precise definition . . . to judge a being who has weighed on my head and my shoulders like a heavy stone for thirty-eight of my forty-two years.

Sword of the West? A sword, all right. But a sword dripping blood from its point to its hilt. The blood of repression, of judgments, of purges; blood of the Spaniards and blood, especially for me, of Euskadi, the Basque people he persecuted fiercely in a special way from 1936 on.

A patriot? For him. Always according to his directions, and like a true tyrant, marking in blood and fire what your flag, your salute, your principles, your anthems, your past, your present, your future had to be. That is to say, no more nor less than his flag, his salute, his principles, his anthems, his past, his present, and his future.

Intelligent? . . . He appeared with an absolutely false image of intelligence, experience, and wisdom to take hold of the destinies of the fatherland with "a firm hand." When in reality it was nothing more or less than the acts of a lunatic Galician, cynical instead of intelligent. . . .

Prophetic vision? Events usually demonstrated the opposite, and on those few occasions when he unwittingly did something right that prevented even greater bloodshed for the country, like, for example, Spain's entry into the Second World War, he held himself up as an example to our generation and those to come of his great political vision. . . .

For all these reasons, I can only judge Franco as a tyrannical man—crazy, bloody, repulsively cold, full of contradictions and complexes, nefarious for the history of Spain, a true dictator in the broadest and most degrading sense of the term. In short, a thorn that I have had driven into the deepest part of my soul as long as I can remember, and whose removal, one joyful November 20, caused happiness to swell up in me, as in millions of other Spaniards, along with the sense of a clear and light air that we have not had a chance to breathe in almost the last forty years.

QUESTION 2: In your opinion, what are the positive aspects of the general's work? What are the negative aspects?

ECHARRI: If it is indeed true that its positive aspects can be found in the dams built during his rule . . . etc., each and every one of these aspects can be clearly rebutted if we begin by asking: at the cost of how much blood spilled by his weapons was he able to build . . . his mausoleum, as if he were a pharaoh. . . . The highways and the country emerged from the ashes into which he had mostly converted our national soil, but this would have happened just the same without his presence, and who knows, perhaps even better. . . .

Behind all this, ignorance proved much stronger than an educational effort neither planned nor carried out. Envy and aggressiveness were the basis of prosperity in the country; agrarian reform—as always—was only a promise; good health was harmed and delayed by poverty and the prevailing filth; scholarship was considered the work of Masons and atheists, and was thus prohibited, while corruption in all its forms grew and dominated the country. . . .

General Franco, the caudillo, the generalissimo will never be remembered by the Spaniards or by history for his positive achievements, which scarcely existed, but rather for the blood that always stained his hands and that always darkened any act otherwise worthy of praise. He will be remembered, undoubtedly, for the forty years of backwardness he cost the country.

QUESTION 3: To what would you attribute his staying in power for so long?

ECHARRI: The answer is easy and obvious. Franco, after winning his war, found a country that was falling apart and lacked enough strength to resist his designs as a tyrant. Nevertheless, from the first armed action of the guerrilla fighters just after the war through his final days almost forty years later there was always, among the Spanish people, resistance, which, even though crushed by the general's boot, never stopped offering an eloquent and worthy attitude of protest for a single moment. . . .

QUESTION 4: Do you believe that Franco respected "human rights," or that he violated them in a systematic, relentless, and bloody way?

ECHARRI: General Franco was completely ignorant of human rights. . . . The dictator only respected his own rights, those that emanated from his personal code as an insurrectionist, a tyrant, an absurd moralist, and a man of blood.

QUESTION 5: Do you believe that we Spaniards are now more united than in 1936, or do you see signs of equally profound divisions?

ECHARRI: Indeed General Franco not only spoke with obsessive insistence of "the unity of the men and the lands of Spain," but he was also convinced . . . that "the peoples of Spain," as he often called them, adored him, and he believed that this unity that he persistently tried to impose on people was a reality.

This is so true that in Euskadi—where perhaps he had come to be hated more strongly than in any other place, although it was nothing but the compensation for the great hatred that the dictator had for the Basques—he had the audacity to say upon his return from a trip to Bilbao in 1964: "From Bilbao I return very impressed and satisfied. . . . The people of Bilbao showed they were by my side, and everything said about separatism, discontent with my policies, etc., is a lie that the tireless minority circulates, but does not reflect the opinion of the people of Bilbao. . . ." Declarations such as this, totally lacking in reality and logic, are the kinds of things that in the specific case of Euskadi strengthen, year after year, the idea of independence and the hatred toward a Francoism that instead of trying to unite, merely ends up marking and increasing the differences.

Rafael García Serrano

Born in 1917 in Pamplona, Rafael García Serrano was educated in that city and in Madrid. After fighting for the Nationalists in the Civil War, he went on to a career as a writer of fiction, winning various prizes for his work.

QUESTION 1: How would you define the general's personality?

GARCÍA SERRANO: No one can doubt Franco's patriotism, because they would appear as imbeciles. It so happens that his patriotism was national and ambitious, while that of today is tribal and borders on the comical. He was intelligent and astute, and, like any man, he was susceptible to error. Personally, I think he merits a very high rating as a soldier, as a politician, and as a statesman. . . .

QUESTION 2: In your opinion, what are the positive aspects of the general's work? What are the negative aspects?

GARCÍA SERRANO: Positive aspects? All of them. If you look at Spain's problems before 1936, and then the destruction of the war, the international isolation, and the general misery of Europe resulting from the Second World War . . . we can get a clear picture of the material value of his work. Under the Bourbons and the two Republics, our heavy industry was [backward] . . . and Franco placed us in the ninth position among all the industrialized countries in the world, counting from the top, not the bottom, as we will have to do soon if God does not help us. . . .

QUESTION 3: To what would you attribute his staying in power for so long?

GARCÍA SERRANO: Franco's staying in power rested exclusively on the consent of a majority of the Spanish people. . . . There was never any serious opposition, and the so-called maquis [guerrilla fighters] were but the latest version of the banditry that all civil wars leave behind. . . . It will be up to historians to decide whether the Spanish people were made up of an immense herd of sheep that put up with Franco meekly, or rather of people who understood . . . the positive policy of that man, who cared more about fundamental and collective liberties and about the common good and the well-being of all the Spaniards than about what people would say after his death. . . . The problem with the generalissimo is that he did not last long enough in power, and he made the error of dying, to the benefit of his political successors. . . .

QUESTION 4: Do you believe that Franco respected "human rights," or that he violated them in a systematic, relentless, and bloody way?

GARCÍA SERRANO: I am convinced that Franco respected "human rights" more than any president of the U.S.A., more than [French presidents Charles] de Gaulle or [Valéry] Giscard [d'Estaing], more than the antifascists in power in Italy, more than the Jews of Israel, . . . and more than the EEC, the UN, the CIA, the English, NATO, the Warsaw Pact, COMECON. . . .

QUESTION 5: Do you believe that we Spaniards are now more united than in 1936, or do you see signs of equally profound divisions?

GARCÍA SERRANO: The history of our fatherland oscillates between unity and tribalism. Franco . . . was a partisan of unity among the men, lands, and classes of Spain. . . . But in the end, as always happens, we are now back to tribalism. A grave error. We will pay for it.

73. King Juan Carlos, Speech on the Coup d'État (1981)

Given Spain's long history of military *pronunciamientos*, as well as its years of living under Franco's military dictatorship, many Spaniards wondered whether the democracy established after Franco's death would last or would prove truly democratic. For the first few years, Spain took crucial steps toward democracy, but fears of a military coup persisted as Spaniards took advantage of the new liberties, and as the new state granted the regions increasing autonomy—long a sensitive subject for the military.

On February 23, 1981, a group of army officers marched into the Congress and declared their intention to take over the state. Over the next few hours events were fluid, and much depended on what attitude the king would take toward the coup. At 1:15 A.M. on February 24, Juan Carlos appeared on television and gave the following speech, which proved crucial to ending the affair.

SOURCE: "La noche más larga del rey," *Cambio 16* 483 (March 2, 1981): 23. Reprinted by permission of *Cambio 16.*

In addressing myself to all of the Spanish people in the extraordinary circumstances we are experiencing at this moment, I ask everyone for the greatest calm and confidence, and I inform everyone that I have sent the captains general of the military regions, maritime zones, and aerial regions the following order:

In the face of the situation created by the events that have unfolded in the Palace of the Congress, and in order to avoid any possible confusion, I confirm that I have ordered the civil authorities and the joint chiefs of staff to take all necessary measures to maintain constitutional order, within existing legal frameworks.

Any military measure that circumstances seem to require must have the approval of the joint chiefs of staff. The Crown, symbol of the permanence and unity of the fatherland, cannot in any way tolerate actions or attitudes of persons who would seek to intervene by force in the democratic process outlined by the constitution voted by the Spanish people in a referendum.

74. Felipe González, Interview on the NATO Referendum (1986)

Soon after the Socialists' 1982 election victory, it was clear that under Prime Minister Felipe González, the Socialists would not implement a Marxist revolution, and indeed a major theme of the post-Franco era has been the moderation of the parties of both left and right. Yet many party militants stood well to the left of González's government.

Passions on the left ran particularly high over relations with the United States. Although a certain level of anti-Americanism was commonly found throughout Europe, many Spaniards also still resented Washington's 1953 decision to reach a military agreement with Franco (in which the United States provided Spain with aid in exchange for military bases). American bases continued to irritate many Spaniards in the 1980s, both because of the perceived infringement on Spanish sovereignty and because of practical annoyances such as the noise of airplanes flying low over surrounding towns. Finally, Spaniards knew that three of the main NATO countries had conservative leaders: President Ronald Reagan, Britain's Margaret Thatcher, and West Germany's Helmut Kohl.

In the mid-1980s, the cold war was still very much in progress, and Spain's location at the entry to the Mediterranean gave it great strategic value to NATO. In 1986, Felipe González called a referendum on Spain's membership in NATO. Spain had joined NATO when the conservatives were still in power in 1982, and at that time the Socialists, who opposed membership in NATO, had demanded a referendum on the question. Once in power, however, González changed his position on Spain's membership in NATO, though he felt compelled to keep his campaign promise to hold a referendum on the matter. On March 12, 1986, with about 60 percent of the electorate voting, some 53 percent voted for membership in NATO while 39 percent voted against it. In this interview with the newsmagazine *Cambio 16*, González explains his thinking on the eve of the vote.

SOURCE: José Manuel Arija, "Si quieren castigarme, haganlo en las elecciones," *Cambio 16* 745 (March 10, 1986): 20–23. Reprinted by permission of *Cambio 16*.

CAMBIO 16: Mr. President, was it worth it to divide the country with this referendum, when agreement was almost total in the parliament?

GONZÁLEZ: The referendum is not dividing the country. . . . It is a question of whether the Atlantic Alliance is appropriate for us. All the rest is fiction. What matters is that the referendum has been convoked entirely responsibly and with clarity of content. But there are people who are scared by the calling of a referendum favored by 70 percent of the citizens. . . .

CAMBIO 16: When did you begin to be in favor of the [Atlantic] Alliance; when did your conversion, so to speak, begin?

GONZÁLEZ: It is not a question of a moment of inspiration. . . . It was after arriving in the government, and taking note of many things. For example, that it did not reduce Spain's autonomy in foreign policy, but rather strengthened it, and that it did not reduce the country's credibility, but rather increased it. . . . Spain is now an important player in the construction of European unity. For this reason, it would seem outrageous to me for Spain to get up from the negotiating table at a moment when policies of European peace and security are being discussed.

CAMBIO 16: What can you say to those voters who feel deceived because they voted for the "no" [in voting for the Socialists] and now you are asking them to vote "yes"?

GONZÁLEZ: I believe that very few Spaniards made their choice to vote while thinking in that way. And to those who voted for us for that reason, I say in good faith what I am thinking, and I submit to their judgment in the electoral campaign. But how many votes went to the Communists, who openly called for the "no"? I am prepared to say to the voters: "Listen, I have corrected my position, I am explaining why, and I submit to your judgment." . . .

CAMBIO 16: Don't you think you are asking for too much from some of your militants in asking them to do the opposite of what they are thinking, including to lie?

GONZÁLEZ: It is not true that they are doing the opposite of what they are thinking. We are facing a sentiment that took the European left more than fifteen years of evolution, and we are obliged to do it in three years, because we have very great responsibilities based on our mandate from the people. In Italy, the Communist Party took seventeen years to say "yes" to the Atlantic Alliance as a guarantee of peace and security. . . .

CAMBIO 16: Now we are going to see a vote of punishment for Felipe González. Won't the accumulated grievances against the president end up as "no" votes?

GONZÁLEZ: I ask the citizens, if they wish to cast a vote of punishment of that kind, to reserve it for the general elections. For in that case they are not damaging this government, they are damaging a project for Spain's foreign policy, which needs to be fundamentally solidified.

CAMBIO 16: Mr. President, do you realize that you have ceased to be untouchable, as you were previously?

GONZÁLEZ: Fortunately, I was never untouchable, because such things do not exist in democracies. It is dictatorships that make people untouchable. You have to wait for them to die to be touchable. In democracy it is the opposite: you have to wait for people to die to recognize that they accomplished anything.

CAMBIO 16: The Communists say that if the "no" wins, we will leave the Atlantic Alliance without any consequences. The [conservative] Popular Coalition affirms that even if the "no" wins, we will not leave the Alliance. What do you think of those two positions?

GONZÁLEZ: . . . The debate is not about that. It is about whether or not it is better to stay in the Alliance. Some Communists also add that afterwards, we must break our ties with the Americans. But neither the Italian Communists, nor the Portuguese, nor the French are saying that, because they know what the consequences would be. Nor did Santiago Carrillo [secretary general of the Spanish Communist Party] say that five years ago. Because they know that the balance of power is very important for peace. . . .

CAMBIO 16: And why is the Popular Coalition saying that we will not leave [the Atlantic Alliance] even if the "no" vote wins?

GONZÁLEZ: That is a good question for the leaders of the right. If I state an opinion, I enter into a quarrel I don't want. Because I'm not quarreling with anyone, but simply trying to tell the citizens what is best for Spain. . . .

CAMBIO 16: What might happen if the referendum loses?

GONZÁLEZ: . . . If that hypothesis is confirmed, we will talk about it then. . . . Your own magazine has said that I am practicing blackmail, which is something that has never been my intention. So I will not give in to the temptation to "blackmail." All I will say is that I am democratic and I will respect the expressed will of the majority.

CAMBIO 16: But the citizens also have the right to know what might happen in the event of a negative vote.

GONZÁLEZ: But without any blackmail, please. Because others practice blackmail when they say that nuclear bombs are going to rain down on them and other such stories. Let's be serious. If the "no" vote wins, the government in the Council of Ministers will ask to leave the Atlantic Alliance. I will continue to uphold my positions, but I will uphold the will of the people.

CAMBIO 16: Nevertheless, you have said in a radio interview that if the "no" vote wins, you would have to pay a high political price. Does this mean your resignation?

GONZÁLEZ: I am simply not going to talk about that. I repeat: that is a hypothesis about the future, and the citizen might feel blackmailed. I have never done that in my life.

CAMBIO 16: Without a doubt, if the referendum loses, your standing with the Western countries will be greatly weakened.

GONZÁLEZ: It will create a severe crisis of confidence. But whether you believe me or not, the personal problem does not concern me at all, because if that concerned me I would not be swimming against the current. We are about to undertake an act of sovereignty. This people, as in few occasions in its history, has the sovereign power to decide. . . .

CAMBIO 16: How do you feel when Manuel Fraga, who organized that referendum for Franco in 1966 in which more than 100 percent of the people voted, now speaks of fraud? [Manuel Fraga Iribarne, a government minister and an ambassador during the Franco regime, led one of the main right-wing parties in the early years after Franco's death.]

GONZÁLEZ: Fraga's 1966 referendum belongs to the past, and I have committed myself not to speak of Fraga's past. Fraga speaks dismissively of my conversion to supporting the Atlantic Alliance, as if to reproach me for it. But I thank Fraga for working for Spain from a democratic perspective, because I know that that required a change of position for him, and one must welcome anyone with the capacity for leadership who wishes to help consolidate democracy.

CAMBIO 16: The leaders of the Popular Coalition have spoken of falsifications, manipulations, and other attempts to alter the referendum results. What is your opinion?

GONZÁLEZ: I believe that that will do more damage to them. . . . The majority of the citizens do not believe that. We have already carried out various elections, and this is the third general referendum. Never, never, have we Socialists questioned the legitimacy of a consultation. . . .

CAMBIO 16: Nevertheless, in your campaign you are trying not to criticize the right. You yourself are treating them with kid gloves. Is this to avoid alienating the "yes" votes?

GONZÁLEZ: Absolutely not. It is to construct democracy. And I'm going to confess something to you: if, as I hope, the referendum's result is positive, on the following day I will once again propose that all the political forces in the parliament assume a single foreign policy for Spain. That is to say, I will once again propose . . . that we all be in accord, no matter what the government is, so that our foreign policy may be permanent and fulfill a single purpose. . . .

CAMBIO 16: Do you believe that the Spaniards already understand what is at stake in the referendum?

GONZÁLEZ: Many citizens are coming to understand that. . . . We did not submit our entry into the [European] Common Market to a referendum because we were all in agreement on that, and we have all worked in the same direction, and there was no division in public opinion. But with the Atlantic Alliance that is not the case.

CAMBIO 16: But wasn't Spanish public opinion divided over the Alliance in large part because your party waged a campaign against it in 1981?

GONZÁLEZ: It is possible, and I assume responsibility for any consequences. Sometimes one sends a message with many nuances, and when it is received, including by one's colleagues, the nuances disappear. But there was never a single moment when I did not say, with all clarity, that we had our responsibility in the matter of collective security.

75. La Mesa de Ajuria Enea, Response to ETA (1997)

During the Franco dictatorship, ETA (see reading 69) enjoyed considerable sympathy not only among the Basque people, but also throughout Spain and the rest of the world. But with the advent of democracy after Franco's death in 1975 came a relaxation of Franco's severe restrictions on the use of the Basque language and other manifestations of Basque culture. The 1978 constitution also granted extensive autonomy to the regions in Spain, making ETA's cause look less necessary to many observers both inside and outside the Basque region.

Those changes, combined with ETA's ongoing campaign of political violence, which took several hundred lives by the late 1990s, led to a steep decline in sympathy for ETA. A small minority of residents of the Basque region still supported ETA and Herri Batasuna (People's Unity)—a legal political party associated with ETA—and Herri Batasuna managed to secure enough votes to control about 10 percent of the local governments in the region, but the vast majority of voters in the region supported other parties. In 1988, six Spanish political parties—including the Socialists, the center-right Partido Popular (Popular Party), and the moderate Partido Nacional Vasco (National Basque Party)—signed an accord to cooperate against ETA. That coalition was known as the Mesa de Ajuria Enea.

One of ETA's longstanding demands was the transfer of its imprisoned members from jails in other parts of Spain to those in the Basque region, and in the summer of 1997 it was holding two hostages as part of an effort to force such a transfer. In July of that year, one of the hostages was released on payment of a large ransom, and the other, José Antonio Ortega Lara, was rescued in a raid by the Civil Guard. Enraged over that raid, ETA responded by kidnapping an obscure employee of a consulting firm and a member of the local town council in the Basque town of Ermua, twenty-nine year old Miguel Angel Blanco Garrido, a part-time rock musician and a low-ranking member of the governing Popular Party. ETA set a deadline of forty-eight hours for the transfer of the prisoners, and when that deadline passed, ETA killed Mr. Blanco Garrido.

That act touched off a wave of massive demonstrations against ETA, as several million citizens gathered in towns throughout Spain. Angry Spaniards also assaulted Herri Batasuna headquarters throughout the Basque country, and when tiny numbers of pro-Herri Batasuna (and presumably pro-ETA) counterdemonstrators took to the streets, the police had to intervene to protect them from furious onlookers. Expressing the views of many in the days after Mr. Blanco Garrido's murder, the Mesa de Ajuria Enea issued the following statement.

SOURCE: *El País* (Madrid), July 14, 1997.

1. In the first place, we offer our most heartfelt condolences to the members of Miguel Angel's family. In these two tragic days we have had the opportunity to get to know them and to listen to them. We have come to experience their infinite sadness. They know quite well that they are not

alone. Never has a Spanish family been so supported in its grief by so many people. We will not forget you, and you should know, for it may bring you some consolation, that the memory of your dignity and your fortitude will comfort us and will serve as an inspiration for us. Rest in peace, Miguel Angel.

2. We are shattered and anguished. We are also profoundly disappointed. We were aware of ETA's inhuman cruelty, but we could not believe it would sink to this level of degradation. We had seen the pleading faces of Miguel Angel's parents. We had heard the still-hopeful prayers of his sister Marimar. We had also heard the continual and insistent clamor of an entire people. We had witnessed their impressive demonstrations. Because of all that we had come to hope that this time ETA would have, if not the humanity, at least the intelligence and shrewdness not to carry out its death threat.

Even memories of our history had occurred to us. We remembered, in recent days, how more than twenty-five years ago, in the midst of Franco's dictatorship, the clamor of this people managed to touch the heart of the old dictator, securing from him the commutation of the death sentence of those convicted in that infamous trial in Burgos. [See reading 69.]

What worked with the old dictator proved to be in vain with this detested ETA. They kidnapped Miguel Angel without cause and without trial. God knows where they kept him hidden and in great distress for two days. And with his face uncovered and his hands bound, without even giving him a blindfold so he would not see the faces of his murderers, they executed him with two shots in the back of the neck. We did not expect such cruelty, nor such evil. We will never be able to forget.

3. Because of this evil murder, ETA is now more isolated than ever. It has placed itself outside this people and against this people. If yesterday people did not like ETA, today they hate it. ETA has dealt a deathblow to our desires for dialogue and reconciliation. We do not know if we will ever be able to recover them.

Nevertheless, despite being abandoned by the people, ETA continues to have accomplices among us. Fewer than before, no doubt, but still too many. Today we wish to denounce them. They are called Herri Batasuna. In recent days, we have all heard their resounding silence. We cannot fail to consider them accomplices of this evil murder. And thus we denounce them.

After the rescue of Ortega Lara, they promised a prompt reprisal. And now we are suffering from that. From now on, we will assume that all of their threats will be carried out. They themselves have forced us to believe either that those who lead that coalition are in on the planning of the crime, or that they inspire it or provoke it with their words.

Their followers should keep this in mind. Their support and their silence also make them accomplices. The time has come for them to make decisions. The people demand it of them. They need them. They cannot believe that they are living alongside so many people for whom this evil murder does not produce a word of protest, a gesture of compassion, a cry of condemnation.

We will thus be waiting, and we will act accordingly. We cannot act jointly to defend any cause, no matter how legitimate, with people who have made themselves accomplices of such an abominable murder through their words of support or their cowardly silence.

4. Society today feels indignation and rage. It is for good reason. We share those feelings. We wish, nevertheless, to remind people that there are two sentiments, two attitudes that we must avoid at all cost, no matter how hard it may be: a desire for revenge, and a sense of desperation.

A desire for revenge is their reaction, not ours. The murder of Miguel Angel was an act of revenge. Serenity, a civic spirit, and dignity have been the reaction that we, the immense majority, have shown during these difficult moments. We must follow that course. We do not demand vengeance, but rather justice. And we wish to assure everyone that justice will come down with all its force on those who have committed this murder. May no one doubt that. Nor will we fall into desperation. ETA's crime was not an act of strength, but rather a sign of its lowly nature and its desperation. Today ETA is weaker than yesterday, more alone than yesterday, more circumscribed than yesterday.

Democratic society, on the other hand—and we say this with full conviction—is stronger, more united, firmer than ever. The demonstration yesterday in Bilbao was not in vain; it was not a fruitless effort. It demonstrated, among other things, that this battle, however difficult it may be, will be won by this immense majority that was so fully represented in the streets yesterday. And it will win with the only weapons it has: unity in democracy, a strict application of the law, and the ethical superiority of its behavior.

5. We will thus channel our legitimate indignation through peaceful means. We are going to show them our power.

For this purpose, and immediately, we propose and encourage the following actions:

a) Today, Sunday, at eight in the evening, we invite all citizens to gather in the three capitals of the [autonomous] community to join the family of Miguel Angel in its grief and to condemn his murder. Plaza Moyúa in Bilbao, that of Gipuzkoa in Donostia, and [the Plaza] Virgen Blanca in Vitoria-Gasteiz will be converted today into sites for the expression of our feelings.

b) In conjunction with the unions, we also call for a work stoppage of one hour tomorrow, Monday, at noon, in all workplaces, for a public gathering of all workers in the neighborhoods of their respective places of employment.

c) We invite all the municipal governments to hold plenary sessions of condolence and condemnation tomorrow, Monday, at noon, and to organize whatever civic actions they find most appropriate for expressing the citizenry's feelings of repulsion in their respective municipalities. We also propose that in those sessions they express their support for this communiqué.

The members of the Mesa de Ajuria Enea will go this afternoon to the mourning chapel set up at the town hall of Ermua, and tomorrow at noon they will attend the funeral that will be held in the parish church of Ermua. . . .

Finally, we wish to thank all the Basque citizens, as well as all of those of the Spanish state, for the impressive expressions of solidarity they have given to the family of Miguel Angel and to the whole Basque people.

76. SOS Racismo, *Annual Report on Racism in the Spanish State* (1999)

Although in recent years Spain has received fewer immigrants than some of its northern neighbors, the flow of migrants has nonetheless grown large enough to provoke serious social and political tensions. Whereas employers in search of an inexpensive labor supply have generally welcomed this immigration, many other Spaniards have grown alarmed at the flow of illegal immigrants, particularly those making the short but perilous sea voyage from Morocco, and as tensions have increased so have incidents of discrimination and violence against immigrants and ethnic minorities. An important part of Spain's response to these problems—as well as to ongoing discrimination against the country's Gypsy community—has been the rise of a new organization, SOS Racismo, which by the late 1990s had branches in over a dozen Spanish cities.

Although the problems SOS Racismo seeks to resolve are hardly unique to Spain—indeed the organization first appeared in France and now has branches throughout Europe—there are certain aspects of Spain's history that are essential to understanding the problems of racism and xenophobia that surfaced in the country at the end of the twentieth century. First is the path that Spain took some five centuries ago, when the newly formed state pursued political and cultural unity by expelling the Jews in 1492 and by gradually forcing the country's Muslims either to convert or to leave the country. A rigid insistence on religious and cultural uniformity continued with the measures that the Inquisition and other royal and ecclesiastical authorities took against Protestants, heterodox Catholics, and Gypsies. In pursuing greater political unity, then, Spain's leaders deliberately promoted cultural, religious, and ethnic homogeneity, and the legacy of such policies was a population largely unaccustomed to living alongside people from other cultures and faiths.

It is also worth noting that until very recently, Spain had been a country of emigration, not immigration. Even after Franco's death in 1975, the weakness of Spain's economy and a persistently high official unemployment rate kept immigration rates very low by western European standards. With the country's increasing prosperity, however, immigrants from Europe, Latin America, and Africa began to arrive in increasing numbers, and by the 1990s, immigration, xenophobia, and racism had become urgent topics of public discussion.

The report refers to Ceuta and Melilla, two enclaves of Spanish territory in Morocco, where North African immigrants often seek entry to Spain.

SOURCE: SOS Racismo, *Informe anual 1999 sobre el racismo en el estado español* (Barcelona: Icaria Editorial, 1999), 207–13. Reprinted by permission of SOS Racismo.

This year again, we cannot affirm that our society is less racist than in previous editions of the report. This is not only because the data gathered in the present report do not offer any grounds for optimism, but also because SOS

Racismo's annual report is not so much a precise index of the prevailing degree of racism, but rather an instrument for denouncing and raising consciousness—yet one that nonetheless reflects the structure of racism in the Spanish state while also giving an idea of its extent. The report, it should be emphasized, is not simply a compilation of the most flagrant cases of racism and xenophobia that happened in 1998. In a certain form, the cases indicate certain acts (some more common than others) by people who do not always perceive them as racist. . . . What we can establish from the outset is that in relation to previous years, we note the persistence of cases of racism and xenophobia, of discrimination based on origins, skin color, and socioeconomic level; also abuses by the police, as well as an institutional racism expressed through discriminatory laws, barely integrative policies, abuses of power on the part of some functionaries and authorities, etc.

Those who suffer primarily from institutional and social racism are those belonging to the Gypsy community, most particularly those of a low socioeconomic level. To daily forms of discrimination—for which the very society in which we all live is largely responsible—one may add the preponderance of some forms that are administrative in nature, and which exacerbate the marginalization of the Gypsy people; [these forms] sometimes spring from aid workers' misconceptions, which keep [the Gypsies] from gaining effective access to their rights.

Although the Gypsy community is the group that is most rejected by the rest of society, immigrants also suffer from a racism and xenophobia fundamentally constructed upon cultural prejudices and often resting on ideas that show a basic ignorance. There are essentially three of these ideas: first, that there is a large number of immigrants in the Spanish state. Yet the number of foreigners in Spain makes up scarcely 2 percent of the total population—with about 600,000 legal immigrants and around 100,000 lacking papers—very far from the 6 to 9 percent in other European countries. The second idea involves considering only those from outside the European Union to be immigrants, overlooking the fact that immigrants from other countries of the European Union make up 43 percent of the immigrants in Spain. Finally, there is the question of the supposed competition for jobs because of immigrants coming from countries of the South, an idea that is as widespread as it is false: according to a study by the CIS carried out in 1996, 45 percent of the immigrants at that time were unemployed; of the rest, only half had written employment contracts, and the wages of those who were working were between 30,000 and 100,000 pesetas a month. On the other hand, a study by IMSERSO carried out in 1997 shows that 60 percent of the population were convinced that immigrants from EU countries had no effect on employment, even in the case of those who held skilled positions that were prestigious and well paid.

The population of immigrants from outside the [European] Community is not homogeneous; their professional and personal situation depends on their administrative status. Nevertheless, with or without papers, much of the discrimination they suffer is the product of legislation that regulates their stay in the Spanish state, as well as of the implementation of specific policies by administrative entities. They thus find themselves relegated by law to a few areas of employment—services (mainly domestic service), construction, and agriculture—that are most often rejected by native workers because of their precariousness, low pay, and limited prestige. The working conditions tend to be very hard, sometimes amounting to exploitation, and the workers' condition of defenselessness is often worsened by legislation; in the case of those whose immigration status is legal, [their defenselessness exists] because keeping their jobs is crucial to renewing their residence permits; in the case of those who lack legal immigration status, [their defenselessness exists] because denouncing their employers may bring detention and expulsion from the country. Given that there are, in practice, no legal means of entry, and that there are clearly insufficient mechanisms through which undocumented immigrants can normalize their status once they are here, the law itself creates a vicious circle that only benefits those who take advantage of the immigrants' defenselessness: exploiters and organized crime.

In the section on living conditions, we observe that many of these persons are rejected by their neighbors or cheated by the landlords who rent to them, in what is a daily form of discrimination that is not always perceived as such. Health care constitutes another area where discrimination is common and originates in existing legislation: in theory, only minors and immigrants with legal residence, employment status, and social security have access to the public health system in conditions equal to those of the rest of the citizens. A revealing example is the case of the lack of health care for minors. . . . If not even all of those who have a recognized right to health care can effectively exercise it, what is there to say about all of those who are denied such a fundamental right? As in many other areas, it is those professionals who come in daily contact with immigrants whose rights to health care have not been recognized who end up making up for the deficiencies in the law, at the cost of exceptional personal efforts of their own. The management of the questions that affect this group of persons is left in society's hands, obscuring the fact that the problem is fundamentally and predominantly political. Something similar takes place in the educational realm, where a certain inequality is evident: less than 10 percent of the children of immigrant families attend private schools, and within public schools, they are concentrated in a few places; yet the problem is not only the . . . schools' refusal to accept them; in this case one must also recall the political dimension. At any rate, it would be a mistake to think that all these forms of discrimination are solely linked to immigration, for in reality the so-called second generations, who go on being identified as "immigrants" despite never having been immigrants, also suffer from them.

One of the most extensive manifestations of institutional, but also social, racism involves the criminalization of foreigners and the consequent pressure to which they are subjected by the police. This type of racism has increased significantly in recent years, since the Popular Party (PP) has come to power, and it has reached its greatest extent in 1997 and 1998. Police pressure on foreigners from outside the European Union takes several forms: an increase in police harassment, a rise in arrests and expulsions, the construction of the Ceuta wall [see below], the persecution of North African youths in that city, the situation of the Calamocarro and La Granja [detention] camps, the persistence of the system of internment centers, irregularities in expulsion cases, etc.

The increase in police pressure can be perceived perfectly well through figures on arrests and expulsions carried out in recent years (see Table 1). If, in the first year of the PP government (1996), the figure for arrests rose by 5,000 over the previous year, it doubled again in the following year. In 1998 the number of arrests stabilized at 40,710. Nevertheless, the arrests did not translate, in any case, into a proportional rise in the number of expulsions. . . . The reasons why this spectacular increase in arrests has not led to more expulsions are simple, and they show that the government's true intention is to increase the pressure on immigrants by subjecting them to a continuous police control that does not lead to their subsequent expulsion; [the failure of arrests to yield expulsions happens] because of economic reasons (to pay for the return trip of a North African is relatively cheap, but to expel a Latin American or a sub-Saharan African is much less so), or because of a greater sensitivity on the part of judges, who perceive how unjustified many

TABLE 1. Numbers of Immigrants Arrested and Expulsions Carried Out, by Years

	1995	1996	1997	1998
Arrests	15,416	20,690	41,441	40,710
Expulsions	4,875	4,837	4,750	5,525

Source: Ministry of the Presidency.

arrests are [and thus] do not support them, or because of the affected persons' greater knowledge of their rights.

According to sources from the Directory General of the Police, the number of persons turned away at the various Spanish borders because of a lack of travel documents or identity papers, visas, or sufficient economic means was, in 1998, 7,870. By sea routes came 936 stowaways, and in the Straits of Gibraltar, 140 small boats were intercepted, with 1,824 immigrants aboard. The number of those immediately turned back without going through the formal process of expulsion also increased, the product of greater police control over the passage of illegal immigrants in small trucks heading toward other countries in the European Union. At the Catalan border with France, for example, these cases of immediate turning back increased 130 percent; in the entire Spanish state, 17,198 such cases were carried out.

The construction of a new wall in Ceuta is another aspect of the government's policy of police repression, which consists of making the borders impassable to impede the flow of immigration and to increase police control over immigrants who are already in the country. Thus as an effect of governmental policy, the spending of 3.5 billion pesetas to furnish the Ceuta wall with cutting-edge technology that impedes immigration and detects those who attempt it—optical and acoustic sensors, video cameras, control towers, halogen spotlights, etc.—complements the spending required for new internment centers for foreigners in various parts of the Spanish state. Paradoxically, this policy of sealing the borders stands in contradiction, first of all, with the certainty of those in charge of carrying it out that such policies would be useless and ineffective. The Director General of the Civil Guard, López Valdivieso, warned in August 1998, in noting the rise in the flow of immigrants during the summer months, that police measures did not constitute a check on immigration; secondly, this policy also stands in contradiction with the recognition by political forces that immigration is a necessary phenomenon: economically, because the entry of manual laborers is essential for compensating for the future lack of workers and to sustain the public pensions system; yet also, and above all, as a factor for social progress, as has been recognized in statements of motives for various bills for a new Alien Act. . . .

Physical aggression constitutes one of the most extreme and crude forms that racism takes. Such behavior is bad enough whoever engages in it, but the fact that agents of the security services are involved in brutal beatings, as a multitude of cases in this report shows, indicates that something has not been working properly in the training that these persons have received, and perhaps the very values of a state of law have not been disseminated as they should within the security forces. Thus it must be pointed out that in trials for racist or xenophobic acts, the sensitivity of the tribunals concerned has remained insufficient. Significantly, there is still great reluctance to punish police excesses; in those cases in which an immigrant accuses the police of mistreatment and is at the same time accused by the police of resisting arrest, the verdict tends to be the conviction of the immigrant. Nevertheless, some progress has been made. . . .

Finally, as noted at the outset, some of the discrimination that affects immigrants has its origins . . . in the norms promulgated to regulate their stay in the Spanish state. The 1985 Law of Rights and Liberties of Foreigners in Spain, criticized by SOS Racismo from the beginning, is the best example of this "normative racism," in that it places a priority on police control over persons not considered citizens, and whom it criminalizes without any crime being committed—something that is unheard of in a democratic state of law. Fourteen years after it came into force, it seems that there is political consensus on the need to change the Alien Act, which was already obsolete when it was promulgated. The reality is that the law has turned out to be doubly ineffective; in the first place, [it has failed] to regulate the situation of thousands of persons condemned to marginality, and [it has also failed] to control flows of migration, which was the original purpose envisioned for it.

SOS Racismo continues to follow with great interest the various bills intended to replace the current legislation that are presented in parliament. Aware of the opportunity that parliamentary discussion represents, SOS Racismo does not want its proposals to be forgotten amid political debate. We believe that the Annual Report constitutes a very suitable framework for offering a brief reminder of what these concrete proposals are:

- the recognition of rights from the perspective of increasing equality, that is, the gradual disappearance of current deficits of rights in comparison with foreigners from the European Union, and, eventually, with [Spanish] nationals;
- an end to the current dichotomy between residence and work permits and the creation of a single permit that recognizes all rights without limit;
- the replacement of the policy of contingents, which is in reality a covert form of legalization, with another policy, which is universal and shows solidarity, and which admits the important contribution of immigration and recognizes the right of every human being to live in dignity and to relocate in full freedom. . . .
- recourse to penalties such as expulsion and forced return only in exceptional cases, applying them only in especially grave cases. . . ;

- a distribution of administrative assignments that favors integration and moves away from the current focus on the police, which only contributes to the fallacious identification of foreigners as delinquents; this includes, among other measures, . . . creating a Secretariat of State for Immigration. . . ;
- finally, without forgetting the European realm, the end of policies of sealing borders, to which the Spanish government has devoted a great amount of resources in the cities of Ceuta and Melilla. Europe cannot be constructed by building walls around it, but rather by creating common immigration policies that recognize rights and liberties, beginning with the right of free circulation. Identifying immigrants with terrorists and drug traffickers . . . supposes the very opposite and makes immigration a form of punishment rather than a right.

The norms and policies that the various governmental entities adopt and the persistence or end of institutional racism are crucial factors in two ways. In the first place, [they are crucial] because citizens' perceptions of the phenomenon of migration are very much influenced by the way in which governmental entities handle it and by the kind of measures they adopt. Secondly, because it is from these norms and policies that a more or less integrative framework for immigrants and their surroundings will emerge. In reality, at the heart of the debate is not so much a given law or certain specific policies, but rather the model of society that we want to construct as we look to the future. In this sense, access to full citizenship for many people who now—after years of having roots in our country—can no longer be considered immigrants but who still lack the most basic rights and any hopes for the future of even minimal stability; and the awareness of the multicultural quality that exists in our society are two of the axes of the debate that should take place in the next few years in the Spanish state as well as in the rest of the countries of Europe, and in European institutions themselves. We here at SOS Racismo think that denunciations, while being a very important element of our work, are not enough by themselves. The raising of awareness is the second of this association's missions. That is why we wish to use these pages to promote reflection and discussion, in the conviction that only an exchange of ideas will allow for real progress in questions as delicate and fundamental as these.

Bibliography

General Histories of Spain in English

Alvarez Junco, José, and Adrian Shubert, eds. *Spanish History Since 1808*. London: Arnold, 2000.
Carr, Raymond. *Modern Spain, 1875–1980*. Oxford: Oxford University Press, 1980.
———. *Spain, 1808–1975*. Oxford: Clarendon Press, 1982.
———, ed. *Spain: A History*. Oxford: Oxford University Press, 2000.
Esdaile, Charles J. *Spain in the Liberal Age: From Constitution to Civil War, 1808–1939*. Oxford: Blackwell, 2000.
Herr, Richard. *A Historical Essay on Modern Spain*. Berkeley: University of California Press, 1971.
Hooper, John. *The New Spaniards*. London and New York: Penguin Books, 1995.
Madariaga, Salvador de. *Spain: A Modern History*. New York: Praeger, 1958.
Payne, Stanley G. *A History of Spain and Portugal*. 2 vols. Madison: University of Wisconsin Press, 1973.
Pierson, Peter. *The History of Spain*. Westport, Conn.: Greenwood Press, 1999.
Romero Salvado, Francisco J. *Twentieth-Century Spain: Politics and Society in Spain, 1898–1998*. New York: St. Martin's Press, 1999.
Ross, Christopher J. *Spain, 1812–1996: Modern History for Modern Languages*. London: Arnold, 2000.
Shubert, Adrian. *A Social History of Modern Spain*. London: Unwin Hyman, 1990.

Collections of Historical Documents

Aguado, A. María et al., eds., *Textos para la historia de las mujeres en España*. Madrid: Cátedra, 1994.
Díaz-Plaja, Fernando, ed. *La España franquista en sus documentos (La posguerra española en sus documentos)*. Madrid: Plaza and Janés, 1976.
———. *Historia de España en sus documentos: Siglo XIX*. Madrid: Cátedra, 1983.
———. *Historia de España en sus documentos: Siglo XX*. Madrid: Instituto de Estudios Políticos, 1960.
———. *Historia de España en sus documentos: El Siglo XX, Dictadura . . . República (1923–1936)*. Madrid: Instituto de Estudios Políticos, 1965.
———. *Historia de España en sus documentos: El Siglo XX, La Guerra (1936–39)*. Madrid: Gráficas Faro, 1963.
———. *La posguerra española en sus documentos*. Madrid: Plaza and Janés, 1970.
García-Gallo, Alfonso, ed. *Manual de historia del derecho español*, 3rd ed. 2 vols. Madrid: A.G.E.S.A., 1967.
Tamañas, Ramon, ed. *España, 1931–1975: Una antología histórica*. Barcelona: Editora Planeta, 1980.

Specialized Studies

Aguilar, Paloma, *Memory and Amnesia: the Role of the Spanish Civil War in the Transition to Democracy*. Trans. Mark Oakley. New York: Berghahn Books, 2002.

Balcells, Albert and Geoffrey J. Walker, eds. *Catalan Nationalism: Past and Present*. trans. Jacqueline Hall. New York: St. Martin's Press, 1996.

Balfour, Sebastian. *The End of the Spanish Empire, 1898–1923*. Oxford: Clarendon Press, 1997.

Beevor, Antony. *The Spanish Civil War*. London: Orbis, 1982.

Ben-Ami, Shlomo. *The Origins of the Second Republic in Spain*. Oxford: Oxford University Press, 1978.

Bethell, Leslie, ed. *The Independence of Latin America*. Cambridge: Cambridge University Press, 1987.

Bookchin, Murray. *The Spanish Anarchists: The Heroic Years, 1868–1936*. New York: Free Life Editions, 1977.

Boyd, Carolyn P. *Historia Patria: Politics, History, and National Identity in Spain, 1875–1975*. Princeton, N.J.: Princeton University Press, 1997.

——. *Praetorian Politics in Liberal Spain*. Chapel Hill: University of North Carolina Press, 1979.

Brenan, Gerald. *The Spanish Labyrinth: An Account of the Social and Political Background of the Spanish Civil War*. 2nd ed. Cambridge: Cambridge University Press, 1971.

Callahan, William J. *The Catholic Church in Spain, 1875–1998*. Washington, D.C.: Catholic University of America Press, 2000.

——. *Church, Politics, and Society in Spain, 1750–1874*. Cambridge, Mass.: Harvard University Press, 1984.

Carr, Raymond. *The Civil War in Spain, 1936–39*. London: Weidenfeld and Nicolson, 1986.

Carr, Raymond and Juan Pablo Fusi. *Spain: Dictatorship to Democracy*. 2d ed. London: Allen and Unwin, 1981.

Clark, Robert. *The Basque Insurgents: ETA, 1952–1980*. Madison: University of Wisconsin Press, 1980.

Clark, Robert. *The Basques, the Franco Years, and Beyond*. Reno: University of Nevada Press, 1979.

Conversi, Daniele. *The Basques, the Catalans, and Spain: Alternative Routes to Nationalist Modernization*. London: Hurst, 1997.

Ellwood, Sheelagh. *Franco*. London and New York: Longman, 1994.

Enders, Victoria Loree and Pamela Beth Radcliff, eds. *Constructing Spanish Womanhood: Female Identity in Modern Spain*. Albany: State University of New York Press, 1999.

Esenwein, George and Adrian Shubert. *Spain at War: The Spanish Civil War in Context, 1931–1939*. London and New York: Longman, 1995.

Gillespie, Richard. *The Spanish Socialist Party: A History of Factionalism*. Oxford: Oxford University Press, 1990.

Gilmour, David. *The Transformation of Spain: From Franco to the Constitutional Monarchy*. London: Quartet, 1985.

Hilt, Douglas. *The Troubled Trinity: Godoy and the Spanish Monarchs*. Tuscaloosa: University of Alabama Press, 1987.

Holguín, Sandie. *Creating Spaniards: Culture and National Identity in Republican Spain*. Madison: University of Wisconsin Press, 2002.

Jackson, Gabriel. *The Spanish Republic and the Civil War, 1931–1939*. Princeton, N.J.: Princeton University Press, 1965.

Kaplan, Temma. *Red City, Blue Period: Social Movements in Picasso's Barcelona*. Berkeley: University of California Press, 1992.

Lannon, Frances. *Privilege, Persecution, and Prophecy: The Catholic Church in Spain, 1875–1975*. Oxford: Oxford University Press, 1987.

Lewis, James E. *The American Union and the Problem of Neighborhood: The United States and the Collapse of the Spanish Empire, 1783–1829*. Chapel Hill: University of North Carolina Press, 1998.

Lynch, John. *The Spanish American Revolutions, 1808–1826*. 2d ed. New York: W. W. Norton, 1986.

Malefakis, Edward. *Agrarian Reform and Peasant Revolution in Spain: Origins of the Civil War*. New Haven, Conn.: Yale University Press, 1970.

Mintz, Jerome R. *The Anarchists of Casas Viejas*. Chicago: University of Chicago Press, 1982.

Morcillo, Aurora G. *True Catholic Womanhood: Gender Ideology in Franco's Spain*. De Kalb: Northern Illinois University Press, 2000.

Payne, Stanley G. *Basque Nationalism*. Reno: University of Nevada Press, 1975.

———. *Fascism in Spain, 1923–1977*. Madison: University of Wisconsin Press, 1999.

———. *The Franco Regime*. Madison: University of Wisconsin Press, 1987.

———. *Politics and the Military in Modern Spain*. Stanford, Calif.: Stanford University Press, 1967.

———. *Spain's First Democracy: The Second Republic, 1931–1936*. Madison: University of Wisconsin Press, 1993.

———. *Spanish Catholicism: An Historical Overview*. Madison: University of Wisconsin Press, 1984.

———. *The Spanish Revolution*. New York: W. W. Norton, 1970.

Pérez-Díaz, Victor M. *The Return of Civil Society: The Emergence of Democratic Spain*. Cambridge, Mass.: Harvard University Press, 1993.

Pike, Frederick B. *Hispanismo, 1898–1936: Spanish Conservatives and Liberals and Their Relations with Spanish America*. Notre Dame, Ind.: University of Notre Dame Press, 1971.

Preston, Paul. *The Coming of the Spanish Civil War: Reform, Reaction, and Revolution in the Second Republic*. London: Routledge, 1994.

———. *Franco: A Biography*. London: HarperCollins, 1993.

———. *The Politics of Revenge: Fascism and the Military in Twentieth-Century Spain*. London: Unwin Hyman, 1990.

———, ed. *Revolution and War in Spain, 1931–1939*. London: Methuen, 1984.

Ringrose, David R. *Spain, Europe, and the "Spanish Miracle," 1700–1900*. Cambridge: Cambridge University Press, 1996.

Robinson, Richard A. H. *The Origins of Franco's Spain: The Right, the Republic and Revolution, 1931–1936*. Newton Abbot: David and Charles, 1970.

Schmitt-Nowara, Christopher. *Empire and Antislavery: Spain, Cuba, and Puerto Rico, 1833–1874*. Pittsburgh: University of Pittsburgh Press, 1999.

Seidman, Michael, *Republic of Egos: A Social History of the Spanish Civil War*. Madison: University of Wisconsin Press, 2002.

Shaw, Donald. *The Generation of 1898 in Spain*. London: E. Benn, 1975.

Smith, Angel, ed. *Red Barcelona: Social Protest and Labour Mobilization in the Twentieth Century*. London: Routledge, 2002.

Sullivan, J. *ETA and Basque Nationalism: The Fight for Euskadi, 1890–1986*. London and New York: Routledge, 1988.

Thomas, Hugh. *The Spanish Civil War*. New York: Harper and Row, 1961.

Tone, John Lawrence. *The Fatal Knot: The Guerrilla War in Navarre and the Defeat of Napoleon in Spain*. Chapel Hill: University of North Carolina Press, 1994.

Ullman, Joan Connelly. *The Tragic Week: A Study of Anticlericalism in Spain, 1875–1912*. Cambridge, Mass.: Harvard University Press, 1968.

Whealey, Robert H. *Hitler and Spain: The Nazi Role in the Spanish Civil War, 1936–1939*. Lexington: University of Kentucky Press, 1989.

Index

Boldface indicates readings.

CPSIA information can be obtained
at www.ICGtesting.com
Printed in the USA
LVHW031327280719
625631LV00003B/403

9 780812 218466